T0312036

The Heart-Centered Teacher

"I will speak to you of what I've learned and what I'm still struggling with, professionally and personally, not just as a teacher and colleague but also as a wife, daughter, mother, grandmother, friend, and concerned citizen. I want to lift you up—to nourish your heart, mind, and spirit."

—Regie Routman

How do we find hope and possibility in challenging times? How do we bring our truest selves into our teaching and personal lives? In this unique, inspiring book, beloved author Regie Routman artfully blends stories and strategies to show how we can introduce more joy and gratitude in our classrooms and in our lives.

Regie invites us to focus on what matters most in our work and in our relationships with those we hold dear. She shares ideas and practical takeaways for teaching, learning, and living:

- Seeing and celebrating each learner's gifts and strengths
- Creating a storytelling culture
- Ensuring equitable opportunities for all
- Co-creating welcoming spaces and routines
- Developing professional knowledge
- Championing the reading-writing connection
- Fostering resilience and hope
- Taking care of ourselves and our students
- Making a worthy difference.

"Here's what I know for sure," writes Regie. "Living a good life is about developing, nurturing, and sustaining caring relationships—in our teaching lives, our home lives, and in the happy intersection of both." Wherever you are on your journey, no matter what loss or hardship you may face, *The Heart-Centered Teacher* will offer you a refreshing chance to pause, take a breath, and reflect on how you and your students can live more compassionate, generous, and authentic lives.

REGIE ROUTMAN has more than 50 years of experience teaching, coaching, and leading in diverse, underperforming schools and classrooms across the U.S. and Canada. Her many research-based books and resources have supported hundreds of thousands of educators to create and sustain intellectual, joyful, and equitable school cultures where all learners can thrive. For full information on Regie's books, articles, podcasts, videos, and resources, go to www.regieroutman.org and @regieroutman on Twitter.

The
Heart-Centered
Teacher

RESTORING HOPE, JOY, AND POSSIBILITY
IN UNCERTAIN TIMES

Regie Routman

Routledge
Taylor & Francis Group

NEW YORK AND LONDON

Designed cover image: Toby Gordon

First published 2024
by Routledge
605 Third Avenue, New York, NY 10158

and by Routledge
4 Park Square, Milton Park, Abingdon, Oxon, OX14 4RN

Routledge is an imprint of the Taylor & Francis Group, an informa business

© 2024 Regie Routman

Library of Congress Cataloging-in-Publication Data
Names: Routman, Regie, author.
Title: The heart-centered teacher : restoring hope, joy, and possibility in uncertain times / Regie Routman.
Description: New York, NY : Routledge, 2024. | Includes bibliographical references. | Identifiers: LCCN 2023010877 | ISBN 9781032463438 (hardback) | ISBN 9781032445502 (paperback) | ISBN 9781003381242 (ebook) Subjects: LCSH: Effective teaching. | Teaching—Psychological aspects. | Teacher-student relationships. | School environment. | Teachers—Job satisfaction.
Classification: LCC LB1025.3 .R68 2024 | DDC 371.102—dc23/eng/20230517
LC record available at https://lccn.loc.gov/2023010877

ISBN: 9781032463438 (hbk)
ISBN: 9781032445502 (pbk)
ISBN: 9781003381242 (ebk)

DOI: 10.4324/9781003381242

Typeset in Minion Pro
by codeMantra

For Sandra Figueroa
With love and admiration

About the Cover

Coffee table in author's living room, with fresh flowers and a fractured plate, showcasing the beauty and fragility of life. Painting by Toby Gordon.

About the Notes and References

To keep this book reader-friendly, we have created two sections in the back: Notes and References and Quotations.

- The **Notes** (starting on page 264) include explanations that may require further discussion or authors not mentioned in the text. They are notated by a superscript in the text and then listed in the Notes section.

- The **References and Quotations** (starting on page 268) include bibliographic information to help you find referenced material, authors cited, and quotations easily.

- Any statement or idea not attributed in the text is based on my own years of experience and observation as a teacher, researcher, and leader.

Online Resources to Further Support Teaching, Learning, and Living

On the author's website, regieroutman.org, you'll find practical resources supplementing many topics in this book, as well as a Study Guide for use as a discussion starter in book clubs or workshops and/or for self-reflection. Other resources include instructional strategies for teaching readers and writers, working with English learners, and professional learning. Resources include but are not limited to:

- Videos
- Conversational seminars
- Articles and commentaries
- Instructional approaches
- Teaching handouts
- Routledge Eye on Education author page
- Recipes

Contents

Gratitudes

To educators everywhere who give their hearts and minds to teaching in spite of daily challenges. You still focus on every student's success and welfare. This book is for you, with much love and heartfelt thanks for the great work you do.

In *The Heart-Centered Teacher* I write about "Becoming a Significant Influencer." Here I want to call out the many educators, friends, and influencers who have impacted the content and spirit of this book and who have enhanced my life and wellbeing. This book is for you, in gratitude for your support and loving-kindness over many years.

I want to start at the top, with my beloved husband Frank, my closest friend, supporter, truthteller, ally, and joyful companion. This book would not exist without your daily encouragement, generosity, and love. Your feedback and our conversations during the year-of-writing were invaluable for keeping me grounded and gratified. My deepest appreciation and love go to you—always.

To my Seattle family, my daughter-in-law Claudine and my granddaughters Katie and Brooke, you enrich my life every day, even as we move forward together without Peter. I admire the way each of you faces the world with grace, generosity, and humor and that you share those gifts with me. Your astute feedback made this a stronger book. I am full of gratitude and love for each of you.

To Peter's Band of Brothers—for your thoughtful response and input on the Shaker Heights, Ohio, integration story and your friendship with Peter over decades—Matt Hartley, Jonathan Garvin, Keith Austin Willacy, Ken Talley, and David Brown, I am deeply grateful for your contribution to this book and to Peter's quality of life. And, special thanks to Keith who spoke the word "heart-centered" in response to what I'd written, which prompted the title word I'd been searching for.

Huge thanks and recognition to my son Peter's dear friend and high school journalism colleague, Amy Rosewater Halushka, who has established in Peter's memory—through the Shaker Schools Foundation—the Shaker Legacy Writing Center for students-as-writers at Shaker Heights, OH High School.

To my sister Amy Bushman for your loving kindness every day. Although we don't see each other often, our bond is strong, and I am so grateful to have you in my life.

To Sandra Figueroa, a sister-of-my-heart, inspirational educator, co-writer in the video based *Transforming Our Teaching* literacy series, and loving partner in work and in life. Our collaboration and precious friendship have made me a better teacher, leader, and human being. So grateful for you.

To Harriet Cooper—my longest held, best-friend-forever, since we met as college freshmen and have been inseparable ever since—I am indebted to you forever. You know me and accept me as I am and have always championed my work. I love you with all my heart.

To Judy Gurland, we bonded together as counselors at Masonic Camp 7 in Tallman, New York, when we were 15 years old and have been lifelong friends ever since. So appreciative of our wonderful friendship.

To my editor, Lauren Davis, it has been my great fortune and privilege to have you as my partner in writing and publishing this book. Here's what I love about you: your gentleness, your grasp of what I am trying to say, your sensitivity to honoring and respecting my language and intentions, your openness and flexibility. The first questions you asked me were: "How would you like us to work together?" "What do you need?" "How can I support your efforts?" You have been a glorious gift, for which I am deeply grateful. I could not have written this book without your magnificent support.

To John Norton, aka Connector, and illustrious MiddleWeb publisher, for your ongoing contributions to literacy, for being my defacto agent and big supporter, and especially for introducing me to Lauren Davis at Routledge Eye on Education. A huge thank you.

To Maura Sullivan, for your amazing strategizing and marketing efforts on this book and for our steadfast, loving friendship over many years. A big round of applause to you, dearest friend. This book is stronger for your wise insights and splendid contributions.

To my stellar, former editors/publishers: Andrea Butler, Philippa Stratton, Lois Bridges, Wendy Murray, Toby Gordon, Alan Huisman, and Stefani Roth. You lifted me up and supported me to write the best books I could. All of you became treasured friends, and I am deeply grateful to each one of you.

To the outstanding principals I collaborated with in multiple residencies over many years: Devon Isherwood, Kim Ball, Greta Salmi, Marilyn Jerde, Trena Speirs, Barb Ide, and Sue Marlatt. Thank you for welcoming me into your life and into your heart, and for sharing your school, teachers, and students with me.

To my esteemed Winnipeg colleagues Allyson Matzcuk, Jason Drysdale, Celia Caetano-Gomes, Trish Richardson, and countless others. Our joyful work together has been a crowning achievement and the most significant, long-term collaboration in my career. I am deeply grateful.

To Judy Wallis, for being my collaborator and dear friend over many decades and for pushing my thinking around literacy and learning. Loving thanks.

To Chad Blake, for your generosity, friendship, and our meaningful collaboration. Appreciative thanks and much love to you.

To Claudia Mason, for welcoming Frank and me to Seattle, introducing us to Chinook's at Salmon Bay, and for our close and loving friendship. Heartfelt thanks.

To Mary Howard, for your generosity, cheerleading spirit, and deep friendship. We met on Twitter and have been close friends ever since. I am full of gratitude for all your support.

To Gail Boushey, for our loving friendship, professionally and personally; our Zoom conversations; and the wonderful wine and chocolate. All delightful and generous gifts! Thank you.

To Matt Renwick, for organizing and sustaining my website, for pulling together many of the Resources that accompany this book, and mostly for being a treasured colleague and close friend. Loving thanks for all.

To dear neighbors and cherished friends in Seattle who have also enriched my life: Beth Johnson, Noel Angell, Emory Bundy, Sylvia Johnson, Tree Swenson, Margaret Cristofalo, Jenifer Katahira, Diana Stewart, Keith Ledgerwood—plus many dear friends from our years living in the Cleveland, Ohio, area. I love and appreciate each of you.

To those who have generously supported my work over the years and at varying locales: Nancy McLean, Linda Cooper, Pat Carls, Ray Coutu, Peggy Sherman, Valentina Gonzalez, Tan Huynh, Larry Ferlazzo, June Abbott, Diane Canepa, Di Buskie, Stephen Perepeluk, Jaclyn Karabinas, Genny Ostertag, and too many more to name them all. Much gratitude.

To James Crossley of Madison Books, for adding beauty and books into our community and into my life. You have enriched my life in so many ways. A big thank you.

To MaryBeth Nicklaus, for sharing your students' stories with me, welcoming me into your home and school life, and for your loving friendship. I appreciate you.

To Mike Gibbons, for always finding value in my work and thinking. I remain grateful for your support over many years.

To Jim Burnette, for enthusiastically supporting my work over decades. Appreciative thanks.

To Delores Groves, my former principal, who took a chance on my 1983 "book flood" proposal to ensure *all* first graders at Moreland School, in Shaker Heights, Ohio, learned to read and to experience the joy of reading and writing. My love and gratitude to you for that lifechanging support.

So many people responded to this text, most often through my reading sections aloud to them over the phone. For all of you, I am profoundly grateful. In particular, written response from Shelia Valencia, Dorsey Hammond, and Denise Nessel gave me a solid perspective where I needed it.

Finally, much gratitude to the Routledge Eye on Education production and design team who worked tirelessly to make this a beautiful, readable, engaging book. Deepest thanks to the cover designer Emma Capel, the copyeditor Lorraine Savage, and the production editor Elizabeth Spicer.

Regie Routman

The
Heart-Centered
Teacher

Living a Heart-Centered Life

A Letter to Readers

My goal, dear reader is to write to you like I'm talking to you, as a fellow traveler on life's winding road, to share my journey with candor and humility. I will speak to you of what I've learned and what I'm still struggling with, professionally and personally, not just as a teacher and colleague but also as a wife, daughter, mother, grandmother, friend, and concerned citizen. I want to lift you up—to nourish your heart, mind, and spirit. We so often find ourselves with little control over what life brings us so we must, each one of us, do what we can to live our lives to the fullest—and support our students and loved ones to do the same—and, also, to leave the world a little bit better than we found it.

The book you now hold in your hands or are about to listen to is full of empowering possibilities and ideas for living a more hopeful, generous, meaningful life—at work, at home, in school, or wherever you are. This book is part memoir, part essay, part life lessons, and part guide to literacy approaches for teaching readers and writers—with all of it grounded in story. The book's tone and content are meant to be personal, inviting, and inspiring and to focus on what matters most in our work and relationships with children and those we hold dear. This book is for teachers at all levels of experience, in any school environment, and for all of us who seek to lead more integrated and satisfying lives. In other words, this book is for you.

After two years of the Covid-19 pandemic and three years after our son Peter died, I found myself floundering with the direction of my life. I didn't want to do things just to keep busy; I wanted life to matter in a way that would be useful to others and that would bring fulfillment, healing, and peace of mind. I had already written many books for teachers and leaders and was thinking about writing another, a book to tie all my work together in a professional and personal way. While teaching and living have always been challenging, these last few years have shown how vulnerable we all are, how social-emotional wellbeing is necessary for effective teaching and learning, and how forces outside our control can wreak havoc on all aspects of our lives and of our students'.

It is part of the human experience to have our hearts broken—by people, by the loss of a loved one, by ongoing inequities, by democratic institutions. At this moment in time, the whole world feels broken. And yet. Living a good life is still possible—and necessary. Heart-centeredness is a way into the good life and is a major theme of this book. It is that peaceful state where we live our core values with compassion, generosity, and authenticity—even in the midst of sadness and strife. In a heart-centered life, we take care of ourselves and others as we seek to establish and sustain loving-kindness, trusting relationships, and daily gratitude. We have respectful conversations where we "see" and hear the "other," not just with our minds but with our hearts. In a heart-centered life, teaching, learning, and living are interwoven and seamlessly integrated. We become our truest selves.

Stories are at the center of our lives—personal stories, other people's stories, literature of all kinds, and stories of history, diversity, and resilience. Stories help make reality orderly and coherent in a manner that can help us understand our complicated world. The longer I teach, read, write, and live life, the more I am convinced that stories form the bedrock of who we were, who we are, and who we might become. We— as teachers, family members, peers, policy makers—often play an outsize role for determining what stories get told, which stories are valued, and who gets to tell the story. "Truth"—how we define it, believe it, stretch it, or distort it—matters a lot for our own and our students' knowledge of history and social justice; awareness of global, national, and local challenges; and for the opportunities we make possible for our students and ourselves—or not.

Much of living a good life is in part how we value, tell, and reshape our stories to become the authors of our own lives. Learning is a human experience and a vulnerable one. Both students and teachers need to feel safe and protected in order to tell their stories. While we may feel like some pieces of life are broken, cohering those fragments into a new and promising narrative—much like the cover image of the cracked plate lovingly made whole—is what we strive to do for our students and ourselves.

The Heart-Centered Teacher: Restoring Hope, Joy, and Possibility in Uncertain Times is intended to support you, your students, and your loved ones to "put down the roots of happiness," to nurture those roots and to live life more intentionally, prioritizing what matters most—in this moment, in this day, in this life. In that endeavor, my hope is to guide you, as best I can, in creating infrastructures of opportunity—intellectually, emotionally, and socially—so that we and all our students might live and learn more reasonably, equitably, and joyfully. I will be spiritually by your side, on your journey, cheering you on.

With deep admiration and respect,

CHAPTER 1
Loving Our Students

❖ Loving our students—and those we hold dear

❖ Seeing and celebrating each learner's gifts

❖ Showing the love—and expanding our definition of love

DOI: 10.4324/9781003381242-1

Loving our students—and those we hold dear

I used to think it was important to bond with every student in order for them to learn from us, but now I think we need to love each one of them. I learned that lesson working with Ted—as I will call him here—a 53-year-old adult man whom I tutored in reading during the pandemic. At the end of a lesson, after we'd been working together a few months and he was progressing well, he said, "Peace, thank you, I love you." He had been saying "Peace, thank you" for some time but not "I love you." I was stunned and, truth be told, a bit uncomfortable. I don't ever recall having a student say, "I love you," and I didn't know how to respond. I had come to care for Ted very much, but did I love him? Ted's words that day got me thinking about what it means to love a student—and everyone we hold dear.

We have been living through extraordinarily stressful times, causing a huge number of us to become more fragile, anxious, and fearful. The pandemic, war, climate change, politics, violence, and other catastrophes have made love more necessary, and have made it clear we need to expand our universe to include all of us, and to see diversity as our strength. In these uncertain times, we need more understanding, compassion, and nurturing. We need to feel safe and cherished. We need to know we can count on teachers and others to have our backs, to be there for us, to calm us and soothe our wounded souls, and to give us second chances.

Perhaps most of all, we need to be seen. Then "I love you" means, "I see you. I know who you are. I am here for you. I appreciate your gifts. I respect you." One can say with conviction "I love you" and not really "see" and accept the beloved with all their flaws, inadequacies, and limitations. "Seeing" means looking through lenses that capitalize on strengths, rejecting a mentality of differences-as-deficits, and providing equitable opportunities for all. "Seeing" means we ensure that students and their families see themselves and their cultures equitably and respectfully represented in the curriculum, books, and resources we promote and use in daily teaching, learning, and living. "Seeing" means I understand you, and to be fully understood is a profound, life-affirming experience.

A broader meaning of "I love you" encompasses acceptance and listening with compassion, support, and good deeds. Then "I love you" means "You are welcome here and safe here; you can become your truest self." Such a full definition requires grace and graciousness, generosity and goodness, patience and positivity. So, yes, I did love Ted, and it was he who paved the way for opening my heart fully to him. I did see him, and the longer we worked together, the clearer and deeper my sight became. And because Ted felt fully seen and accepted, he opened his heart to me.

But let's start at the beginning of our journey together, which began with our first lesson—Ted and I getting to know each other. A bit of background here first. Ted had just lost his full-time job as a custodian in a large marketplace. Understandably, he was distraught and anxious at losing the daily routines he enjoyed and depended on. He liked his job, and he was good at it. He enjoyed camaraderie with his co-workers, and he liked giving a helping hand to the elderly at the marketplace. But now, unexpectedly, he was at a loss for how to fill his days and what to do with his life, living alone with his cat in an apartment, in the middle of a pandemic. He called me out of the blue. We had never spoken by phone before. He got right to the point: "I'm wondering if you'd be willing to tutor me so I can improve as a reader and writer and have a more interesting life." I immediately said "yes." And so began our twice-weekly learning sessions.

I didn't know Ted well. While he was an extended family member, I only saw him a couple of times a year at holiday gatherings. I knew he was "street smart" (his words), had an ironic sense of humor, and had limited reading and writing skills. Every year when I sent him a birthday card, I hand printed a simple message on the card but never knew if he could read it. I did not want to pepper him with questions about his past education and what he could or could not read and write. I wanted to start with his strengths and interests and use them to further meaningful literacy development. At that time, I had no idea how I would teach Ted, but I knew with certainty that I would teach him and that he would become a reader. In my many decades of teaching reading, I had never failed to teach a child to read.

At the same time, I knew from many decades of teaching in schools— almost all of them underperforming schools with diverse populations— that teacher-student relationships are key to students' success and that we'd have to begin there—getting acquainted, building trust, finding and celebrating his strengths and interests, and using our conversations to determine our learning curriculum. So in our first sessions, we just talked at his comfort level. I learned he listened daily to National Public Radio and was interested and informed on politics, sports, and the news in general; how important his cat Rosie was to him; and that he loved music and had a CD player. Knowing his interests framed the texts we read, although at the beginning—before I had recognized how important it was for him to choose almost all the texts—I was doing the choosing.

It's important to note up front here that we had no technology except our two phones. Ted had never texted, emailed, or touched a computer. I refused to see those factors as unworkable impediments and, instead, chose to consider our "phone only" approach as a challenging opportunity. Also, while we both had iPhones, due to a hill behind my house that interrupts reception, I had to use my land line for our sessions so there was no workable FaceTime, Zoom, or other visual contact. And, of course, because of the raging pandemic, in-person tutoring wasn't possible.

I will explain in detail in Chapter 6 "Championing the Reading/Writing Connection" the how, what, and why of my reading work with Ted, my lesson planning, the importance of his choosing almost all of the texts to read, and the implications for all readers who learn differently and those I have come to call "up-and-coming readers." But for now, I want to focus on expanding the definition of love we've been talking about to also include "tough love." By tough love, I mean pairing and balancing loving concern with strictness with the goal of yielding more responsible actions on the part of the learner. It's important to note that I didn't begin with "tough love." I activated it once our relationship felt trusting and secure. Ted already knew I held high expectations for him, and after a while I believed he was ready to hold those high expectations for himself.

One of the first things with Ted I got "tough" on was showing up for our work looking and feeling ready to go—that is, attending to daily hygiene, dressing, and eating breakfast before we met, even on those days when he felt stressed. We began each of our tutoring sessions with a daily check-in. He would feel the need to talk a bit about what was going on in his life; only after he released some of his anxiety could we start our actual learning work. When I'd been working with Ted for a month or so, in our daily check-in, during our "How are you doing today?", he responded that he was tired, was still in his pajamas, and had not eaten breakfast yet. I suggested he take the time to get ready for our sessions the way I do. "You know, Ted," I told him. "I take our work together seriously even when I'm tired. I've had a shower, eaten breakfast, gotten dressed, combed my hair. I'm ready to go to work." A few days later he texted me right before our scheduled session with a photo of himself fully dressed, looking quite dashing and proud of himself. His text read: "Hey kiddo. I got dressed for you today." I couldn't stop smiling. (Let me add here that a friend of Ted's had just taught him to text by using his voice, something I hadn't thought to do, which made any communicating between sessions easier.)

I also practiced tough love with Ted by holding him accountable for showing up on time. Ted had taken on the responsibility of calling me at 10 AM every Tuesday and Wednesday for our 45-minute sessions, although we had begun with 20-minute sessions and then 30-minute sessions until he built up stamina. I made a big deal of Ted calling me on time and initially thanked him for doing so, but then he began to call a minute late, two minutes late, and as much as five minutes past our agreed-upon 10 AM time, so I said to him, "You know Ted. I set aside this time specifically for you, and I am ready to get to work on time as a matter of respect for you and also because our time together is limited and important. I expect you to be on time every day." Message received. He was never late again, and after many months, he said, "Have you noticed that I'm never late calling you?" to which I replied, "Yes, I have noticed." Enough said. No need to praise him, which I've been known to overdo; his reward was his sense of self-satisfaction coming from his pride of being responsible.

In another instance of "tough love" early on in our sessions, Ted canceled at the last minute. Ten minutes past our scheduled time, he called to say that his beloved cat was sick and that he had to take her to the vet. He was understandably worried. I appreciated his concerns and wished him a good outcome. A week later (when his cat was fine), he called ten minutes past our meeting time to say he was too tired to meet today, that he'd been taking care of his cat and he'd been dealing with some "hard things." To which I replied, "You know, Ted, I'm tired today too. I know life can be hard. It's like that for me too. But we made a commitment to each other, and I expect you to honor that, to show up at our appointed time." After that, he arranged all his appointments, for himself and for his cat, around our scheduled weekly sessions. He just did it, and I never commented on it, but I took it as an indication that he prioritized our sessions together.

While taking a tough love stance worked well for optimizing our working routines, such as honoring our agreed-upon tutoring times and showing up on time, a "tough love" stance was initially problematic when it involved his reading progress—in particular, his preparedness and commitment to improving his reading. After we'd been working together for about six months and Ted was coming unprepared to our sessions more than a couple of times, I took a tough love stance when it was apparent he hadn't "practiced" before our session. Practice meant that he listened to agreed-upon pages in the audiobook we were also reading in print. I said to him, "Your reading isn't going to improve much just because we're meeting together. You've got to spend time on your own listening to the chapter and following along with your eyes. You'll need to do that at least a couple of times or until your reading is smooth." To my surprise and chagrin, he called me five minutes early for our next scheduled session and told me, "My biggest worry with you being all firm is that I'm going to lose you as my teacher." I assured him that would never happen, that I would be his teacher for as long as he liked, that I would always be available to support him. But his words left me heartbroken that I had caused him so much distress. I had not anticipated the impact my words might have in his lifelong, vulnerable area—reading. It made me realize that tough love, especially when sensitive issues are involved, needs to be accompanied with tenderness and carefully chosen words, and that every day—as best we can—we need to be aware of and sensitive to each learner's uniqueness and vulnerabilities in becoming literate.

Truthfully, sometimes "tough love"—related to independent practice— worked to improve Ted's reading and sometimes it didn't, but he did learn that I always knew when he hadn't done his homework and that it was up to him to take his reading more seriously—or not. He also knew, because I told him so, that the reason I held high expectations for him was because he was smart and capable and could progress faster if he put in the practice time between our sessions.

These days Ted is back to working full time at his old job, and we keep in touch, mostly by phone. Working with Ted is a gift that stays with me. While ostensibly I was teaching him, he was also teaching me. He taught me to be a better listener and to think deeply about what mattered most in our sessions together. He taught me patience and gratitude. He showed me what it means to fully "see" the gifts of each person, especially one who learns differently. Our work together grounded me, enriched my life, and added predictability during uncertain times. My deep interest in Ted's welfare and optimal learning took me away from myself and my worries. Teaching does that; the nobleness of our profession is life giving.

Living with so much upheaval and uncertainty has increased the intensity of students' emotions and needs, adding additional challenges and struggles to daily teaching, learning, and living. Educators, families, caregivers—all of us—are exhausted and depleted from coping with increasing emotional and academic demands and expectations while doing our best to provide expert leadership, teaching, and guidance—often with minimal or temporary relief and support. Teachers and students alike are struggling with mental health issues. Online teaching, not seeing friends, and being expected to do more with less have taken a heavy toll. Many students have less academic stamina, have become more attached to their digital and virtual worlds, and are feeling the toll of social distancing and the "ramifications of the Covid years."[1] So it's critical we choose and apply our language, texts, and curriculum with care and sensitivity to our students, families, and all those we hold dear.

The truth is we are all fragile. It is not just learning loss that is at issue but loss of health, loss of life as we knew it, and loss of some predictability about how we can structure our days and live our best lives. As for our underserved students—students of color, students with specialized academic needs, students of poverty, students without stable housing—it's even tougher than usual. Loving all these students means focusing on possibilities instead of limitations and providing support structures and hope for their academic and emotional futures. It means letting go of difference as deficit. It does not mean we work to become superheroes.

If students feel safe and loved and are gaining new knowledge and a measure of independence, then we are doing more than enough. Let me say that again. If we are putting forth our best efforts in teaching and supporting our students to become more capable, thoughtful, and independent as learners and human beings, that has to be enough—even when we are not meeting the needs of all our students and we know we are falling short. We are only human. If we do not also take care of our own health and family, we won't be much good to our students. So, cherished reader, love your students and dear ones as best you can, but also ensure you put aside some time and energy to look after yourself in ways that bring you peace and pleasure. My hope is that reading or listening to this book will encourage and support you to live your life more reasonably, radiantly, and resiliently.

Seeing and celebrating each learner's gifts

So how do we recognize, value, and protect each learner's gifts? First of all, it takes "seeing" each person as fully human and doing our part to ensure their right to equitable and excellent care—educationally, emotionally, mentally, and physically. It takes flexibility, openness, and courage to change course when new, reliable, and valid knowledge becomes available. It also means we teach with the assumption that all kids can learn and that it's our job to find a way in, to reach every child.

We are, each of us, limited by what we "see" and believe. But, I believe, each of us—in our own way—must stand up to power when an injustice causes severe harm. A case in point is the tragic story of the Flint, Michigan, water crisis, powerfully told in *What the Eyes Don't See: A Story of Crisis, Resistance, and Hope in an American City*, by Mona Hanna-Attisha. The book's title comes from a line the author attributes to D. H. Lawrence: "The eyes don't see what the mind doesn't know." Think about that for a moment.

Hanna-Attisha was a pediatrician, "seeing" first-hand the poisonous effects of lead in the city's drinking water on children's brains, but she wasn't taken seriously until she exposed the truth through extensive, irrefutable research. Because city and state officials could not "see" the toxins, they publicly deemed the water safe for consumption. Let's be clear. Indifference, callousness, and racism played a role here as well and, more recently, in a similar crisis in Jackson, Mississippi. Then as now, it was primarily the most vulnerable populations that were impacted—children, minorities, and families living in poverty. Most officials had also chosen not to "see," to turn a blind eye to a lethal, environmental injustice, the systematic neglect that had been going on for years.

In Flint, it was Hanna-Attisha's standing up to power with public proof, documents, overwhelming evidence, and an insistent, clear voice that officials and the public could "see" and understand, that ultimately forced officials to *begin* to rectify the situation. In Jackson, it was national news coverage that finally opened the nation's eyes and conscience to an appalling disregard for a human right—safe drinking water. Think about what that means for how we live our lives and perceive and interact with others. If we don't know why a person is behaving in an unusual way or have knowledge of that person's background and living conditions, what we glean about the person, issue, or situation is limited and constrained.

"The eyes don't see what the mind doesn't know." I've thought a lot about what that statement means for our students and loved ones and how inflexible and rigid attitudes, accompanied by low expectations, limit possibilities and progress. That's why deep, professional learning that respects and honors each learner's strengths and interests is so vital. When we get locked into following a script or rigid program, when we adopt a mindset focused on limitations, we make it less likely we will tap into each learner's gifts and possibilities. Here's a personal example of how not seeing and valuing a person's unique talent can stymy health and progress.

When my dad was transported by medical air ambulance from a New York City hospital to a rehabilitation hospital in Seattle after a severe stroke, he had to learn to speak all over again. Among the specialists he saw regularly was a speech therapist who saw him daily. My dad, who was then only saying a couple of words, was expected to repeat back short phrases and short sentences, exactly as spoken by the therapist. None of this made any sense to my dad; I suspect he found the program beneath his intelligence. It wasn't exactly that he refused to cooperate; he couldn't see the purpose of the exercises, so his efforts were lackluster. One day, out of the blue when I was talking to my dad, he came out with a one-liner, a funny joke. I was ecstatic and could hardly wait to tell the speech therapist, who was unimpressed as indicated by his stern look and response: "He needs to follow the program I have him on. I am not interested in jokes." My heart sunk. I tried to explain that showing a sense of humor was a sign of cognition and intelligence. My dad continued to tell short jokes, mostly one-liners, and I knew then he was mentally okay. That was his old spirit kicking in. Being a joke teller was part of who he was. I encouraged Dad to "show off" and tell a couple of his jokes to the therapist, thinking the therapist would finally see my father's competence, but he never did. He kept on with his program and my dad kept on with being disengaged.

My father, in essence, was being punished for his divergent thinking. His therapist withheld any praise or support for Dad's sense of humor and individuality. Only the right-answer response the therapist held was considered of value. Sadly, this is too often the case for many of our students, especially those who are marginalized and attend under-resourced schools, that is, schools where professional learning is not a priority, where implicit bias and low expectations prevail, and where programs substitute for a curriculum that meets the interests and needs of all learners. Human beings don't fit neatly into a program, nor should we want them to. What makes us human is our uniqueness, and we need to seek out and value the gifts each one of us has. But too often we are expected to follow a prescribed program without deviation. Never mind that some students don't benefit much, and for these students they're not learning very much. Never mind that some are being turned off to learning, perhaps for the long term. Even when a program is required, think of it as a tool, a framework to be tinkered with, to suit the needs of your population. Anything less is malpractice. Each and every student deserves the dignity and respect of being truly "seen."

One of my favorite stories of "seeing" involves my dearest friend Harriet, whom I've known and loved since our college days. She gave birth to Seth, her first child, when she was 24 years old. It was a normal pregnancy, so it was a shock to learn that her son was a child with Down Syndrome. She was devastated and cried nonstop for days; her grief penetrated to her soul. This was 55 years ago, and the first thing Harriet's doctor told her after the birth was that she would need to institutionalize her son. To which she replied, "I don't know what world you're living in, but it's not my world. Seth is not going into an institution." Despite that stated conviction, Harriet felt hopeless and without a plan. And that's when a kind nurse stepped in and showed a glimpse of what the future could be for Seth. The nurse showed Harriet a photo of an adorable, pigtailed, kindergarten student holding a book and sitting in a room with other students. The little girl was a child with Down Syndrome, and she was the daughter of the nurse. And just like that, Harriet could "see" possibilities instead of limitations. She realized she had a choice, and she decided to do something positive with that choice. Her expectations and actions on Seth's behalf went from nothing is possible to everything may be possible.

Today, kids and adults with Down Syndrome do what other people do—participate in sports, travel, work, use a cellphone, drive, enjoy their lives to the fullest. And this is largely true for Seth as well. He lives in a small group home with Chuck, Harriet's special-needs brother whom Seth grew up with. He adores his Uncle Chuck, his mom, and his whole big, loving family, along with Sandy who is his group home manager. They all adore him right back and love spending time with him. He is funny, sweet, kind, and sees the world in uncomplicated ways. He has been an inspiration and joy to all who know him. Harriet says he is her easiest and happiest child and always makes her smile. She calls him "my shining light."

"If you can't envision the possibilities, it's not going to happen." That's what Harriet told me when we recently spoke. It's as true for dealing with health issues and how we live our lives as it is for teaching kids. If we believe the best that we can give our students is a one-size-fits-all program, or if we go along with that dictum, our students are not going to reach their full potential. If we believe that students need an instructional assistant with them at every moment in order to stay focused, we are saying this student is not capable. If we believe that students can't handle choice in their reading and writing, we deny them a full range of genres, authors, history, and cultures. When we don't see a person's gifts, we limit what's possible. We stymie their achievement. We take away their human rights.

So dear reader and listener, ask yourself this question, with a particular student or loved one in mind: "What are they good at?" and, if the answer to that question is not obvious, then search, look hard, and ask yourself: "What *might* they be good at?" if we have the will to provide tailored guidance, support, and encouragement. Once teachers and our loved ones "see," value, and capitalize on each learner's unique talents and strengths, it changes them—and us. Possibilities override limitations. Pride of accomplishment replaces failure. Effort leads to excellence. Joy is present, the best gift of all.

Showing the love—and expanding our definition of love

L et's expand our definition of love to embrace the diversity of learners and the belief that all learners are curious, capable, and want to learn. Then, an essential part of our work includes providing, as best we can, safe learning spaces that include acceptance, trust, and kindness. It also means, as we've been discussing, finding each learner's unique gifts and celebrating them. Love also means disrupting the poverty of low expectations that pervades many schools and classrooms, and letting go of the pandemic as an excuse for students falling behind.

Learning loss has always been a factor in urban education and in areas where kids have been historically underserved. It's just more obvious now. So it's important we focus not on the loss but on what we can do, right now, in this moment to create a love for learning that sparks effort and excellence, that we create possibilities learners might not yet see for themselves, and that we instill hope for a promising future.

Scholar and researcher P. David Pearson wisely notes:

> A teacher's job is always to bridge from the known to the new. There really is no other choice.
>
> > Kids are who they are.
> > They know what they know.
> > They bring what they bring.
>
> Wishing that they know something more or something different won't make it so. Our job as teachers is to help them transform what they bring into curricular resources rather than instructional inconveniences.

There are so many ways we can let students and their families know how much we care about them and how much we are committed to their success and wellbeing. There are lots of options and actions we can take that reduce stress, provide equitable learning opportunities, and accelerate learning. Many such actions and tips are relatively easy to implement. I'm a big believer in simplicity—not making things simple, but making things manageable and worthwhile for all parties involved.

First of all, beginning with a strengths-based perspective is paramount. That means seeing each learner—whether student, teacher, or leader—through a positive lens. So often we see through a deficit lens. Certainly, that was true for me when I began teaching. I focused on learners' weaknesses and needs before their strengths and interests. I did not first see the learner in front of me from a strengths-based stance. It wasn't until I became a Reading Recovery teacher and learned to notice, name, and notate what the student could do that my mindset began to shift. If the student could only write the first letter of his name, that's what I wrote down. I did not write down all the things he could *not yet* do. It was a hard habit to break. I was so used to needs-based recording and thinking. That mind shift to first noticing, appreciating, and celebrating what the learner could do eventually carried over into all my relationships and made me a better and more empathetic companion, colleague, and teacher. That new mindset also helped me ditch the label a learner had been given—with its accompanying, deficit-based identifiers—and truly see each learner's uniqueness in front of me.

Establishing relationships that respect the dignity, culture, language, interests, and strengths of the learner—as we've discussed earlier in this chapter with my getting to know Ted—is not a difficult thing to do. If we make it a priority, we can make it happen. We must make it happen. One of the ways we can forge connections and a sense of belonging is by sharing our stories and honoring learners' stories, which is the focus of the next chapter. Students who feel that we know them and care about them are likely to be more engaged in learning. Trusting relationships anchor a healthy and thriving classroom and school culture. Without that trust, learning is likely to be compromised and limited. As well, a focus on learners' social-emotional wellbeing, even as we focus on academic learning, is a necessity. Loving care is what we all need first and foremost.

Honoring students' names is an easy way to show respect, which is crucial to students' sense of wellbeing. Students learn better and feel better emotionally when we say their names correctly, and that includes calling students by their preferred names and pronouns. I am sensitive to pronouncing names correctly as my name Regie is often mispronounced as "Reggie" instead of "Regee." I tell students, "If I mispronounce your name, please tell me. Saying your name correctly is important to me. It's a sign of respect for who you are." Also, as much as is feasible, greet students by name in a brief, daily check-in, even just a simple "Hello, James" or "Good Morning, Laticia" or "Hi, Carla." Every interaction we have with a child matters.

Actively listening to our students and our loved ones is a precious and necessary gift, whether the person talking is 5 or 50. If we want to know and truly "see" our students and develop mutual understandings, we need to make a conscious and respectful effort to actively listen to what they are saying and not saying—and to limit teacher talk. If we are instead thinking about what we're going to say next, and I have certainly been guilty here, we cannot give full attention to the speaker's words and the meaning behind those words. There are simple actions we can take as active listeners to contribute to a speaker's comfort and trust level, such as remaining undistracted, occasionally nodding our heads, leaning in, or just offering a smile.

Related to smiles, there's a difference between mouth smilers and eye smilers; you can fake a mouth smile, but an eye smile is the real deal. One of the surprises of wearing masks during the pandemic and beyond is how I have noticed eye smilers. I bet you have too. The eyes have a sparkle; they seem to light up; there might also be a crinkling just below or beside the eyes. You instinctively grasp that the smile is genuine and that it's meant for you. It's one of the things I love best about my husband Frank. He has always been an eye smiler.

Practicing radical empathy is another way to show love. Being deliberately aware of other people's realities, actively noticing and listening to another person's situation with understanding, and taking action to support that person goes beyond just empathy to what is called radical empathy. Mental health issues among children, teenagers, and adults have greatly increased. Many of us and those we hold dear have experienced anxiety, depression, grief, and confusion. Understanding how fragile so many of us are means extending as much loving-kindness and support as we can muster to colleagues, students, and their families.

Honoring students as intellectuals means we assume they are capable of understanding complex texts and concepts *if* we provide the necessary supports and encouragement—relevance, background information, reading texts aloud, reading texts together—and lots of opportunities to scaffold conversations with students to optimize their understanding. (See page 154 for specifics on scaffolded conversations.) Sadly, I have never been in a school where expectations are too high. Almost without exception, and especially in high needs schools, educators often equate poverty with low expectations for what students can learn and accomplish. What are we doing to find our students' gifts and to mentor them to take on intellectual endeavors? I never thought of myself as an education scholar until I had written many thoroughly-researched books. Looking back, I now realize that writing was my way to prove to myself I was smart, at least in that one area.

Creating a love for learning is one way to ensure we maximize student and teacher learning. Provide more choice and agency over their learning. Find out what students are passionate about and carve out time for students to follow that passion. Make school assignments relevant, reasonable, and timely. Be sensitive to tasks, such as giving assignments that require technology and Wi-Fi when access might be lacking. That includes homework, where the research has been clear and consistent for decades. Homework is appropriate for practicing what has already been taught. It is not appropriate to expect parents and caretakers to be available or able to help students.

Personalizing the learning and the learning space makes it easier to do "the work." As is manageable, permit students to personalize their spaces like most of us do. My desk in the room where I write has photos, shells, small objects, and personal mementos on it, which comfort me during the hard act of writing. For example, I have a beautiful hand painted mug, a gift from my favorite aunt, where I house my pencils and pens; I have a hand-crafted, tiny blue elephant from a generous colleague; I have a few Post-it Notes on the wall with wise statements on living a full life. Take a look at your space, whether it's at home or at work. What can you do to make it cozier, friendlier, and provide a sense of calm? Even if students are moving from classroom to classroom each day, consider allowing them to keep a small, favorite object with them.

Giving students all the information they need to be informed participants in our complex world is another way of letting our students and their families know we will equitably and lovingly educate each one of them. Preparing them well for their future is an obligation. Being an informed citizen means we understand history and its lessons, we can think critically, participate in meaningful conversations, communicate clearly, and demonstrate empathy and compassion for others. More about all that in our discussion of "Pursuing truth through literature" in Chapter 2 and "Curriculum as conversation" in Chapter 3.

Doing less testing is another way to love our students; not everything important can be measured. Anxiety levels for many of us are higher these days, in part due to learning disruptions in the pandemic and beyond, more family stress, and more uncertainty about life in general. Tests can add pressure to students' wellbeing, even for those of us who are "good" students. For example, when I was in middle school, I remember feeling sick before any kind of a big test despite the fact that I was an "excellent" student according to my grades. Nonetheless, I developed stomach pains on the day of the test and would tell my parents I didn't feel well enough to go to school. I never told them, then or as an adult, that it was the looming test that made me so anxious I literally felt sick to my stomach. As well, some of us are just poor test takers. I'm one of them as reflected by my less than stellar SAT scores.

Also, instead of formal tests, let's provide more formative assessments and give students second chances and opportunities. Focus less on data, grading, and late homework, and more on the quality of the work that is eventually turned in. Kindness, flexibility, and understanding do encourage us, our colleagues, and our students to do better work. And, speaking of second chances, consider giving more leeway for when tasks need to be done. Our son Peter was a big procrastinator. I got tired of reminding him to mow the lawn every week. So, I made it easier for him by allowing that as long as he successfully completed the task by the end of the weekend, before sunset, that was acceptable. And, no surprise, he waited until the last minute, but he always got the job done well. This was true for his school assignments as well.

Giving more choices in everything—room layout, assignments, rubrics, seating, required reading and writing—can be game changing. Do provide more choices, for example, in organizing the classroom library, in topics to be studied, and in presenting "the work." Much of giving choice is what I call "choice within structure," that is, there are specific parameters; it's not just anything goes. Giving students choice is a way of sharing the power and giving the message, "This is our classroom and learning space" and not "This is my classroom and teaching space." For students whose complex lives don't allow much agency or control, choice provides dignity, freedom, and expanded opportunities.

Providing feedback—information on how we are doing to reach a clear goal—is a necessity for affirming learners and supporting them as they move forward. The language we use here is paramount. Giving specific feedback that is welcome, timely, useful, and actionable is an artform and an act of love that requires great skill and care. For example, in writing this book, my editor kept her initial feedback to focusing on the big ideas and highlighting the specific, memorable language I used to get those ideas across to the reader. That allowed and encouraged me to have the energy to keep on writing. Then, once we were both confident the material was solid and readable, we delved into the nitty-gritty details, which I was now ready to handle with gusto. Too often, and I've been guilty here myself, our quickness to critique and suggest improvements—before acknowledging strengths and efforts—can discourage learners from risk taking and applying best efforts.

How we use language in everyday events and in giving feedback is also paramount for setting a positive, aspirational, and equitable tone in the classroom and in our lives. Agreeing on acceptable and welcome conversation is paramount. My husband Frank and I have learned over the years that a peaceful start to the day sets a positive tone that often determines how the day will go. To that end, we do our best to make breakfast a problem-free zone with no talk of "ills and bills," annoyances, or personal grievances. We savor our coffee, read the newspaper, and enjoy our breakfast. In the same way, we want to positively start our workdays by greeting students and colleagues by name and with positive language. Again, the start to the day matters. "So good to see you" and "Glad you're here today" can be easier on someone having a bad day than "How are you?" which can compel some of us to say "fine" when we're not so fine.

Giving second chances promotes resilience. To ensure students turn in their best work and efforts, make it possible for them to redo something, have a deadline extended, or retake a test. Every one of us needs to have some sense of fulfillment and purpose, to know that our contributions—no matter how small—matter in this life, and that if we "mess up" we will be given another chance. I subscribe to an apprenticeship-based view of learning, that is, "Do the best you can. I'll help you with the rest." See, also, in Chapter 10, "Fostering Resilience." Also, related to giving second chances are disciplinary measures. Let's keep in mind that some students who are acting out or not doing the work may be hungry, sleep deprived, depressed, and/or overwhelmed. When possible, try showing the love—meeting the student with compassion and empathy even as a punitive measure might be necessary.

All of what we've been talking about in this section, "Showing the love—and expanding our definition of love" promotes social and emotional wellbeing, which must be an integral part of all teaching, learning, and living—not separate from it. In addition to thinking about meeting academic goals, let's think about how we can support and affirm students so that what happens in school and in class elevates learners' sense of self, efficacy, and wellbeing. Not only that. The attitudes, actions, and tips just discussed can help build a promising intellectual and social-emotional foundation upon which every student feels cherished, seen, and eager to learn. Isn't that what we all want for every learner?

CHAPTER 2
Telling Our Stories

- ❖ Telling our stories—and validating our lives
- ❖ Creating a storytelling culture
- ❖ Pursuing truth through literature

DOI: 10.4324/9781003381242-2

Telling our stories—and validating our lives

Every life is a memoir of love, loss, and longing. Who gets to tell our story, how the story gets told, and what is included or excluded has the power to influence and determine our worth, our dreams, our safety, and our future. The stories we hear, tell, discover, and believe shape our lives in ways that are visible and invisible. Who gets to determine our truth? Who helps uncover it or keep it buried? Who celebrates or denigrates our story? Stories seem especially important now as the world seems in chaos, uncertainty, and fear—so much of it out of our control. We all have a primal need to create stories to make sense of our lives, to give a narrative to the good as well as to the despair and uncertainty.

I believe it is our job as educators and family members to validate the uniqueness of each child's life and to believe in our heart and mind that our students come to us with valuable resources—their culture, their knowledge, their language, their stories. Neurologist and naturalist Oliver Sacks writes:

> We have, each of us, a life-story, an inner narrative—whose community, whose sense, *is* our lives. It might be said that each of us constructs and lives, a "narrative," and that narrative *is* us, our identities... Biologically, physiologically, we are all not so different from each other: historically, as narratives—we are each of us unique.[1]

In my family, my parents decided my story. The narrative they laid out for me was this one: I would go to college primarily to find a husband. I would study to become a teacher or a nurse, as "something to fall back on." My main purpose in life would be as a full-time wife and mother—like my mom. I never questioned that story until I was in my 20s, married with two young children, and feeling at loose ends. I wanted more. I loved my husband and kids, but I needed to do something for me, something that engaged my intellect as well as my heart. I set out to change my life story, to rewrite the script of my life. That re-storying was the beginning of my journey to becoming a more confident woman, one willing to risk conflict and discomfort to achieve personal and professional goals.

I went back to college and got a Master's degree in Education as a reading specialist and teacher of students with learning disabilities. I got a part-time job in a high poverty school tutoring students who were failing to thrive as readers. When a full-time reading specialist position became available at that school, I was offered the job and I took it. Not surprisingly for the times, my husband shared the same beliefs my parents did, that a woman's place was in the home taking care of him and the children. So as you might imagine, changing my story—without his permission or approval—caused a rift and a reckoning that was deeply uncomfortable for us both. To his everlasting credit, he opened his heart and mind to gradually transition from a fixed story of our how we would live our lives to a fluid and equitable story, one that came to value my work and goals alongside his own. He came to experience and believe I could be a loving wife and mother—and work outside of the home. Eventually, my guy not only accepted my full-time working and all the exciting places my teaching and writing career has taken me, but he also became (and has remained) my biggest and most devoted champion.

The messages and stories we hear, receive, and perceive, as young children and throughout our lives, reside deep within us and have the power to restrain us, sustain us, and/or help us soar. In some ways, I am still working to reclaim my story. Not being encouraged to see possibilities for my own life story slowed my growing into maturity and wholeness. Because my parents' expectations for me were so minimal, I sold myself short. It took me a long time to develop enough confidence to become the author of my own story, to make my voice heard, to find the courage to take a stand on important issues, to write and speak out publicly.

I grew up being told who I was, not just at home but also at school, where teachers complimented me for my neat handwriting, my ability to get along with others, and for getting my work done well and on time. I don't ever remember being celebrated for my uniqueness or even thinking about it. Perhaps that's why I have few vivid memories of schooling and why I feel so strongly about the need and hunger for stories in all aspects of our lives. Think: What can I do to help this child, student, person, or loved one value, revise, affirm, and set right their life story, and, ultimately, to provide hope for a bright, future story? Stories have the potential to make our lives more orderly, manageable—and even beautiful.

One thing we can all do is ensure our children and students have the opportunity to listen to, read, and write stories that validate who they are—their lives, their families, their culture, language, histories. As Rudine Sims Bishop, Professor Emeritus at Ohio State University, famously wrote many years ago, the stories and books that are available to learners must be "mirrors, windows, and sliding glass doors" so that children see themselves reflected in stories and can look through, see, and enter other worlds that may be unknown to them. Bishop notes that the diversity of stories is not just important for marginalized children but for all children. We know the stories that children hear and read impact their self-worth, how they view others, and what they intuit that may or may not be possible for them. Many stories that children have the opportunity to read can be written by the children themselves and become part of a diverse classroom library. Their own stories in familiar language are easy and engaging to read.

I have no memories of being read to as a child, and I did not become an avid reader until I was in my late teens, inspired by books my grandmother read aloud to me. However, the stories I treasured most were the ones my grandmother told me. I regularly stayed overnight in her small apartment, and she regaled me with tales from her past. Many of her stories she had written down, often on scraps of paper she kept in a cardboard box. I can still picture her taking the tattered box down from her closet and reading aloud snippets of her life. She hoped one day to publish those stories but lacked the confidence, repeatedly telling me, "I'm not a real writer." But of course she was! Like our students and us, she just needed someone to encourage her that those stories mattered, not just to her but also to others.

One story that left a deep impression on me was how she did not have the courage to marry the penniless man she passionately loved but married my grandfather instead, a kind and successful businessman, only to lose him to cancer—and to lose all his money, as well, during the Great Depression. As a young widow and mother of three daughters, she worked at various jobs to make ends meet—mostly as a milliner who made and sold beautiful hats, and also as a talented jewelry designer and seller of her stunning creations. Although she had dropped out of school in 6th grade to help support her family—her parents and six sisters—she was a born entrepreneur. I loved listening to my grandmother's stories; those stories were a way into her life, and I felt privileged she shared them with me.

When our students enter our schools, do we seek out and celebrate their stories, their culture, their identities, their history, their families? Do we make stories central to our and their historical and personal curriculum? Do we honor the storyteller and their stories? And if not, why not? Are we using stories to help them reclaim their lives? Do we value the tradition of oral storytelling, now popularized through podcasts, interviews, and audiobooks, and bring these into our lives and into the classroom?

Storytelling and stories can also bring a community—at school, in the classroom, in the workplace—together in a way that creates a safer, happier, more productive space. Along with ensuring a viable curriculum and safe space for all students, we need to help students envision and develop a life story of what's possible for them. I had no help with that, and neither do many of our students. All the more reason that we must make diverse and culturally relevant libraries the center of our classrooms, schools, and communities. Students and our children need to feel—and stories play an outsize role here—that they are smart enough, beautiful enough, worthy enough. We need to find ways for them and us to tell our stories through personal narratives, journals, podcasts, videos, music with lyrics, raps, hip-hop, poetry, plays, dance, graphic texts, sketch-noting, photographs, illustrations, photo montages, wordless books, multimedia, original formats, and other venues. One way we love our students and create a trusting, empathetic culture is to hear our students' stories—and provide some choice in the way they tell them— and to see the world through their eyes and experiences. To be seen and heard is to be validated.

To begin, keep the storytelling process simple by having students write about topics such as "What's most important about me?" or "What do I do really well?" or "What do I want you to know about me?" Open ended topics like these allow a lot of leeway and choice in what students choose to reveal—or not. Of course, you'll want to first do your thinking-writing demonstration aloud on one of these topics, or something similar, in front of your students.

An interesting footnote on creating stories: It's been fascinating to observe how television has become a powerhouse for developing and promoting original podcasts and podcast series on all manner of topics connected to history, biography, original stories, and much more. Keith Morrison, veteran correspondent for *Dateline*, notes:

> When we figured out how to do it, by golly, it was just a delight— maybe that's the wrong word to use for murder mysteries… But doing these stories via podcast has been more pleasurable than most things I've done in my ridiculously long career.[2]

Podcasts are perfect for the school and classroom. In making their own podcasts, students can add music, sound effects, and other flourishes as they write, rewrite, and practice their content message before recording their podcast for their audience. All the researching, writing, rereading, and revising required to make an excellent podcast expand learners' literacy skills and knowledge.

For our marginalized students and students who grew up economically and/or emotionally challenged, stories are a way in to "seeing" and "seeking" new possibilities in school and in life. That is as true for us as teachers and adult learners as it is for our students. When I wrote *Literacy Essentials: Engagement, Excellence, and Equity for All Learners*, it was important to me to integrate personal and professional stories into the text, to make stories as necessary to the text as they are to living a full and happy life. Literacy, learning, and living are intertwined; they always have been. It has been telling, writing, and recording those stories that have helped me to appreciate the intersection of my professional and personal lives and to see myself more fully, to use my stories to define and to re-define myself. Just as we teach the whole child, it is the whole teacher our students want and cherish. It took me a long time to believe my stories mattered, but my grandmother's storytelling voice was whispering in my ear, "You can do this. You need to do this." And you, dear reader, can do this too. No one has told your story in your own voice, speaking your truths.

Our lived experiences and those of our students matter—a lot. Stories validate us, humanize us, help us make sense of our lives, and show us what might be possible. Telling our stories is an act of bravery, celebration, and hope. As Toni Morrison poignantly says:

> The theme you choose may change or simply elude you, but being your own story means you can always choose the tone. It also means that you can invent the language to say who you are and what you mean. But then, I am a teller of stories and therefore an optimist, a believer in the ethical bend of the human heart, a believer in the mind's disgust with fraud and its appetite for truth, a believer in the ferocity of beauty. So, from my point of view, which is that of a storyteller, I see your life as already artful, waiting, just waiting and ready for you to make it art.

Stories are all about the human condition. Stories allow us to be vulnerable, to be seen, to affirm our uniqueness, and to heal our wounds and trauma. We need to empower students, family, and friends to honor and tell their stories and to reclaim their life story. Personal storytelling is uniquely positioned to support the social-emotional growth that plays a pivotal role in preparing students for life readiness, whether that be college, career, or some self-chosen endeavor. Importantly, our stories invite us to become the authors of our own lives.

Jason Reynolds, award-winning author of novels and poetry for middle grades and young adults, says, "I get an opportunity to write Black kids into the world." In a CBS interview with Jane Pauley, he encourages students to embrace their stories:

> To me, reading becomes a lot more palatable if young people realize that the stories/the books that exist within them are as valuable as the books that exist on the outside of them, and we have to be able to imagine stories that don't exist.

For some terrific ideas and inspiration on storytelling, see, listen to, and read award-winning author Chimamanda Ngozi Adiche, including her TED Talk, "The danger of a single story," and founder of Story Corps, Dave Isey, including his TED Talk, "Everyone around you has a story the world needs." For great guidelines and resources, including podcasts, see *The Moth* (themoth.org), an international, non-profit organization dedicated to the art and craft of storytelling. Their books, *How to Tell a Story* (2022), *Occasional Magic: True Stories About Defying the Impossible* (2019), and *All These Wonders: True Stories About Facing the Unknown* (2017) are outstanding educational resources, especially for older students and adults. So is StoryCorpsU, a terrific program for guiding middle and high school students to tell their stories through an interview process.[3]

Even as we follow required standards and curriculum, our primary job must be to find a way in, to use each student's strengths and interests to provide hope for their futures. The pandemic and its aftermath have been life-altering for all of us, but for those students whose lives were already filled with trauma, I believe we're compelled as responsible educators to reorder our teaching and our lives and to pay attention to their stories. Focusing on learning loss is not productive. This is the time to practice radical empathy, to lovingly care for people, to seek out their gifts and their strengths. This is the time to listen to, validate, and encourage stories.

Students—and all of us who live and breathe—need to know that our lives matter, that we are uniquely human, and that change is possible. Telling our stories acknowledges who we are as we speak truths to our setbacks and our successes, our heartbreak, and our hopes. In doing so we affirm and celebrate our past, current, and future selves with heightened self-awareness, courage, and dignity. Storytelling is distinctively suited to these worthy ends. And to new beginnings.

Creating a storytelling culture

When our granddaughters entered their teenage years, there were times we became invisible to them. We would walk into their home on invitation from their parents, and the girls would physically see us, but it was as if we weren't there. They would walk right by us without acknowledging our presence. Or they would hear our voices but remain upstairs until one of their parents said, "Grandma and Papa" are here. Only then would they dutifully come downstairs, offer a brief "Hi" and disappear. None of this is unusual behavior for a teen, but it was disconcerting. We had a close relationship with these two darling girls, and it felt like we were losing it. They didn't talk on the phone, and they didn't do email. They texted; I learned to text as a way to communicate with them, but our texting was infrequent and limiting. What to do?

I created what we still call "coffee and conversation" even though I was the coffee drinker, and they mostly drank tea. Every couple of months, I would arrange a separate, one-on-one meeting with each granddaughter. At the end of a school day, I would pick up my granddaughter at an agreed upon location close to their high school. We'd head off to a nearby café or coffee house, where we'd put devices away, sip our drinks, enjoy a pastry, and just talk. Genuine, back and forth conversation where they told me about their lives, and we connected on a personal level. At first, the conversations were mostly reporting of happenings—what was going on in their classes, how band practice was going (one played piano; one played the violin), how much homework they had, who their friends were, and what they were doing as a family. But eventually as we both grew more comfortable with these get togethers, stories—theirs and mine—became the heart of our conversations. This became especially true once each granddaughter went off to college and chose to continue our conversations, coffee cups in hand, via Zoom.

For example, they might tell a story of a tough time they were having with a friend. I might tell a story from my life that related to their issue. I tried to avoid giving direct advice; I used the story to help them see possibilities for the decision or actions they might decide to take—or not. We still talked a lot about their classes, what they were learning and thinking about, and also about their hopes and dreams. We talked about the books we were reading and made book recommendations to each other. As they matured, they increasingly wanted to know what I was up to and how their Papa (who occasionally dropped in for a "guest appearance") was doing.

After her freshman year in college, I asked Brooke what she most strongly remembers and values from our "coffee and conversations." I had no idea what she might say; without hesitation she elaborated on two life stories—one mine, one hers—that still resonate for her.

> A few years ago, you told me the story about a divisive family incident in your life and how a fiction book you read mirrored your experience and provided perspective. As a young person still trying to figure things out, it made me feel special to learn something so significant in your life and, also, that we weren't just talking about my life.

> And then recently, when I was having difficulty with one of my suite mates and feeling trapped by my anger, it was very comforting to hear you say that I'm not crazy for feeling angry but that anger might not be serving me well, that it might end up hurting me more than anyone else. I saw I had a choice in what actions I might take. By using context from your life, you were able to then give me that advice and connect it to my current issue.

I asked Katie the same question. She spoke about how the sharing of personal stories helped her see some of those closest to her as fully, actualized people, beyond "mom as mom, and grandparents as grandma and grandpa."

Sharing our stories made me see parallels in my own life. I learned who you and Papa are, not just as grandparents but as friends and mentors, people in my life who have been through things like everybody else. Those extended conversations, when you can learn about each other—humanizing persons in all their complexities—is, I think, a pretty beautiful thing.

To be clear, I have included this story to show how setting the stage for genuine conversations can lift the level of talk and bring closeness between people of all ages. In particular, when we share our stories with our friends and loved ones, we have the opportunity to see them—and have them see us—in new and genuine ways. Getting to know each other through stories and conversations makes teaching and learning more effective and joyful. In my residency work in classrooms, where I am demonstrating and coaching for both students and teachers, I always introduce myself with stories from my life as well as stories I read aloud from enchanting picture books—stories that delight, inform, and celebrate our diversity. I also read aloud and share stories and books related to the content we are teaching, studying, and learning about.

We took "coffee and conversation" to a new storytelling level when we brought our granddaughters on vacation with us one summer. We drove from Seattle to a beachside village on the Oregon coast, a spot Frank and I loved that we wanted to share with them. The accommodations were modest and comfortable. The beach was walkable and beautiful; the kitchen was outfitted for cooking; free bikes and free movies were available; and the sunsets were spectacular.

A jolting surprise was that the 14-year-old's most cherished companion on our vacation was her cell phone—never out of reach and almost always in use. She was physically present but emotionally absent. That's when I created "cocktail hour" before dinner: "wonderful drinks for everyone, special appetizers, telling stories, and no devices allowed."

I pulled out all the stops telling a riveting story that surprised and impressed the girls. But when encouraged to tell their own stories, at first, they said, "We don't have any stories." But slowly and with encouragement, they each began to tell a story, and over the years, returning with them to this favorite spot, the stories became integral to our time together. I can still picture Brooke on the beach just before sunset one night, dramatically and in unsparing detail, going all out to express how and why she detested her first and only camp experience. We laughed until the tears came down.

Storytelling has to be modeled. My grandmother did that for me. She regaled me with tales from her life, stories I cherish and remember to this day. We need to do the same for our own children and students. Regardless of the age of the learners, telling our stories can go a long way to ensuring a heart and mind connection with others, necessary for understanding and empathizing with others' lived lives and experiences. The power of stories has the potential to deepen literacy learning, humanize us, and give enhanced meaning to our lives.

Start your own storytelling with stories you know will appeal to your audience and that will also give learners ideas for their own writing. Students of all ages have loved my stories of Norman, a female cat (go figure) who roamed our neighborhood when we first moved into our Seattle home. While the cat was technically homeless, several neighbors let us know the cat "belonged" with the house—and the implied message, "That cat belongs to you." That message was punctuated by the enormous bag of cat food the former owners left us in the otherwise empty kitchen. Neither my husband Frank nor I like cats, so we quickly dismissed cat-owner possibility. And yet, it was late November, and the days and nights were cold. We worried about the cat.

My kind-hearted husband was especially concerned. He added a heating pad and one of his old sweaters to the plastic box just outside our kitchen door, where Norman was used to sleeping. Frank was also worried that the regular, dry cat food we were giving Norman was too boring a diet, so he augmented her diet with a packed in oil, gourmet tuna fish. Slowly, over many months, we fell in love with Norman and got used to her antics, including her occasional walk-abouts where she would disappear for a couple of days. Eventually, our acceptance was total. She sat on my lap when I ate breakfast each morning. I petted a cat for the first time in my life—and enjoyed it. She eventually became an indoor cat who had the run of our place, including settling herself for most of the day on our off-white couch. Who would have thought?

When I tell my Norman stories, and there are many, I pull out all the stops. Just as when I read aloud, I make storytelling a performance. We tend to remember performances, whether it's live theatre or a dramatic reading of a book. And, if we want students to feel free and encouraged to tell their stories, we need to model that by sharing some of our own and using those stories to jumpstart storytelling in the classroom.

As appropriate, I also tell stories of tough times—stories of struggle, hope, and resilience, and stories where things didn't turn out so well. Life can be hard. Endurance takes courage, energy, and loving support. Listening to, reading, or telling a heart and mind story—and then making time and space for conversation—help build a thriving storytelling culture.

Use storytelling to bond with your colleagues. It's easier to build trusting relationships when we take time to get to know each other. Not just professionally, but personally too. A team-building activity that is non-threatening and enjoyable, plus has the potential to improve the culture and comfort of your workplace, is to take a bit of time and have colleagues write "One small thing my colleagues don't know about me." I model that first by talking about a few light-hearted possibilities: I eat handfuls of semi-sweet chocolate chips every day; I don't own a pair of sneakers, except for playing tennis; I haven't bought a new item of clothing since the pandemic began. Each of these particulars has an accompanying story, upon which I elaborate. Then I choose one to write about.

Teachers have written about riding a motorcycle for relaxation and enjoyment, being famous in their family for homemade pecan pie, and taking ballroom dancing lessons at the age of 50—to name just a few stories that have emerged. It only takes about 20 minutes for each member of the group to write their short story, which are usually not more than a paragraph or two. Teachers are given a few days to revise and turn in a word-processed copy, along with a photo headshot, to a teacher volunteer who binds it all into a booklet, in which each teacher has their own page. Knowing each other better, even in these small ways, is reassuring and helps bind people together. We are all human; we all have stories to tell.

While the audience for "One small thing my colleagues don't know about me" is our fellow colleagues, we have also done similar booklets—"What's most important to know about (fill in name of staff member)"—where the audience is parents, caregivers, and/or families new to the school. This is a powerful welcome to the school, and most often custodians, secretaries, and support staff are also included here. Teachers might also choose to include students as a part of that audience. Of course, writing with a specific audience in mind changes the content, language, and tone, and writers become aware of that and adjust accordingly. Several copies of the completed booklets are kept on hand in the principal's office and are always in demand. In particular, when students are part of the intended audience, they love reading about—and getting to know—all the teachers and staff at their school. Something similar could be done by students for their classmates once you and they co-establish guidelines and model the process.

A storytelling culture includes putting stories at the center of the curriculum, and most of these stories will have been written by fiction and nonfiction writers, essayists, journalists, poets, opinion writers, biographers, historians, scientists, and more—and will include both professional and student writers and illustrators. We don't yet live in a post-racial society, so we need to create spaces and places where all people feel safe to tell their stories and have choice and access to reading stories by diverse authors. In the next chapter, "Promoting Equitable Opportunities," we will discuss hearing all the voices, curriculum as conversation, book banning and censorship, and a story about a school district's integration efforts that were life-changing for many.

Pursuing truth through literature

Beyond our personal stories that are integral to literacy, learning, and living a good life, stories of our past history are necessary for making the present more equitable and for ensuring a good life is possible for all of us. History and all life, after all, are about his-story, her-story, and their-story. Who tells the story and whether or not the teller is a reliable narrator make all the difference in the "truths" we receive. Stories shape facts and impact our understanding of reality, so it's imperative we have trustworthy narrators, a challenging ask in today's times where social media, media literacy, and news outlets cannot always be relied on as accurate sources.

Renowned historian Doris Kearns Goodwin "speaks to the power of story for communicating the truth and combatting lies."[4] Truth requires grounding in historical facts, not in isolation, but taught within a historical context. Such context is necessary for creating opportunities for deep engagement and conversations that promote respectful deliberation of ideas. Truth also requires accessing, reading, and working with excellent resources. Those resources include, but are not limited to, primary sources, first person accounts, autobiographies, videos, documentaries, and online offerings. Librarians, informed teachers, and other experts are crucial here for teaching media literacy and for getting diverse books and stories by reliable narrators into students' hands. Storytelling shapes facts and impacts our understanding of reality, so it's imperative we get our information from credible sources.

Among other sources, I rely daily on professor of American history Heather Cox Richardson and her "Letters from an American" for thoughtful analysis of today's political landscape regarding national and world news. I also rely on Maria Popova's weekly email digest, "The Marginalian," as solace for the heart, mind, and soul in our search for meaning in our lives. But primarily, I rely on literature. By literature, I mean wonderfully written prose or verse whether it be books of fiction or nonfiction, articles in magazines or news sources, essays, poetry, and more. I also include here my reliance on visual texts and information from storytellers who are artists, photographers, and documentarians who employ film, video, graphics, podcasts, and other media to tell a complete story, augment a written one, and/or visually express the human experience, emotions, and thoughts.

Like many of you I am concerned about maintaining our democracy. To that end, I am fulfilling my need to hear, read, view, share, question, and talk about stories that reflect various viewpoints on subjects such as climate change, equity in education, and—in particular—the history of enslaved people in America and how that history continues to limit and deny people "life, liberty, and the pursuit of happiness."

Developing a more diverse and compassionate worldview depends on us knowing the facts, intelligently arguing the issues, and being able to question stories and integrate them into a wider, more diverse worldview. Here we need to know and discuss stories not just about hardship, violence, and fragility, but also about love, humor, and living a good life. Not enough stories, picture books, documentaries, movies, and multimedia projects celebrate the contributions and lives of people who have most often been marginalized. For example, lots of stories about history don't include women, especially Black women such as Fannie Lou Hamer, a trailblazer from Mississippi who fought for civil and voting rights.

Before discussing stories and books that have impacted my knowledge of history, especially as related to our nation's complicated story on racism, let me emphasize that I am not an historian or a student of history. My views and perspectives are, therefore, necessarily limited. That said, *The 1619 Project: A New Origin Story* has had a particularly profound effect on my understanding that the one who tells the story has the power to decide who belongs and who doesn't, whose voice is heard and which voices are suppressed, whose lives are deemed to matter and whose lives do not. My eyes have been opened wide to the history of enslaved people and of persistent inequalities that shape human lives today. Reading *The 1619 Project* caused me to revise the story of what I knew. Author and editor Nikole Hannah-Jones asks us to consider: What happens when we do not begin with the Mayflower but with the slave ship and tell American history from that perspective?

The Sum of Us: What Racism Costs Everyone and How We Can Prosper Together by Heather McGhee, an expert in economic and social policy, has also been transformative. As well, McGhee has a TED Talk, "Racism Has a Cost for Everyone." She frames her book and TED Talk around her extensive research, which debunks the common belief that for one group to benefit (for example, immigrants, minorities), another group will lose something (whites, people of privilege). Or, put another way, it's the belief that one group's ascension is another group's demise.

This book has stayed with me. For all my years as an educator, working almost entirely in high poverty schools where expectations for students—most often Black and brown—are typically low, I have never understood why we continue to fail as a country to see and act upon the fact that if we equitably educate everyone's children well—with excellent teachers, adequate funding, and first-rate resources—everyone in society benefits and our incarceration rates would dramatically fall. The cost of our entrenched school segregation is disturbingly high; the benefits of diversity extend to everyone.

A few other books that have altered my understanding of history and been a call to action—especially as related to confronting the causes and effects of structural racism and poverty—include, but are not limited to *Caste: The Origins of Our Discontents* by Isabel Wilkerson, *How to Be an Antiracist* by Ibram X. Kendi, *Between the World and Me* by Ta-Nehisi Coates, and *How the Word Is Passed* by Clint Smith. Smith asks a crucial question: *"How do you tell a story that has been told the wrong way for so long?"* Regardless of the subject matter you teach, think about how to include some study and discussion of the inequitable systems that personally impact so many of our students' lives.

Stories must include all of us. Otherwise, we have an incoherent history of who we are as a people, a misunderstanding that works against finding and understanding truth. That incompleteness—which includes deletion of stories we or others choose not to tell or to omit, either by design or by accident—works against equity, human rights, and human dignity. We can and must do better.

CHAPTER 3

Promoting Equitable Opportunities

- ❖ Conversations—hearing all the voices
- ❖ Curriculum as conversation
- ❖ Confronting book banning and censorship
- ❖ An integration story (Shaker Heights, Ohio)

DOI: 10.4324/9781003381242-3

Conversations—hearing all the voices

Respectful and meaningful conversations promote empathy, resilience, and stronger relationships. As James Britton famously wrote, "Reading and writing float on a sea of talk." Douglas Barnes later modified that statement to "learning floats on a sea of talk." My dear friend and civic education professor Walter Parker has written, "classroom discussion is the best pedagogy for strengthening both knowledge and voice."[1] For optimal relationships and optimal learning, the quality and depth of conversations matter—a lot.

Elevating talk to the level of conversation does not occur automatically. It has to be modeled, practiced, and nurtured so all participants feel safe and encouraged to speak their thoughts. As I was not raised with a good model for conversation, that inadequate model followed me into the classroom. I did most of the talking, involving my students in question-and-answer talk (I talk; you mostly listen)—until I knew better.

My dad was an interrupter. If he had something to say, even when someone was talking, he'd just insert his thoughts into the conversation. He was a big talker and had lots of opinions. I don't believe he realized he was being rude when his voice was the most persistent one. He was a businessman, a boss; he was used to controlling and taking over. Unfortunately, I learned from his model. To be frank, it was often the only way I could get a word in when he was speaking, to make my less insistent voice heard. The downside was that becoming an interrupter worked against my becoming an attentive listener, and that impacted my relationships and my teaching.

Figuring out how to have conversations that enhance relationships, teaching, and learning is tricky business. Such conversations are respectful to all parties involved, value active listening—often before speaking—and depend on the moment and setting we're in at the time. So much depends on how and where we've been raised, what messages we receive, and our past practices and beliefs. For example, I'm a proud New Yorker, born and raised there. Go into a major New York City department store, and it's perfectly okay, if not expected, to say something like "Excuse me. Can you tell me where the shoe department is?" And the salesperson, who might be in cosmetics or handbags, will pause as she is helping a client and kindly offer a brief response, such as, "You'll want to go to the fourth floor." End of conversation. But when we moved to Seattle two decades ago, and I went into Nordstrom, Seattle's flagship department store, the response to a similar question was an icy: "Madam, you see I am with a customer. You'll need to wait until I'm free." My interruption was considered rude. I only needed that one encounter to change my behavior. What was acceptable in New York was unacceptable in Seattle.

However, sometimes interrupting can be way of invigorating conversations. It all depends on the speaker's intentions, past habits, how well we know the speaker, and again the culture we've grown up in and that culture's norms. In Japan and in Sweden, for example, interrupting a speaker is considered quite rude, but in France and Italy interruptions and asking questions while a speaker is talking are commonplace and ingrained in the culture. That's how it is for my dearest friend Harriet and me, both of us born and bred New Yorkers. We routinely interject our thoughts into a conversation while the other is speaking as the way we communicate with each other. Our weekly phone conversations are peppered with frequent "interrupting" as an effective, enjoyable way we enrich our conversations and expand on each other's meaning.

The way we speak with each other is what linguistics professor Deborah Tannen calls "cooperative overlapping." Harriet and I have been talking to each other in that manner since our college days. However, I've learned, sometimes painfully, that these "interrupter conversations" are generally not favored by others, that in most situations these interjections are considered impolite and disrespectful. I am still striving to be a better listener and infrequent interrupter in most settings. I am especially careful when I don't know someone well and, also, when I'm in a workplace environment. For example, I've noticed that interrupting in schools and other workplaces makes it hard for introverted, shy, or low confidence people to participate in the conversation. That's why a pause or silent "wait time" of five to ten seconds or inviting someone by name to offer up their thoughts is so important. Scaffolded conversations, which I discuss in Chapter 6, are particularly effective in supporting tentative speakers such as English learners.

I've further noticed that as a teacher, parent, family member, or friend, the reason a person takes over the talking and what that talking is about might simply be related to enthusiasm about the topic and accepted cultural norms. But in other cases, doing most of the talking might be related to disrespect for the listener's point of view, self-importance, awkwardness, loneliness, or reasons I haven't considered. For friends or family who live alone, which may not be by choice but possibly because they've lost a loved one, I understand and empathize with their need to talk about every medical appointment and ailment in detail. No issue for me there. But if they're basically healthy, I might remind them of the "organ recital" which, if you're not old enough to have encountered the term, refers to parts of the human body, not the instrument. It means, among my older friends, that we mostly agree that we will not dominate the conversation (for more than several minutes) going on about our medical ailments. Such talk precludes more interesting talk. Such talk shuts down interesting conversation and storytelling.

So, what does this mean for how we speak and interact with our colleagues, friends, family members, and students? Conversations, I believe, are at the heart of all worthwhile learning exchanges. Who gets to do the talking and how and what we talk about is an equity issue. Whose voice gets to be raised and listened to is often tied to power, race, rigid rules, and precedent. Who gets to tell the story is sometimes more important than the story itself. Whose voices are silenced speaks volumes about what we believe, what we're willing to fight for, our politics, our hopes, and our fears. Optimally, we want the conversations we have with our families, students, colleagues, friends, and all those we hold dear to enhance and enrich our relationships, understanding, compassion, and knowledge as well as empathy and resilience. So it's vital we establish norms with our students, family, and friends that encourage hearing all the voices. We all want to be heard. To be truly seen and heard is to be understood.

Storytelling and conversation go together. When we invite learners into the conversation through storytelling—across the curriculum and across our lives—the culture dynamic shifts. Stories we tell, hear, read, write, and talk about have the power to open up a conversation that includes all of us. Well-told stories from history, science, literature, mathematics, the arts, diverse cultures, and our lives—telling, hearing, reading, and discussing them—are a productive way to engage all learners in a community of inquiry and rich conversation. Esau McCaulley, assistant professor at Wheaton College, fondly recalls how his high school history teacher positively impacted his life:

> Most students who fall in love with learning do so not because of any particular curriculum but because they encounter a teacher who gives them permission to think… This ability to hold fair and stirring conversation is the gift that all great teachers have. It is impossible to legislate.

And, stirring conversation requires an emotionally safe and respectful culture that guides and supports equitable, conversational dynamics.

One way to promote thriving conversations is to establish partner and/ or small groups where students can speak freely to and with each other.

Thalia Wheatley, professor and social neuroscientist at Dartmouth College, has documented that small group conversations can promote student voice and agency and help a group come to consensus. "Conversation is our greatest tool for aligning minds. By sharing thoughts with others, we can sift out what we are thinking. We don't think in a vacuum but with other people."[2]

Of course, you'll first want to establish guidelines for communal dialogue, that is, how to have meaningful conversation that invites and honors each student's voice and encourages deep thinking. For example, teaching students to ask open-ended questions, which expand possibilities, rather than have closed conversations, which tend to have one right answer and therefore shut down conversations, is a must. So are good posture, eye contact, gestures, and behaviors that let the speaker know we have their full attention. Any student-to-student structure will first need to be modeled, practiced, and discussed with teacher guidance. To work well, the social-emotional part of successful conversations will also need to be part of this practice and include such elements as respect, attentive listening, inviting a speaker to participate or further explain—and what all that equitably looks like and sounds like. Setting aside such time is worth it. Maria Popova said:

> … real conversations (much like a good book, which requires the same investment and rewards with the same intimacy of insight) are among the few ways to invite meaningful ideas into our lives, for we don't arrive at meaning via sound bites and status updates. Lest we forget, William James was right—conversation is how "bound energies are let loose." True thinking—the kind of deliberate reflection that welcomes wisdom—takes time.[3]

Asking questions in a manner that encourages students to make their voices heard and providing a safe emotional and mental space for authentic give-and-take discussion is part of creating an infrastructure of opportunity—at home, at school, and in the workplace.

Posing questions as statements can feel less like an interrogation for students and children who believe a teacher or parent is seeking a "right" answer. For example, I might say something like:

"Let's talk about the part of the story (text, poem, illustration, video, podcast) that most captured your attention?" and/or

"There are a lot of issues here. Let's discuss one that especially impacted you—or not." and/or

"I'm wondering what questions the story might have raised for you?" and/or

"Say more about that." "Explain what you're thinking about…"

Aim to give students authority by not repeating what they say, by providing wait time, by being non-judgmental, and by building on their responses to affirm their thinking and to encourage deeper thinking.

Researchers and educators Dorsey Hammond and Denise Nessel note: "One of the most effective ways to improve the quality of student talk is to change the nature of teacher talk." And part of that change is handing over more responsibility to learners and making safe spaces for everyone to enter the conversation. In that regard, ensure that most conversations are learner-centered and not, primarily, whole-class talk led by the teacher.

In promoting equitable opportunities for all learners, it's also imperative that we include English learners and welcome and amplify their voices so they can enter the conversation. To that end, ensure speaking, listening, reading, and writing opportunities include scaffolded activities with linguistic support. Multilingual educator, Valentina Gonzalez, suggests many ways to ensure instruction is accessible and actionable for English learners—promoting peer-to-peer discussion, responding to open-ended questions, reading side-by-side versions of a text in student's primary language and in English, and having daily opportunities to write, to list just several. In my book *Literacy Essentials,* I provide many ways to support English learners, and that information is part of the free resources that accompany this book. Recognizing that our future will have a large, multilingual workforce, bilingualism is a necessity. In my home state of Washington, the plan is to enroll all K–8 students in bilingual programs by 2040.

Finally, keep in mind that the person who does most of the talking has the power to open up or shut down any conversation. From my experience, we teachers and adults—parents too—tend to dominate the conversation. I think back to my dad at the dinner table each night. He did most of the talking and did not regularly invite our participation, and so we were mostly silent. And sadly that is often the case in the classroom. *Talk only rises to the level of conversation when there is a meaningful exchange of ideas and observations, an informal and respectful give and take discussion.* Let's prioritize creating a classroom environment that puts conversation at the heart and center of teaching and learning.

Curriculum as conversation

*W*hat *if we thought of curriculum primarily as a dialogue and not a document?* I have chosen to put conversation at the center of teaching, learning, and living as it's the quality of talk and what content, stories, and voices are included—or not—that expand or limit our thinking and actions. Raising our children and our students to be open to other viewpoints, civic minded, and compassionate for the less fortunate is necessary for becoming fully human and for sustaining our fragile democracy.

All learning involves conversation. That conversation might be with ourself, a colleague, a mentor, an apprentice, a friend, a student, or an author's words on the page. So let's start by discussing what we mean by conversations. In my book *Conversations: Strategies for Teaching, Learning, and Evaluating*, I quote scholar Arthur Applebee from his exceptionally thoughtful *Curriculum as Conversation*:

> Rather than beginning with an exhaustive inventory of the structure of the subject matter, we begin with a consideration of the conversations that matter... The question then becomes, how can we orchestrate these conversations so that students can enter into them?

Applying "curriculum as conversation" requires a rethinking of curriculum. *In Literacy Essentials: Engagement, Excellence, and Equity for* All *Learners*, I write:

> Curriculum is more than content. Curriculum includes all we do to create and sustain an intellectual classroom and school culture that fosters inquiry and invites all students on an intellectual adventure... Curriculum as thinking about real-world issues must apply to all students, not just our high-performing ones.

Curriculum as thinking means conversation as dialogue, which is different than debate. In a conversation, we are not generally trying to convince another person or seeking "answers"; we are having an exchange of ideas, which can only happen when we listen attentively and respectfully with a genuine interest in what our conversation partner or partners have to say. The nature of teacher talk, where we do most of the talking and agenda setting, works against students freely raising their voices. Also, if we are not seeking, welcoming, and hearing student voices, then we are not fostering conversations that lead to thoughtful learning and learner empowerment.

Fostering conversations that matter requires a classroom and school culture of respectful and trusting relationships. Parker Palmer writes in *The Courage to Teach*, "In fact, only when people can speak their minds does education have a chance to happen." I believe this is true for both our personal and professional conversations. Until we feel emotionally safe enough to speak what we truly believe, that is, that our voices will be heard, honored, and received without judgment, are we likely to be open to scrutiny and considering other points of view. I believe this to be true for learners of all ages. If we're preparing students to live in a diverse, multicultural, multilingual society, they need to be able to talk about race, ethnicity, gender, and social justice without fear of reprisal. They need to feel a sense of belonging, validation, and acceptance. They need, for example when studying history, reliable narrators who help us get to the truth.

Most of us, and I include myself, have been ill prepared to share content knowledge and teach lessons related to contentious issues we never learned about or experienced ourselves and to talk about those issues with our students in a way that encourages compelling questions and constructive dialogue, not necessarily "answers." Many states, trying to remedy that, now have or are working on developing materials designed to teach K–12 students an accurate and nuanced history, for example, of Indigenous Peoples.

Let's modify Applebee's question "how can we orchestrate these conversations so that students can enter into them?" to include conversations in multiple settings: *"How can we orchestrate conversations to ensure the topic and setting invite all voices to be heard?"* The classroom and school—and home—must be safe and welcoming places where we do all we can to support students to become their truest and best selves, not just places to master standards, curriculum, and/or do well on tests. Ultimately, we want our conversations—and our education process—to elevate our lives. The following story shows how a concentration on living the good life has the potential to make quality of life possible for all learners.

While in the midst of writing this section, I received an email from Jason Drysdale, an assistant superintendent in Winnipeg, Manitoba, whom I have known, admired, and worked with for over a decade. Among other things he shared with me was the new *Manitoba Framework for Learning* with its Guiding Principles and Global Competencies, a document so magnificent in its Vision and scope that it took my breath away. It is not just a document for teaching and learning; it is a master plan for living a good life.

First of all, the document's Vision is focused on The Good Life, which, coincidentally, is an overriding theme and big question of this book: "How can each of us and our loved ones lead a fulfilling, hopeful, civic-minded life in spite of the adversity and loss that accompany every life?" To see that phrase, The Good Life, as the dominant purpose and goal in an official, provincial document gave me hope and filled me with optimism. It was the first time I have seen education equated with our full humanity. It is important to note here that in Manitoba, the concept of The Good Life is directly linked to and drawn from Indigenous Peoples—*Mino Bimaadiziwin*; this means the good life in Anishinabemowin—which is one of the common Indigenous languages spoken in Manitoba.

All the specifics in this multi-layered Framework flow from "The Good Life" and "flourishing life," two terms which are used repeatedly throughout the Framework. The vision offered in The Manitoba Education and Early Childhood Learning document is the same vision I share for this book: "students are prepared to reach their full potential and to live **The Good Life**" in which they

> have hope, belonging, meaning, and purpose; have a voice; feel safe and supported; are prepared for their individual path beyond graduation; have capacity to play an active role in shaping their future and be active citizens; live in relationships with others and the natural world; honour and respect indigenous ways of knowing, being, and doing with a commitment to and understanding of Truth and Reconciliation.[4]

There is no mention of test prep and testing, textbooks, standards, or curriculum specifics. Instead, we encounter multi-faceted and interdependent "Global Competencies": Creativity, Citizenship, Connection to Self, Critical Thinking, Collaboration, and Communication. Each of these fundamental competences subsume that meaningful conversation around important concepts, along with critical thinking and analysis, are a necessary path to fulfilling those goals. Creating authentic learning experiences, principles for implementation, action research, and continuous evaluation are also part of the plan. So, while the plan focuses on student academic achievement, the curriculum focus resides alongside social, emotional, and equity goals that translate to policy.

Seeking out meaningfulness, worthiness, and doing good for others, high ideals for living **The Good Life**, permeate the Manitoba document. As Jason Drysdale notes in an email:

> I think it holds HUGE promise for education in Manitoba. It is responsive, learner focused, big idea focused, linked to credible research (Fullan and Hargreaves) and respects teacher autonomy.

The intent is that this will be used to frame all of the specific curriculum renewal going forward in Manitoba—this is exciting!!

The Manitoba Framework is accompanied by curricula documents including the English Language Arts Curriculum. Implementation of this curriculum is supported by the comprehensive "Reading, Writing, and Oral Communication Learning Progressions" for K–3[5] and a separate, related document for grades 4–6. These superb, research-based documents provide essential support to new teachers, teachers new to a grade level, and all teachers who want to grow professionally. The documents, created by project lead, Allyson Matczuk, Early Literacy Consultant, with feedback from many educators, provide the specific, observable behaviors for a student that teachers can use to guide their instruction while recognizing "There is no set sequence since every learner's personal literacy processing is unique."

Matczuk states, "While literacy is broader than reading, writing, and oral language, the document answers questions teachers have. It gives them a place to start." I have read the document, and it is masterful for providing high expectations that most students can reach, emphasizing that "Competencies in language develop AT THE SAME TIME as reading and writing," and recognizing that language is a system for developing whole-to-part-to-whole teaching relationships for effective communication.

How do we ensure that the content we teach and the concepts we discuss are worthy of students' time and talk? I am reminded of and still troubled by my granddaughter's Advanced Placement history class in her junior year in high school. The entire course was, and still is, dedicated to passing the AP history exam, and the content was delivered almost exclusively through the huge textbook which "covered" hundreds of years of American history. (The prep guide notes: "The AP US History exam involves critical reading, writing, and in-depth analysis. It's not just about memorizing names and dates, but rather interpreting historical evidence quickly and accurately, recalling outside information on a topic, and synthesizing your ideas into a coherent argument.") All worthy goals but, realistically, there isn't much time for them. My granddaughter did well on the test, but she didn't learn much of worth and doesn't recall much about American history. Sadly, none of those classes were devoted to discussions and exploratory talk around the upcoming Presidential election, the resegregating of public schools, or other pressing equity issues. More recently, there have been concerns about what many perceive as AP courses' inadequate handling of the African American experience.[6] How was this class preparing students to be activist, knowledgeable, empathetic citizens? It wasn't. The broad context learners need to understand historical facts with perspective and to recognize, question, and discuss their own biases and beliefs was missing.

Reflecting on the course, my granddaughter notes:

> Teachers have to follow such a standardized, specific curriculum that there's no time to give certain topics the weight they deserve. Due to this, we moved along extremely rapidly—even major events like world wars were consolidated into just a week or less of study. Another problem is that so much of the focus of class revolves around learning the actual format of the test, which is hyper specific to the designations of College Board (AP organization) and doesn't really meaningfully build many skills. You can only do well on the test if you know how to follow this format precisely and quickly so as to finish everything within the strict time limit. Because the test is structured around one three-hour test, it's not surprising that the material never is fully engaged with critically.

Here's where teachers can and must be a powerful and necessary influence. Without thoughtful dialogue and an educated populace, we are doomed to repeat the mistakes of history. We are overdue—in the U.S., Canada, and many other countries—for earnestly confronting our dark past. It feels like we are just at the beginning of that journey, which includes fully recognizing and honoring the contributions of enslaved peoples and Indigenous Peoples for their rich cultures, language, heritage, cuisines, music, art, history, and so much more. It means recognizing their will to survive and resilience as not just admirable but astonishing. It means seeking to understand the horrors they faced and dealing with the past in all its complexity. The job of the school is to provide a full history—of the past as well as the present, the unforgiveable as well as the great, the unjust and well as the just—so we may graduate thoughtful, future voters and citizens who actively assume responsibility for creating a more equitable, habitable, inclusive society. "Citizenship is not a spectator sport."[7]

Crucial as well is finding a way to negotiate the curriculum, that is, to provide students some options and choices within required content and standards. Not only are we then sharing the power with students, but we are also acknowledging the democratic principle that people, even young people, deserve some say in what they are being asked to learn and do. The children's interests, needs, curiosity, and knowledge are all taken into consideration, which make it more likely learners will approach any inquiry or work with a sense of purpose.

To be clear, there may be no choice on the topic of study, but how the topic is taught and learned can be collaboratively negotiated, at least in part. It might be as minor as something akin to the limited choice wise parents offer their children, such as, "Would you prefer this or that (food, activity, item of clothing)?" There is no option given for "neither one." In school, the limited choice, what I call "choice within structure," might be related to writing topic and format, number of sources required for a research paper, options for presenting student learning, date assignment is due. As two specific examples, negotiating the curriculum might be 1) co-creating a rubric for goal setting and/or requirements for completion of a project, or 2) self-grading, to be used along with the formal report card. When students have a voice in what they will be learning and achieving, their engagement, motivation, and efforts increase—along with their achievement and enjoyment.

How well students and our children cope with and find fulfillment in their current and future lives depends, at least in part, on how skillfully they can summon their voices as concerned and knowledgeable citizens who actively seek to participate in equitable solutions for local and global issues, such as climate change, housing, poverty, equity, and social justice. Even if these issues are not included in our district and provincial standards, teachers of every subject must find a way to include a culturally responsive, real-world curriculum and teach our students how and why to become civic minded, starting in preschool. Learners are never too young to participate in curriculum as conversation. For example, with our guidance, even our youngest learners can discuss, understand, and apply recycling efforts as a necessity for prudent living in our classrooms, school, home, and even our planet. They can also discuss and advocate for some action related to fairness and justice, for example, how to make recess on the playground and lunch time work more effectively and enjoyably for all participants. Curriculum works best when it starts with the child, inspires curiosity, includes everyone, and gives students some agency in their lives.

As I was completing the writing of *Literacy Essentials: Engagement, Excellence, and Equity for* All *Learners*, the 2016 Presidential election had just ended. Democracy was on the ballot then, as it always has been. Alarmed by the complacency and failure to vote by more than 50% of eligible voters in the United States, I added an *Afterword* to the book, "The Need for Civic Engagement." It felt more urgent than ever that civic engagement and civics education be part of all teaching and learning. I wrote:

> Getting our students ready to be citizens—preparing each of them to become engaged, committed, and intelligent participants in a democracy—may be our most crucial responsibility of all. It's no exaggeration to say that the survival of any republic depends on it. "An ignorant people can never remain a free people."

That urgency has only grown more insistent. At this writing, on a global, national, and local scale, there is overwhelming evidence confirming a movement away from democracy and towards autocracy. We are seeing writ large the silencing of dissenting voices, voter suppression, harsh punishment of peacefully protesting dissidents, and flagrant lies and conspiracy theories used to justify government takeovers that nullify the will and voice of the people. Exhibit A: The January 6, 2021 insurrection at the U.S. Capitol, an attempt that nearly succeeded at upending the rule of law and overturning our Presidential election by any means necessary, including extreme violence. Exhibit B: Russia's unprovoked war, atrocities, and brutal massacre of Ukrainian soldiers and civilians. Exhibit C: The worldwide increase of autocratic leaders. And there is so much more that is deeply concerning—ruling by intimidation, school shootings, police brutality, fear mongering, and systemic social and economic disparities.

Our current backsliding as a democracy seems to be connected to, at least in part, a perceived threat that a growing diverse population of "others" will "replace" and grievously harm "our side." Demographic changes are viewed as threats rather than as opportunities for positive multicultural exchanges and relationships. So it's imperative our children and students know this history, so they can recognize and call out injustices and do the necessary work to transition back to a democratic republic.

Related, increasing calls and actions advocating censorship of language, content, and books are alarming and terrifying—an organized attempt to shut down conversations and thinking related to academic freedom, social justice, civil rights, sexual and gender issues, and other "controversial" causes. At the same time, an urgent concern these days is that teachers are increasingly being given less freedom to teach and less authority to make "acceptable" decisions—on curriculum, content, books, language—even while being held more and more accountable. As a result, freedom of expression is in retreat.

We have a reckoning to do that is long overdue. We have not yet fully wrestled with harsh truths that impact all of us, especially as related to the sorrowful, inhumane history of enslaved people, Indigenous People, ethnic or religious minorities, and marginalized populations that are underserved and ignored. As well, we have not yet confronted and resolved the unacceptable reality that many of our schools remain racially and economically segregated.

At the very least, if we are to live in a democracy that benefits all of us, we need to be having tough conversations around these issues. The conversations are a start. You can't change what you can't first acknowledge. For example, we can't diminish racism and homophobia and inequity until we recognize these injustices and call them out. Let's be asking ourselves and reflecting upon questions like these: "What are we reading, writing, and talking about?" "Whose voices are being amplified, marginalized, or silenced?" "What are we doing to create opportunities for a more livable and joyful future for all students?" "How does what we focus on each day make students feel smart, cherished, safe, and hopeful?"

Creating a "more perfect union" where each person's culture, language, history, and dignity is lifted up and celebrated is something we can at least strive for. Promoting and making time for curriculum as conversation is a start. That thoughtful deliberation on important topics, accompanied by active and compassionate listening, is a necessity for achieving an equitable and excellent education—a human right for each one of us. That means being able to dialogue with people outside of our tribe and comfort zone. Education is our best hope and most effective antidote to hate and violence.

If we and the generations that follow are to make our world a more habitable, generous, and equitable place for all of us, we must have the will, communication skills, and knowledge to provide the non-negotiables that make living The Good Life possible. That means creating infrastructures of opportunity that guarantee ample safety, education, housing, food, health, income, and justice. It means equitably educating all our students well—regardless of ethnicity, background, gender, race, or social status. It means providing and discussing the full history of our past so we can, all of us, live better lives together. It means providing hope for the future.

Confronting book banning and censorship

Let's begin this discussion of teaching and reckoning with our history of book banning with two quotes from Clint Smith, award-winning author and advocate:

> Banning books that expose students to the atrocities and inequities of our world does not protect them. If anything, it leaves them less equipped to understand why our society looks the way that it does today. Teaching these histories honestly helps them make sense of who we are.[8]

> Whether it's slavery, the Holocaust, or the genocides of indigenous peoples across the world, literature can help us cultivate public memory so that it doesn't happen again. We should be expanding curriculum to include more of these books, and certainly not pulling them out.[9]

Book banning and other forms of censorship are part of an effort to limit what teachers can say and what children can read and talk about. Such a move denigrates our faith in children, teachers, and our public schools. Suppressing and silencing certain voices is not just disrespectful and hurtful; it is inhumane. With knowledgeable teacher guidance, students are capable of learning about our country's racial history—and other disturbing issues that cause discomfort and controversy. Gaining a full understanding of what happened, why it happened, and how we can and must do better, for all of us, is necessary for restoring and sustaining an inclusive democracy.

While diverse books have always come under attack, and we've had previous book bans, the latest book bans are influencing teaching, learning, and our freedom of speech and choice in a manner that cannot be ignored. The particular books that offend people change over time, so it's mandatory we demand access to all kinds of books, even ones we personally may not approve.

I hadn't expected to be writing about book banning in the 2020s, but we are living through different and difficult times. The unprecedented rise of book banning is a well-coordinated effort to remove "inappropriate" books from many of our school and public libraries. But who decides? Who determines which voices and stories are worthy of being heard, read, and discussed? It often feels like forces outside of our control—school boards, legislators, politicians, the courts—are making consequential decisions about our lives and our children's lives that are best left to librarians, parents, teachers, families, students, and ourselves. The unspoken belief is that librarians and teachers can't be trusted, that we need monitoring and policing by people with little or no experience in education.

I am certainly not an expert on this fraught issue but as an avid reader, an advocate for democracy, and a freedom lover, I feel the need to make my voice heard. Let's be frank: book banning is about controlling, limiting, and excluding access to information—ideas, history, facts, and opinions deemed controversial and unacceptable—and most of those protestations are related to race and racism, sexual and gender identity, LGBTQ issues, and marginalized populations. Importantly, the greater number of books written by, for, and about the LGBTQ community and beyond has made it easier to mitigate a sense of isolation and assume our true identities. That's why book banning and censorship are so harmful. They limit possibilities for re-envisioning and being accepted for who we are and for becoming our authentic selves.

Also, some parents, political groups, and others complain that the language in books causes harm; therefore, book censorship is necessary. I've never seen any research to confirm that "harm." While it's a rite of passage for many of us—coming across books or language in our childhood we're not mature enough to handle or read yet—I'd say the language worries are overblown. I remember at about age 12, coming across my mother's carefully hidden copy of *Lady Chatterley's Lover* by D. H. Lawrence. I can still recall the two lines that shocked me. But harmed me, no. After sneak reading a few parts of the book, I put it back in its hiding place, realizing I was too young to be reading it. I did pick it up as a young adult; it was still a bit shocking in its explicitness, but I found it very well written and the characters well developed and fascinating. I did go on to read and savor more books by D. H. Lawrence, a highly acclaimed—and provocative—author known for exploring the nature of relationships.

Censorship of books, news, and information sources undermines our rights to intellectual freedom, historical facts, and the rule of law. Here's what I know to be true from teaching and living. Censorship and book banning deprive readers of multiple perspectives, which necessarily limits our thinking and compassion for others. For example, if we are truly to become a self-governing democracy, then Black history, Indigenous history, and historically underrepresented groups must all be seen and discussed as American history, Canadian history, or your particular country's history. How else can we expect to move forward together in a way that respects, benefits, and honors the stories and life of each one of us?

In our country that is deeply divided on a whole host of polarizing issues, we need a freer and more expansive flow of factual information and points of view so we can at least try to understand each other, become more empathetic and less dogmatic, and begin to reckon with past injustices. Letting our students think for themselves scares some people, but it's a necessity for maintaining democratic ideals. Letting students in on the horrors of slavery, the Holocaust, abuse, wars, and other human catastrophes and injustices are difficult to read about but are necessary. Intellectual freedom, guaranteed in the First Amendment of the Constitution, is a necessity for creating a fully educated, informed, humane citizenry who can meaningfully contribute to making our local and global worlds more equitable and livable—for all of us.

It's important to see the difference between censorship and concern. Concern is appropriate. I believe censorship is not. It's essential we add books of diversity, not take them away, but at the same time teacher guidance is often needed—to deepen students' understanding of the times, the emotions, the complex issues involved. If instead we pretend that, for example, slavery, racism, and gender identity issues don't exist or don't warrant our attention—by refusing to read and talk about those issues—we do our students a massive disservice. Only knowing our full history—now and in the past—can we prepare our students to navigate the winding paths ahead of them. It is our job as educators to provide the contexts for the facts, language, and descriptions kids are reading about and to open up conversations, not shut them down. It does require teachers—and all who promote reading—to have the sensitivity and knowledge to explain why certain language was used by an author at a particular time in our history and why that language might be perceived as offensive and inappropriate today. Children's author Mark Weakland wrote:

> Removing books from public libraries denies the rights of parents who want their children to be able to access all books, and it limits the ability of students who want to experience many viewpoints. Also, when information is erased, there can be no fully realized discourse. Finally, many libraries have mechanisms in place, from stickers to databases, to stop any given student from checking out a book their parents don't want them to read.[10]

For free support on handling book banning issues, see Pen America at pen.org. Pen America is an excellent organization and leading voice for information and updates on "threats to free expression in education." For banned books specifically, see "Banned in the U.S.A." at pen. org/banned-in-the-usa, a great and useful resource. See, also, from the American Library Association, The ALA's Office for Intellectual Freedom:

> The ALA's Office for Intellectual Freedom (OIF) receives reports from libraries, schools, and the media on attempts to ban books in communities across the country. We compile lists of challenged books in order to inform the public about censorship efforts that affect libraries and schools... The goal of the office is to educate librarians and the general public about the nature and importance of intellectual freedom in libraries.

For free consulting services, "The Office for Intellectual Freedom (OIF) can help you prepare against censorship and implement vital intellectual freedom best practices within your library or school through our consulting services."

Public libraries continue to be an oasis for many—a lifeline for communities, families and students with limited or no access to books, content resources, and the broadband and technology services libraries provide. Equitable access to quality, diverse libraries stocked with literature of all types is one of our best hopes for sustaining our fragile democracy. Book banning, censorship of books, stories, and subject matter—bodes ill for a democracy. You can't avoid controversial issues by censoring or ignoring them. Banning books dumbs down education. Concepts and words such as "equity," "social justice," "inclusion," and "anti-racism" must be reckoned with as part of our history if we are to "form a more perfect union." As educators and concerned citizens, let's do all we can to ensure free flowing access to books and instructional materials. And that includes classroom libraries. (See Chapter 6, "Championing the Reading/Writing Connection: Putting libraries at the center" for establishing equitable classroom libraries with and by students, and see Chapter 10, "Becoming a Significant Influencer" for bringing book abundance to communities with book scarcity.)

Book banning limits and removes possibilities for deep conversation on controversial topics. Books are inseparable from ideas. One action we can take is to support our librarians, who are under siege as never before. We must also do what we can to support all those who are pushing back along with bookstores, authors, and illustrators who celebrate diversity and inclusion through their books. Diversity and inclusion represent the fullness of our strengths and our humanity. Book banning and censorship of information are major disruptors and contributors in how a democracy dies. It doesn't have to be this way.

An integration story
(Shaker Heights, Ohio)

I have always believed in public schools as the cornerstone of a functioning democracy. Having attended an integrated, public elementary school as a child, I wanted the same integrated education and experience for our children. So when my husband accepted a job offer in Cleveland, Ohio, so we could live closer to family, we purposely moved into Shaker Heights, a Cleveland suburb. In the early 1960s, Shaker Heights was one of the first and few examples of a U.S. school district deliberately striving for racial balance through voluntary integration. The Shaker Plan, as it was known, was not just about integration but about Black excellence, and for many that stated opportunity became reality. Our son Peter and his "band of brothers" are models of what was/is possible (and I tell that story of life-long friendships in Chapter 8). Here I will weave my family's story into the history of the times to show the necessity for excellent, integrated public schools as a right and benefit to each of us. As author, economist, and researcher Heather McGhee emphasizes in her remarkable, wise book, *The Sum of Us: What Racism Costs Everyone and How We Can Prosper Together,* racism has a cost for all of us, our fates are linked, "our injury to one is an injury to all."

A bit of local history here. Like other cities and neighborhoods all over the U.S., segregated schools have persisted and promulgated despite being deemed inequitable and unlawful. However, in a deliberate and unusual effort for the times, Black and white couples in the Ludlow neighborhood in Shaker Heights formed a community association, essentially a housing office, to combat racist, exclusionary housing, and mortgage practices. Recognizing that affordable and attractive housing opportunities were key to integrating the schools, the association worked tirelessly to attract and sustain both white and Black home buyers, encouraging new Black home buyers to settle in Ludlow and other parts of Shaker Heights, such as the Lomond neighborhood where we were living and where my children were attending elementary school. Successful racial and economic integration meant that all stakeholders benefited, white students and Black. As Heather McGhee notes in a TED Talk, "Racism is bad for white people too. Racism has a cost for everyone." Looking back, it was diverse students living close by to each other in the neighborhood that made it possible and likely for interracial friendships to flourish. Seeing and appreciating each other's common humanity resulted in enduring friendships, a priceless gift.

Notably, it was in 2nd and 3rd grade at Lomond School where Peter began his lifelong friendship with Jonathan. The friendship happened easily. On his walk to and from school each day, Peter stopped at Jonathan's house to pick him up in the morning. Most often Jonathan wasn't quite ready, and his siblings would shout at him, "Pete's here; hurry up" while Peter would wait patiently and engage in talk with the family. The two boys also walked home from school together and said goodbye to each other every afternoon. Living close by in the same neighborhood and spending lots of time together was the beginning of a cherished friendship that came to span more than 40 years.

Starting in 7th grade, Peter began what would become enduring friendships with several other boys. Those friendships became possible because they wound up in similar classes together. Again, it was the proximity to where they lived that made it effortless to get together outside of school for spontaneous play and games. None of the boys recalls ever having a conversation with each other about race. Matt told me, "We were just a bunch of friends who liked hanging out with each other." Starting in elementary school and junior high—and continuing through college, post-college, work, and just about all of his life—Peter's closest friends, whom I call his "band of brothers," have included Matt who is white and Jonathan, Keith, Harold, and David who are Black. It was the positive integration effort that provided the life-changing opportunity for these boys to grow up together, show up for each other, and stay in close and loving contact throughout their lives.

Notably, these six boys spent their junior and high school years in and out of each other's houses, playing board games, and staying out of trouble. These guys were smart, nerdy, kind, and fun to be with and, probably, somewhat naïve. They didn't yet realize that some of them, as Keith's dad told them, were "going to have a target on their back just for being Black." Their remarkable friendship sustained them. Ken told me, "From being a little kid to a grown man, we have a bond that you can't break. We have all these memories together." (See pages 183–190 for the history, impact, and continuing benefits of that friendship of more than 40 years.)

I believe housing, in particular, was and is key to leveling the playing field in education. Neighborhood housing, not busing—which makes getting together with kids outside of school hours difficult—is a major factor for making successful integration more likely, and this was why the Ludlow Community Association (LCA) focused so heavily on maintaining a racial balance in neighborhoods. For David, the tenacity of his mom, who applied for and received rental assistance through the federal government's Section 8 housing assistance program, changed his life. Authorized by Congress in 1974 on behalf of low-income households, the program paid up to 70% of the rent for those families. That assistance made it possible for David's mom, a single and devoted mom supporting her family, to move into a rental home in Shaker Heights and take advantage of the excellent public schools for her children.

Moving from Cleveland public schools, where David was in the "enrichment" program, he was stunned to learn that instead of being advanced he was, in fact, far behind in academics. He quickly caught up and thrived.

It was like night and day. Moving into Shaker Heights changed the trajectory of my life. It gave me a safe place to be a kid. Once we moved there, I no longer had to worry about basic life necessities. No kid should have to worry about that. Once I stopped worrying about those things, I could concentrate on school. School, friendships, my mom's unrelenting efforts, all those interactions, plus churchgoing—with all those churchgoing ladies—kept me in line.

In 1987, just before David's senior year in high school, Congress stopped the funding benefit for the Section 8 federal housing assistance program. Without subsidized rent, David's mom and her kids were forced to move to a less expensive neighborhood with its lesser quality schools. Then, kindness and generosity stepped in when Dusty Klein, one of David's good friends, and Dusty's family invited David to move in so he could complete his last year of high school in Shaker Heights. David went on to graduate Kent State University, where he began studying architecture and then shifted into information technology. Today he is a successful network engineer for an internet company.

Looking back on the role his teachers played, he notes that while almost all his teachers had high expectations for him, one teacher in particular impacted his learning. He notes that his 5th grade teacher, Mary Ann Mahoney, was the first teacher who took a personal interest in him and repeatedly told him he could do better. David said, "She wouldn't let me slide on anything. 'I know you're smarter than that,' she would tell me." And then David told an unforgettable story:

It was Halloween and she understood that being a low-income kid, my mom couldn't afford a Halloween costume. She took off her full frog-costume jumpsuit and allowed me to walk around in it when everyone was parading around the gym. She did that for me on the spot.

However, while many touted the success of integration, Moreland School where I was teaching was an outlier. That neighborhood remained mostly Black and underserved, and the school experience for those students was uneven at best. Reading scores for Black students in grade 1 were dismal. (I tell that story and how things changed in *Transitions: From Literature to Literacy*.)[11] Even for a time, when Moreland School became a magnet school, with special programs designed to attract white families, the number of whites that chose to commit to Moreland remained low. The school remained heavily segregated with Blacks comprising about 90% of the student body. Moreland School was eventually found to be out of compliance with federal law, and Shaker Heights was court-ordered to integrate all schools in our district. As has been true in our racial history as a country, it was the Black families and students who bore the greatest burden. It was the close knit, Black community that was disrupted, their beautiful school the one forced to close, their students who were bused across the district to unfamiliar neighborhoods, their children that had to make the greatest adjustments. My own job, as a reading specialist and staff developer for the district's five elementary schools, moved from being based at Moreland School to Mercer School, the wealthiest neighborhood in the district. I recall hearing some of the bused Moreland students talk about the "castles" they passed on route to their new school.

Unsurprisingly, relying on busing to ensure Black and white kids attend school together did not yield an equitable education for all. In fact, I vividly remember a two-day, required "racial sensitivity" training that all of us teachers were required to attend. I specifically recall wondering about the after-effects on a kindergarten teacher because parents of Black children routinely complained she was "racist" and requested their child not be in her class. I wondered if a short, intense training would change her. It did not. You cannot change a racist mindset in a brief, crash course. Changing the heart takes much longer. For starters, it takes a willing heart. I would amend the statement in

Chapter 1, "The eyes can't see what the mind doesn't know," so it reads "The eyes can't see what the mind doesn't know and what the heart doesn't feel."

Ultimately, while many see the Shaker Heights plan for integration as having been mostly successful, five decades later the K–12 racial achievement gap still persists. For example, Advanced Placement (AP) classes in the district remain predominantly white in spite of the fact the district is now a "majority minority" district. Anecdotally, a longtime teacher in Shaker Heights reports talk of white flight to private schools or to a neighboring district because of a perception that "Blacks are bringing achievement down," mirroring what has been occurring across the country. Some white families, initially attracted to Shaker's integration plan, are now looking elsewhere. Black families are leaving as well, frustrated that the majority of students performing below grade level are Black. Notably, "The economic gap between Black and white residents is growing."[12] For many years, Shaker Heights was "considered something of a utopia" for its integration and housing efforts, so it's personally disheartening to see so much promise undone, not just there but across our nation.

Similar white flight is occurring in other urban districts, including Seattle, where I live. Roosevelt High School in Seattle, which my granddaughter Katie attended, still struggles with race, diversity, and Black achievement. Seattle has one of the "worst opportunity gaps in the nation" even though Seattle has one of the fastest growing economies. As well, "Seattle was the last city to develop an open housing ordinance."[13] A lack of integrated housing options that make it possible for interracial friendships to develop and flourish in the neighborhoods and schools—like the friendships Peter and his friends experienced—hurts us all in the long run. For democracy to survive and thrive—which requires reducing our nationwide opportunity gap—we must, each of us, do what we can to ensure all children excel and prosper.

Teaching all kids as if they are gifted—and educating teachers to hold high expectations for all students—would go a long way in reducing opportunity gaps. One equitable and commonsense solution might be to ensure all Black students—and all Asian, Hispanic, multicultural, and multilingual populations—receive a "gifted," integrated education. When Peter was wait-listed for entry into the "gifted and talented" program, which began in grade 4 and continued through grade 6, we discussed and decided his best placement was in a neighborhood school in his "regular" class. That way, he could continue to learn from and value the talents, friendships, and diverse backgrounds of his classmates. Notably for us, Peter's most gifted teacher in elementary school—in grade 5—was a female Black teacher, Marty Singleton, his first teacher to fully see Peter's gifts and to celebrate him—his intelligence, his quiet leadership, his keen and unique sense of humor. During and after that school year is when Peter began to thrive in all ways, intellectually and personally.

How gifted kids are selected nationwide is still flawed at best and inequitable at worst. Interestingly enough, Shaker Heights named their one "gifted and talented" class, for grades 4–6, "Special Projects." In a class of 25, Jonathan was one of four Black students and one Asian student from a school district where the student body was close to 50% white, 50% Black, and less than 5% Asian, Hispanic, and other. That Jonathan wound up in the "gifted" program at all is a story in itself. Reflecting on when he was in kindergarten and grade 1, he told me:

> I was automatically put in the "slower kids" group. My mom was furious and talked to my teachers who said, "He can't read, he can't do this, he can't do that." My mom wanted to show them I could read; she had me read aloud to them. Eventually I got moved, but it wasn't easy.

Echoing Jonathan's story and that of many other Black students nationwide, it took Ken's mom's advocacy and actions to convince his teachers and principal that, as Ken puts it, "I was precocious and bright." One of Ken's teachers repeatedly complained about his behaviors, saying he was out of control, bothering other kids, and needed to calm down. It got so bad that the school psychologist was called in to observe Ken. Her conclusion:

> He's bored. He gets all his work done quickly and easily. He's not being provided enough stimulation. He's "bothering" other children because he's done with his work and sees other kids struggling so he helps them. He's a prime candidate for the gifted program. His intellectual level is above his peers.

Ken describes his mom as "a fighter," as being aggressive about keeping an eye out for her children. Once she saw she could get things done by showing up at school and having her say, she was relentless in seeking the best for her kids. Ken says, "Everyone knew her by her first name; they had her on speed dial." Ken did get moved to the "Special Projects" class, but without his mother's efforts it would not have happened. Ken went on to Kenyon College, where he graduated with a studio art degree and a minor in psychology. Today he works for a biomedical firm and continues to pursue his art part-time.

Matt was also in the Special Projects class with Jonathan and Ken, but no special efforts were needed to ensure his entry. He was white, had high test scores, and his teacher recommended him for having "special promise." Matt went on to Syracuse University, where he graduated with a degree in political science and an interest in public policy. These days he works part-time tutoring students in test prep and academics. He lives with his wife Sarah and daughter Grace in the house he grew up in. His primary and most joyful job is raising his precocious daughter who just started kindergarten at Boulevard Elementary. Matt walks Grace to and from school every day, the same school Matt attended as a child.

Keith, like Peter, was not in the Special Projects class, aka, gifted class, but he was plenty smart and entered kindergarten as a reader. Nonetheless, his kindergarten teacher insisted "He can't read" and automatically grouped Keith and all the Black students in the class as non-readers and failed to academically challenge them. It was only when Keith's parents intervened—both of whom had college degrees from top universities and were successful lawyers—and insisted Keith be seen and taught as the talented child that he was, that the situation gradually improved. Keith went on to excel through the grades. He was accepted to several, prestigious universities but chose Dartmouth, which his father had also attended. He says, "It's because of who my parents are as people and the classes I was in that propelled me to excellence." Keith majored in psychology, minored in education, and took a lot of music classes. Currently, under the name of Austin Willacy, he performs music worldwide to bring disparate views into meaningful conversations. He is a talented songwriter, arranger, composer, producer, and recording engineer.

Kids shouldn't have to prove to us they're smart before we treat them as such. It's our job to find, see, and nurture their gifts. It was Jonathan's 2nd grade teacher, Carolyn Booker, who was Black and who held high expectations for all her students, that changed schooling for Jonathan. She was his first teacher to fully see and champion Jonathan's intelligence and potential. Jonathan says, "I remember going from being considered 'slow' to being one of the 'smarter people.'" Jonathan went on to graduate from Yale University and Cornell Law School. He works today as a successful public defender representing indigent clients. Still, that early label of 'slow' was hard to dismiss. He said, "It took a couple of years to feel I belonged at Yale, that it wasn't a mistake."

Strong schools that educate all our students equitably and joyfully are a necessity for the health and wellbeing of our democracy. Our schools and classrooms are where our future voters and leaders learn to think critically, effectively communicate, actively listen to and consider other points of view, and learn about and "see" the larger world beyond their local neighborhood—or not. It's also where learners realize—or not—that they have agency in their lives and that with hard work and expert support they can determine their futures. Ideally, all of the above factors depend on high expectations and students developing trusting relationships with teachers and peers, and some of these need to be people who are not of their "tribe." Although it doesn't solve our problems of racial inequality, schools where the population is diverse and multiracial—like those my children attended—can show what's possible when a community makes a commitment, imperfect as it's bound to be, to excellence for all. I see it as a civic duty that all of us do what we can to ensure all students have equitable opportunities for excellence.

CHAPTER 4

Co-creating a Joyful, Inclusive Culture

- ❖ Creating a welcoming culture
- ❖ Establishing routines, rituals, and celebrations
- ❖ Designing spaces for living, learning, and wellbeing

DOI: 10.4324/9781003381242-4

Creating a welcoming culture

If we focus first on building an equitable and joyful culture of trusting relationships, respect, and celebration of learners' strengths, then all things literacy-wise are possible. That means providing an emotional, social, intellectual culture where students—at least while they're in our care—feel seen, heard, and applauded. It also means nurturing their intellect, academic confidence, creativity—and provoking resilience. The trauma and constant uncertainty many children and their families endure from lack of basic needs—adequate food, shelter, safety, health, and easy access to technology—impede learning. Students need security and predictability to feel safe and to function at their best. The school experience must be that respite, that safe and loving environment that optimizes teaching and learning.

CULTURE IS THE SOUL OF THE SCHOOL

determined by how we

1. treat everyone kindly
2. hold high expectations
3. honor and hear all the voices
4. focus on professional learning
5. employ principled practices
6. intellectually challenge all students
7. celebrate learning

—or not.

Dear reader, what you have just read is a tweet I sent out in August 2018. I share it here, at the beginning of this chapter, because it received one of the largest and most positive responses of any tweet I've ever done. What I've learned over many decades is that the "culture of the school"—which, for me, also means the climate and the environment—is the most important indicator for whether or not teachers, the principal, students, and all members of the school's community will thrive—or not.

Where there is a thriving and equitable school culture, educators put into daily practice all of the mindsets and actions listed above. As well, the emotional, social, and physical tone of the school is one of inclusiveness, trust, and joyfulness. The *physical spaces*, even in old buildings, are clean, safe, and attractive. The bulletin boards, charts, seating, and room design reflect that the school belongs to all of us, students included. The *mental spaces* we create in a thriving culture incite the intellect and encourage risk-taking, choice, and agency for students and teachers. The *emotional spaces* are heart-centered, that is, students feel safe and encouraged to be and become their true selves, to share their passions and their hopes and dreams, and to know they are supported by caring teachers who "see" them and who respect and honor their language and culture. The *social spaces* promote collaboration, celebration, and friendship through seating, room design, and curriculum as conversation. Altogether, a healthy and joyful culture is a place where everyone wants to be and where everyone feels wanted and welcome. When students feel supported and seen, they are more likely to establish connections with their teachers, parents, and their peers—in and out of school. So let's talk about how to create such a culture—and sustain it.

Creating a welcoming, thriving culture is living graciously. In my life, outside of school and work, my husband Frank and I strive to make our living environment as pleasing as we can, for ourselves and for those we welcome into our home. We want our guests to feel cherished and appreciated. We attempt to create spaces that are beautiful, whether it be a vase of fresh flowers or a carefully set table for gracious dining. We set up the seating so it promotes comfort and easy conversation.

All of this gets me thinking about the parallels to the classroom and school environment and making it welcoming for all those who work and visit there. What is the culture we want to create? What can we do to ensure it is a beautiful, welcoming, safe place for learning, for making all voices heard and respected? How do we make everyone feel valued and seen? I will never forget my many years working as an instructional literacy coach when I was in a different building each day of the week, supporting teachers. Sometimes we had after-school meetings where all the teachers worked late. The district would provide dinner and it was, almost always, pizza on paper plates. Yet, as the district's elementary instructional coach for five elementary schools, when I reported monthly at the principals' lunchtime meeting with the superintendent, I saw that those meetings included a catered lunch on china plates. I felt then, as I do now, that it would have been terrific—as a way to show appreciation to teachers for their extra efforts—to provide a wonderful meal on real plates for them, too, at least occasionally.

Debbie Lenhardt Mair is a principal in a high needs elementary school in Winnipeg, Manitoba. While her students live in an economically challenged area, she creates a sumptuous learning and living environment for students and staff. When I visited her school and met with her teachers, I noticed the homey atmosphere in the staff room—comfortable furniture, cozy curtains, and personal touches. What most impressed me was our lunch; we ate at round tables with tablecloths and delicious food served on fancy plates accompanied by real silverware and cloth napkins. Why did that make such an impression on me? To be fussed over like that sent a message of caring, respect, and appreciation. I've never forgotten that setting, and I've never seen anything like it in another school. Mair notes, "Creating a beautiful environment honors all that attend and work in our school. Staff share they feel special, and it provides a positive environment to support good mental health and wellbeing."[1] Especially these days, when so many students, teachers, and families are experiencing or recovering from anxiety, isolation, and/or trauma, creating a beautiful and peaceful environment can be calming and healing.

The first thing I notice when I enter a school is how welcoming it feels to visitors. I look for authenticity and real-world purposes in literacy tasks, collaboration by teachers and students, conversations that go beyond test-taking and skills, and a beautiful, clean, and safe environment. I notice what's in the hallways and on classroom walls and whether what's posted is truly meant to be read by readers or is just posted to fill space. I look at the way desks are arranged in classrooms and the opportunities for students to work together. I notice the quality of the literacy resources and whether or not they're first-rate, worthy of the students' time and respectful of their interests, languages, and cultures. I notice how teachers are dressed, as dressing professionally also imparts a sense of caring about the profession and sets a good example for children. I look for first-rate classroom libraries and comfortable areas for voluntary reading. I notice how respectfully adults talk to each other and to children, and who's doing most of the talking. I listen for a commitment to high expectations and a belief that students can be high achievers. And, always, I look for a sense of enjoyment in teaching and learning and whether or not people are glad to be there.

What I've learned over many years of working in classrooms and schools is that a welcoming and caring culture is a necessity for high, schoolwide achievement and that we all have the opportunity and responsibility to work to make the culture a positive one for learning and for living. The little things do matter—greeting each other warmly, refusing to participate in gossip, having fresh coffee available, taking the time to remember staff members' birthdays, and doing whatever we can to create a more trusting and joyful environment, one where everyone feels appreciated and cherished.

Perhaps most of all, I notice if there are trusting relationships between and among teachers, students, and administrators. Where there is trust, anything is possible. Without it, all aspects of teaching, learning, and living are limited. "Progress moves at the speed of trust." I don't know who to credit for that wise statement, but it's stuck with me. "Progress moves at the speed of trust." If we focus first on building an equitable and joyful culture of trust, respect, and celebration of learners' strengths, then all things literacy wise are possible. Where people in a community establish warm, trusting relationships—whether that community be a school, classroom, home, or homeless shelter—anything is possible.

Establishing routines, rituals, and celebrations

L ike most of you, I need a fair amount of predictability in my life, especially when times are uncertain and life feels out of control. It is then, especially, that I depend on routines and rituals to help ground me and breathe a bit easier. Not only are routines and rituals necessary for optimal and joyful creating and learning; they are essential to our physical, social, and emotional wellbeing. The routines and rituals we adopt can help provide a safer, more peaceful, and serene environment as well as peace of mind. With that goal in mind for you dear reader, let me share some of my routines and rituals that have made it possible to relax, enjoy life more, and be more productive—even if it's just for a moment. As well, rituals are necessary for sustaining a storytelling culture.

As I am writing this section, it's a week before Thanksgiving, one of our family's favorite holidays. Part of the reason we enjoy it so much involves the traditions and rituals we follow each year—stringing cranberries for decorations, setting a beautiful table, making everyone's favorite dish, and adding some new ones. Much of the cooking now is enthusiastically shared with family members and other guests. Especially joyful for me is making the cranberry sauce and the stuffing. The cranberry sauce is my mom's recipe; I can still picture her making it, year after year. After she died, I took over making it, and I have shared the recipe with many friends over the years. Sharing it with loved ones is part of the joy. In fact, our friend Kevin is stopping by tonight to pick up a quart jar. He just texted me, "I will come by for your spectacular cranberry sauce. I have been dreaming of it since I used up my last bit last year." Happy to share the recipe with you as well. It's easy to make. I cook the cranberries with freshly squeezed orange juice instead of water, and add chopped pears, apples, and ample cinnamon.

The stuffing recipe, using homemade croutons, is one I created many years ago and that we all love. Part of that love is knowing that our particular stuffing is now generational and will, most likely, continue to be. Family traditions, especially around food, are one way many of us celebrate our unique holiday cultures. While I was the original stuffing maker, my granddaughters Katie and Brooke made the stuffing with me for many years, and now Katie has taken over that role. Just like in the classroom when we want a great end result, demonstrating how to "do it," and then sharing and guiding the experience with learners bodes well for excellent results. Of course, it's essential that the quality of the ingredients and resources are first-rate.

Thanksgiving is a holiday and ritual I love—for the food, the memories, and gathering around a beautiful table with loved ones. One of my fondest Thanksgiving memories growing up was having my grandmother with us at the extended dining room table, a table that was enhanced by the gorgeous, crocheted tablecloth she had spent eight years creating. During those many years, wherever she was, my grandmother was never without her thread and hooked needles, carefully moving her fingers to form and weave a beautiful, crocheted square. Each square took an hour of delicate needlework to complete and another hour to attach to other crocheted squares or the rectangular linen cloth in the center. I remember her telling me there were well over a thousand crocheted squares, and that didn't include the linen napkins with crocheted borders she also hand made.

My grandmother was a practical person, so she made sure the tablecloth was washable, in a washing machine on a gentle cycle. As the tablecloth is delicate, we only use it every few years. But this year, we can all use some beautification and glamor, so we're thinking about bringing it out again. For our students who may not be gathering with family for a Thanksgiving dinner or other holidays, consider incorporating some kind of ritual in the classroom. For Thanksgiving, it could be as simple as writing poems about what we're grateful for, for more than anything else, this is a holiday about shared gratitude. For other holidays, it might be providing materials for students to create simple, handmade gifts.

Personal routines and rituals help ground me, especially when I'm feeling anxious, or life just feels "too much." Taking a walk, getting out in the garden, listening to music, baking cookies, deep breathing, and exercising all take the edge off—at least for a while. Other rituals I observe that bring me pleasure and satisfaction include keeping a monthly reading record of books read; setting aside sacred time for writing every day; reading before bed; making time for friends; and celebrating birthdays, efforts, and achievements of those I admire—often through handwritten notes. So much of what we do in our personal lives has implications for how to make our classrooms and schools warm and welcoming places. The main thing is that we establish rituals with our students and our children. When life feels chaotic, familiar rituals and routines can help steady and calm us and create a sense of normalcy. In the classroom, it could be kids grabbing a book when they enter the classroom and reading for the joy of it; Friday morning book talks related to favorite books and authors; writing a class-authored thank you letter each month to someone who helps the classroom and school run more smoothly (for example, the principal, the school secretary, the custodian, the crossing guard); and/or the unique celebrations and rituals you and your students devise and carry out.

Creating an orderly space before I begin a new project is a necessary ritual. Before I begin writing a new book or any big writing project, I "clean up" my writing area. I simply cannot begin writing—or any project that demands my full attention—without a well-organized and uncluttered space. The same is true for me in the kitchen. I can't begin cooking a meal in a messy kitchen. However, once I'm "creating," the mess is all part of it, and I can pretty much ignore it. With writing, it's folders and papers in various piles on tables and scattered on the floor, often for months. In the kitchen, it's many ingredients on counters and unwashed dishes; I am not one who cleans up as I go. Once in the process of creating, my focus is on the "doing"; the "mess" doesn't bother me.

So when you think of your important spaces in the classroom, home, or office, what can you routinely do—or continue to do—to make your space and your life more peaceful and productive? Consider involving students and family members in deciding what can work fairly for everyone involved regarding issues such as the use of personal devices, cleaning up, communicating information, how we respectfully talk with and greet each other, and much more.

One unusual and wonderful school ritual I fondly remember was the annual and beloved tradition by Ms. Westbrook, who was the kindergarten teacher for both of our children. For open house in the fall each year, she would greet her students' families wearing a beautiful, white blouse tucked into a floor length full skirt, but this was no ordinary skirt. This was a carefully-stitched-together skirt comprised of adjoining, colorful squares of equal sizes. Each cloth square had been hand drawn with an original picture signed by the kindergartner who created it. All the kids knew the significance of their square being an important part of the meaningful whole. I fondly remember as a parent how welcoming and loving it felt to greet Ms. Westbrook, so splendidly dressed, showcasing an original piece of art from every child in her classroom. I don't remember much about her teaching style, but I loved her personal style which communicated, "Your children matter to me. Each one is unique and dear." All these years later, I easily recall this loving ritual for students and their families.

Incorporating celebrations at the beginning of every staff meeting and/or professional learning meeting sets a positive tone that pays big benefits. It's human nature. We are more likely to be open to dealing with tough issues if we first focus on something that's going well. I have found most teachers are reluctant to publicly share or "brag" about their successes. So, in my weeklong residency work in schools and classrooms, as I notice something wonderful a teacher or student has done, I invite that teacher to share at our end-of-the-day professional learning meeting. I will start by saying something like, "When I was in Loretta's classroom today, I noticed…so I've asked her to share that with you." That celebration might be a poem a writer who struggles wrote; it might be something a teacher had the courage to try for the first time; it might be a shared writing created with students.

Oftentimes, I read aloud a picture book at the start of a professional learning meeting, regardless of grade levels or positions of the participants. That 10 minutes is well spent even if we only have 30–40 minutes together. It's soothing to the soul, introduces us to a story and/ or author/illustrator we might not know about, reaffirms the power of literature, and binds our community together. I recall, several years ago, reading aloud to a group of principals, administrators, and assistant superintendents a favorite picture book, *Adrian Simcox Does NOT Have a Horse* by Marcy Campbell, illustrated by Corinna Luyken. It's a poignant book about bullying, poverty, judging others without knowing their "back story," and—ultimately—the power of kindness and a vivid imagination to set things right. The room went silent when I finished reading and many were smiling, touched by the empathy a genuine, heartwarming story can provide. When I learned it was the birthday of lovely Celia, one of the assistant superintendents in attendance, I gave the book to her, as a gift, with a personal written message. Like many great picture books, this one is a gem for reading aloud and having follow-up conversations—for learners of all ages.

In schools that have a thriving culture, the principal leads a celebration culture. It took me many years, as a teacher-researcher and a practitioner, to realize that without principal and superintendent leadership, which includes deep knowledge of literacy, whole school progress is not sustainable. While it's well known that teachers are the most important factor in a child's learning, it seems to be less well known and accepted that leadership at the top is equally crucial. Time and time again, I have seen a flourishing school culture fall apart in just a few months. A strong and trusted principal leaves and is replaced by a principal who, instead of building on what's working and embracing teachers as partners in learning and leadership, sets off on their own course. Despite the fact that the school had embraced a professional learning culture, without the new principal on board, learning growth is stymied and curtailed. I used to think a highly knowledgeable group of teachers-as-leaders could sustain the gains, but in my experience, that's rarely the case.

Marilyn Jerde is a great example of a principal who created, led, and sustained a celebration of learning culture. I met her during her first year as principal in Westminster, Colorado, where I was privileged to co-lead with her a weeklong writing residency for five consecutive years and to begin what turned out to be a loving, life-long friendship. I recently asked her why she thought the culture—of trust, respect, and academic achievement—had been sustained after she left. She said, "It's not just about getting the job done but nurturing the soul of these people." One of Marilyn's gifts is her ability to recognize and account for nuance in all situations, that situations are rarely black and white. She always provided a gentle touch even when it was necessary to be firm with people. One of her former teachers recalls, "She was inspirational and loving; at the same time, she held teachers accountable to do their job and provided them support." For example, she provided mentors to teachers who were struggling.

As part of the school's learning culture, Marilyn balanced high expectations, goal setting, and ongoing assessment with regular opportunities for celebration. She led professional learning meetings every week, where teachers read and discussed professional articles, met at and across grade levels to discuss research and strategies, and examined and celebrated what was going well across grade levels before focusing on the most pressing needs. The teachers became a community of learners. The more they got to know one another, the more their feelings of trust and support for one another grew. The staff developed routines and rituals for their times together, and celebration was always a cornerstone. As an example, they shared stories of their lives, and one year they published a book together— *Our Stories Come to School*—about something in their life no one else on staff knew. Marilyn says, "The key to celebration is that it has to happen at the right time, with the right people, for the right reason. We all appreciate sincere recognition and validation of our work in schools." She supported teachers fully, filtered out stressors coming from the district that teachers didn't need to know about, and kept the focus on what was right and best for students and teachers.

After five years as a building administrator, Marilyn left the school to become a director at the district level, where she set up and led principal cohort groups. She also mentored and provided support to the new principal who followed her. It was interesting to observe that the positive school culture Marilyn had lovingly nurtured remained unbroken. Teachers knew the joy of being part of a school culture that functioned as a caring community. The staff did everything they could to support the new, inspiring principal so she and they could succeed and sustain the academic gains, the thriving culture, and the rituals they had co-created—and add new ones.

Bittersweet rituals are important too as they remind us of the fragility and impermanence of life, along with the joy, which gets me thinking about blackberries. Our family has been picking wild blackberries in August every year for as long as I can remember.

During blackberry season, I am unbothered by stained purple fingers, prickly scratches, or muddy shoes. Filling up a bucket of blackberries is pure joy. I love the tart, juicy, sweet taste of the berries and being out in the hot sun in the midst of all the wild bramble bushes. I love making blackberry jam and blackberry pie and sharing those fruits of my labor with people I care about. I save about half of what we pick to create a frozen stash for homemade winter delights, such as pancakes topped with blackberries and blackberry tarts.

Most of all, though, when I really think about it, what I most savor are the exquisite memories that blackberry picking evokes—wonderful family times when we picked berries together. Life seemed so uncomplicated then. This year, unpredictably and for the first time, there were no blackberries worth picking. We kept checking our favorite spots, and the berries were dry and withered. Was it climate change, a damp summer with not enough sunshine, or something else? Like so much of life, we don't always know why things happen as they do.

Picking blackberries reminds me that life is sweet and sour, smooth and thorny, and always an adventure—sometimes within easy reach and other times a great challenge. So it is with our teaching—now and then prickly, often challenging, and with moments of pure delight. All the more reason to ground our lives and our work in routines, rituals, and celebrations that create lasting, positive memories—especially important for counteracting the tough days that we, our students, and our loved ones inevitably face.

So I'm thinking about Thanksgiving again. The number of people around our table is smaller than it used to be. We honor those who can no longer join us. We remember them through the stories we celebrate and share. The memories we created together are still intact—pleasurable, nostalgic, and tinged with a bit of pain. Bittersweet, I would say.

Designing spaces for living, learning, and wellbeing

Creating a beautiful, peaceful setting can be soul healing. Calming. Uplifting. I truly believe that. The physical spaces we live in impact our emotional wellbeing and our overall comfort. In fact, our immediate environment influences how well we learn, feel part of a community, take risks, and thrive—or not. Being married to an architect and artist has helped me appreciate, understand, and confront this reality. While there are so many factors in our lives where we have little or no control, we can take steps—even small ones—to organize and enhance our workplace and living spaces in a manner that improves the quality of our lives. Being flexible and open to such change is not easy, but it is possible. Here's a story that sheds some light, literally.

When Frank and I were married just a few years, we moved from Detroit to Boston, where he had accepted a job in an architectural firm. We rented a small, two-bedroom, basement apartment in nearby Waltham, Massachusetts. The combined living room-dining space also included a tiny, see-through kitchen. There was a linoleum floor throughout, which we covered with a white, shaggy rug in the living-dining area—without any thought that white is totally impractical for all the obvious reasons. With donated fabric from my dad, who was in the textile business, I used my sewing machine and modest skills to make lined draperies for the living room and curtains for the bedrooms. It remains the most comprehensive sewing experience of my life, and I am still proud of the "good is good enough" results.

Once we had our major furniture in place—a large sofa with two ottomans (all of which we still have to this day, recovered multiple times) along with a small table and chairs for dining—I assumed all would stay exactly as we'd arranged it. That's how it had always been in the home I grew up in. The sofa, chairs, lamps, paintings, and small items such as an ash tray or candy dish remained frozen in their original placement, never to be moved. My mother loved dependable order and we, her family, never thought to question that immovable stance. By contrast, my creative guy found numerous ways to rearrange things, constantly. It was as if we had endless, movable walls. He unexpectedly and regularly moved everything around, which made me physically and emotionally uncomfortable—knocked me off balance to be truthful. I didn't tell him any of that. I was 23 years old, not confident in my design skills, and I was years away from finding my voice to say what I really thought. So, I tolerated the changes and the discomfort as best I could. Then gradually and surprisingly, I came to welcome the changes and even to embrace the whimsy, the flexibility, the freedom to make a few modifications myself. I came to find each new look and repositioning fun and even exhilarating. A boost on a dreary day. A jolt of ingenuity to replace a stale, tired look. A literal and emotional light added or placed to brighten up a dark corner.

We live in Seattle now, in a house where we both constantly rearrange things to beautify our living space and make it more interesting and more comfortable. I am just as likely to initiate the change as Frank is, and he welcomes and appreciates my ideas. In the winter, we often have heavy, colorful rugs on the wooden floors. When spring approaches, we live with barer floors, fewer rugs, and more neutral colors. While we both regularly move furniture and objects around, as some of our paintings are Frank's original work, I leave the what-goes-on-the-wall decisions to him. Changes to our living space create vitality and freshness, which lifts our mood. We feel lighter, more productive, happier.

Why not do the same in the classroom and design our physical and emotional spaces for inclusiveness, flexibility, and lightness? We honor our students with the care we take in creating a beautiful and equitable school environment. Why should we and our students be relegated to learning in a boring, uninspiring space that remains stagnant for the school year? Why not collaborate with students on how *our* classroom and school might work better for living and learning? Co-creating and crafting a room design with students can add calmness, vibrancy, beauty, and a sense of order and ownership, especially important for students lacking those qualities in their day-to-day lives. Not only that. It's one way of preparing students for change, which is inevitable, and learning not just to accept it but to welcome it. Such design flexibility also needs to extend to how we group students. Too often students see themselves relegated to one fixed group, often with an invisible label that indicates "needs improvement," "disabled," or "low reading group." Make groups truly flexible and balanced by purpose, interests, needs, and gender.

Finally, personalize your spaces. In the room where I write, I have a painting by our dear friend Juliette above my desk. I have pictures of my family everywhere, on my desk, on the walls, and on the window ledge. I have favorite objects on my desk that bring me comfort—a couple of shells from the beach; a small pile of favorite notes and cards from friends and family; a small, wooden bowl—a handcrafted gift from educator and mentor Don Holdaway; and other small, treasured keepsakes from teachers around the world, such as a blue elephant, a glass whale, a wooden carving of an Indigenous child—each with its own special significance. Why not encourage students to personalize their spaces in some way? For many of our students, it may be that school and their classroom is their favored personal space, the place in their lives where they feel most physically and emotionally safe or, if they are homeless or housing insecure, it may be their only predictable, safe space where they can be truly present. Allow them to make it their own in some way.

Start with personalizing the physical space of the classroom. Invite students to sketch, illustrate, and/or graph plans for possibilities, including decluttering the classroom to seek a more peaceful, calming atmosphere. Be sure to include what goes on the walls—the charts, student writing, artwork, and work in progress. Ensure that what goes on the walls represents and serves well the students and the learning going on. Consider eliminating commercially produced charts that add an impersonal feel and that are often written in adult language that students rarely access. Ensure displayed content is student-centered, student-guided, and student-led. As well, design spaces for conversation, which means comfortable seating, cushions, tables, and furniture that can be easily moved and reconfigured. Frequent opportunities for conversations, where all voices are heard and respected, are part of a healthy culture.

Also, not to be minimized are adding simple but important additions like flowers (real, dried, or made of paper by students), plants, and areas for reading and conferring that can make a space more welcoming and personal. Lighting, in particular, changes everything. An inexpensive lamp with a soft glow and other inexpensive means of illumination such as uplights can bathe a dark corner in a light that adds warmth and personality to a room. Frank and I have several, small uplights strategically placed on the floor in our home. Seattle gets lots of dark and dreary days in the winter, and brighter illumination is a spirit lifter.

Ideally, we want to co-create spaces where we and our students, children, and loved ones feel free and encouraged to become their best and truest selves. In such spaces, the physical and emotional elements seamlessly co-exist in an environment where creating, sharing, and learning thrive. When you walk into your home, your classroom, or your school, think: "Does this space reflect the people that inhabit it? Or does it give off a vibe of belonging to one dominant decider?"

When I enter a school, it takes me about three minutes to figure out who the school belongs to and who feels comfortable here—or not. The messages and student work in the hallways and on classroom walls speak volumes about who's in charge, what the expectations are, and who the audience is for "the work." For example, is student work posted in hallways at eye level so students, teachers, and visitors can read and enjoy it, or is it posted high up, serving primarily as decoration? Also, if the work on the walls is meant to be read, is the posted work accompanied by an explanation, written with students, so readers have some context for the work? Take a critical look at the spaces that you and those you care about inhabit and see where and how you might beautify those spaces—visually, physically, and emotionally—to be more inclusive, accessible, and meaningful.

Part of our work as educators is, as best we can, to fill the spaces kids don't have growing up. Creating a space for everyone includes acceptance, love, and trust. A safe and orderly environment is necessary for learning. Just as many of us think of our homes as a sanctuary, think of school as a sanctuary, too, a place and space where all learners—even our most vulnerable ones—can feel protected, hopeful, and able to envision possibilities for their future.

CHAPTER 5

Developing Professional Knowledge

- ❖ Becoming professionally knowledgeable
- ❖ Transforming teaching and learning
- ❖ Considering the science of reading
- ❖ Seeking out mentors

DOI: 10.4324/9781003381242-5

Becoming professionally knowledgeable

Let me say this straight-out. This is a difficult time to be teaching. I know what you're thinking. We're already struggling with teacher burnout, families in crisis, and daily stresses. Developing professional knowledge is not high on the "to do" list. But hear me out. I'm not talking about professional development where an expert offers training on the new commercial reading program, transmits standardized, pre-determined knowledge, and focuses excessively on test scores and data. I'm talking about professional learning, where you and your colleagues get to examine literacy and learning as it relates to your students, at your school, in a collegial setting.

Ideally, it's teachers and leaders forming a schoolwide learning community to examine and discuss their beliefs and practices and engage in authentic learning. It's collaborative knowledge building for the purpose of more effective, equitable, and engaging teaching and learning. The professional learning community, or what I often call the professional *literacy* community, might just be two teachers from the same or different grade levels or subject area disciplines meeting over lunch, a grade level team convening at a common planning time, or an after-school meeting devoted to a common interest or concern. Professional learning done well is enjoyable and makes your life easier, more manageable, and more satisfying.

When I began teaching, my professional knowledge was scanty. I did not yet see knowledge—especially collaborative knowledge—as crucial to being a successful teacher, that is, one who met the interests and needs of all my students in a kind, compassionate, and equitable manner. Based on my undergraduate university "training," I knew how to use a teacher's manual, write a structured lesson plan, and follow directions in the packets of ready-made materials. I did not know how and why different approaches worked. I did not know how to tailor instruction for each student, raise expectations, or teach responsively to the students in front of me. For the first decade or so of my teaching, that seemed to suffice. I believed I was a good teacher, and no one told me differently. I never thought to read a professional book, and that is also the reality for some teachers today.

It was only when it became obvious to me that I was not meeting the needs and interests of the students I was teaching that I reached out for help. At home, with my two young children, I was reading captivating books to and with them, but in school, there was no emphasis on "real" reading and I began to question, "Why not?" My particular work situation at the time was as a reading specialist in a high poverty school, pulling out small groups of primary grade students that were failing to learn to read. The commercial skills program that I was expected to use focused on drilling kids in phonics exercises, skills-in-isolation. That is, except for lots of word work, there was no "reading" involved or expected. There were no actual books! There was also no professional study going on where I was teaching, at least not any I remember. Faculty meetings were devoted to rules, procedures, upcoming events, open house, and the like.

What I needed was high quality professional learning. If you are a teacher, educational leader, literacy advocate, librarian, or deeply concerned and/or involved with kids and literacy, knowing how to teach and support readers and writers so they become competent, self-monitoring, joyful readers and writers requires a solid foundation of theoretical and practical knowledge accompanied by a big dose of compassion and kindness. Parents fit in here too, for their knowledge and behaviors about literacy impact their kids. If, as was true for me years ago, you are in a situation without positive opportunities for quality professional development, professional books are especially important as a way to jumpstart your professional growth.

Also, if you want to continue to be a fully-informed educator, you will find a way to keep up with the latest research, approaches, and trends and then apply your professional judgment to your own teaching/

leading context. In addition to professional books, I read professional journals, news articles, online texts, reputable blogs, and educational research via Twitter. I also listen to podcasts. I want to share with you the authors and books that transformed me as a learner and teacher and that still resonate today. That is, the methodology and research remain solid and applicable. If you do not yet have seminal books and authors who have impacted your teaching and learning, the books I share are still relevant. You will also want to get current recommendations from knowledgeable colleagues and reliable sources.

My first professional reading began out of a need to know. In particular, I was searching for a better way to teach reading. In that search, I learned about the literacy and language work that was going on in New Zealand and Australia, especially the groundbreaking work of Don Holdaway, Brian Cambourne, and Marie Clay. Each was committed to literacy and language learning for *all* children—ensuring optimal conditions for learning, early intervention when needed, and joyful learning. Each wrote in great, replicable detail about creating an equitable and caring learning and language environment, explicitly teaching phonics and other necessary word solving skills in meaningful context, reading for meaning right from the start, assessing learners in the midst of teaching, and mindfully adjusting to meet the interests and needs of the learners. These authors became my early—and lifelong—mentors. Reading and studying their work made it possible for me to develop my own theory of learning for teaching and thinking, which remains integral to the way I approach learners, instruction, and curriculum today.

Above all, the thinking and work of Don Holdaway was transformative. His seminal book, *The Foundations of Literacy* (1979), changed how I looked at literacy, language, and learning. I began to envision what a positive and joyful literacy environment might look like and entail for *all* students, including those in under-resourced schools with large populations of low-income students, Black students, and/or English learners. I still consider this timeless book mandatory reading for gaining a foundation in understanding language learning and fostering it through a strategy-oriented style of teaching. See Chapter 6, "Championing the Reading/Writing Connection," for specifics on Holdaway's "shared-book-experience," a powerful instructional approach that continues to be a mainstay of my teaching—across the curriculum. Along with *The Foundations of Literacy,* Don Holdaway's *Independence in Reading* (1980) and *Stability and Change in Literacy Learning* (1984) also greatly shaped my thinking, especially as related to the human element. That is, first and foremost—before any subject matter—we are teaching unique human beings and relating content to their strengths, knowledge, interests, needs, and culture.

In the mid 1980s, Brian Cambourne's work also provided invaluable insight into the language learning process and inspired my teaching, thinking, and learning. Cambourne's discussion of "conditions for learning"—immersion, demonstration, expectation, responsibility, use, approximation, and response—are necessary conditions for all effective language learning. "Cambourne's conditions," as they are often called, provided me an invaluable visual and mental model for respecting each learner's developmental level, concentrating on strengths, focusing on process, and encouraging "languaging"—opportunities for conversations and interaction—to name just a few principles and beliefs from his model. In *Made for Learning: How the Conditions of Learning Guide Teaching Decisions* (2020), with co-author and American teacher Debra Crouch, Cambourne has updated and expanded his original thinking. The authors challenge us to critically examine the effects of our literacy beliefs, practices, and processes around teaching and learning, and they provide numerous practical ideas and examples for applying the Conditions of Learning for ensuring meaning-making in the classroom. This is a must-read book for all educators!

At the same time that I was studying Brian Cambourne's work, I was fortunate to be in one of the first groups in the U.S. to be trained as a Reading Recovery teacher. Reading Recovery is the brainchild of educator, researcher, and psychologist Marie Clay. The research-based program was developed in New Zealand in the 1970s and is a short-term, one-on-one approach for teaching and accelerating the lowest-performing 1st graders in reading. For most of these readers, the impact is meaningful and long-lasting. Even though I had certification as a reading specialist, it was my Reading Recovery "training" that finally made me a competent and confident reading teacher. Crucially, I learned about the complexity of reading and comprehension monitoring, even for our youngest readers. Practically, I learned how to integrate phonics and word work with reading and writing delightful stories. Clay's work is also notable for its emphasis on the role of early writing behaviors with reading. For all those seeking to become more knowledgeable literacy teachers, I highly recommend reading Marie Clay's *Literacy Lessons Designed for Individuals: 2nd Edition* (2016).

Teaching children to write was an area I knew little about when I began teaching. Like most teachers at the time and still true for many teachers today, I never had a college course on teaching writing. However, in my reading and studying of professional books, Donald Graves' work leaped out. His first book, *Writing: Teachers and Children at Work*, published in 1983, was an eye-opener. This practical text takes the reader through the process of children's development as writers and gives teachers confidence, understanding, and strategies to support children in their writing development. I recall all these years later how while reading Don Graves' book, I realized for the first time—and felt distressed about it—that I didn't know anything personal about most of the students I was teaching and how that connection is necessary to fully support children as writers. In addition to Don Graves' work, around the same time I also embraced the groundbreaking reading and writing work of Nancie Atwell, Donald Murray, Tom Newkirk, and many others.

Dorsey Hammond's work also transformed and validated my teaching and teacher-research at a time when I needed clarity. I met Dorsey at the

1982 International Reading Association Conference, where I attended his session on teaching reading comprehension. I was struck by his sensible, solid, in-depth approach to teaching reading and his unique inclusion of phonics as a core element but not as a singular emphasis. Teaching phonics in isolation was in vogue at the time, so it was refreshing and affirming to see and hear Dorsey's balanced perspective. Determined to learn more, I can still remember approaching him after his presentation and asking him if he'd be speaking anywhere near me, in the Cleveland, Ohio, area. He graciously invited me to attend a workshop at a local college as his guest. I've been learning from him ever since.

His brilliant book, *The Comprehension Experience: Engaging Readers through Effective Inquiry and Discussion* (2011), co-authored with mentor and author Denise Nessel, asks and responds to the essential reading question: "What kind of instruction best supports comprehension?" In the Preface (xiii), the authors write: "We think it's time to decrease the emphasis on skills and strategies and turn our attention to increasing learners' capacity to construct meaning." In the Foreword of the book, which I was honored to write, I state: "*The Comprehension Experience* is about teaching and empowering all students to think and deliberate at high levels while giving us educators the language and examples of exemplary teaching to make that happen" (vii). This classic text remains my favorite and most useful text for teaching reading—and so much more—effectively and joyfully.

Some other literacy notables whose work, thinking, and books I embraced early on were Frank Smith, Ken Goodman and Stephen Krashen. As well, I remain especially indebted to P. David Pearson and Richard Allington for their lifetime of research, its practical application to the classroom, and their respect for teachers. More currently, I also appreciate and have been influenced by the research of John Hattie, Nell Duke, and Linda Darling-Hammond, to name several, along with many literacy practitioners, such as Cris Tovani, Kelly Gallagher, Penny Kittle, Donalyn Miller, Larry Ferlazzo, and so many more.

While professional reading was and is essential for improving our teaching and learning, it is not enough to effect sustainable, worthwhile change. I recognized such change was only possible with ongoing, embedded professional learning that was schoolwide. I learned that lesson in the early 2000s. I was being invited into schools and districts across the U.S. after the staff had read and done a book study on my books *Reading Essentials* and *Writing Essentials*. I distinctly recall being stunned at how limited teachers' literacy knowledge was *in spite of* their professional reading and study. Even though I believed my books were practical and easy to read, what was missing for teacher readers was being able to directly *see* principled practices in action, *hear* the language of responsive teaching and assessment, *analyze* the lesson, and have an opportunity to *"try and apply"* in the classroom—with guidance and support.

That realization was the impetus for creating a weeklong residency model grounded in demonstrations, shared and guided experiences, and coaching in diverse classrooms. Teachers in the school were released to observe, along with the principal, in a primary grade classroom in the morning and an intermediate grade classroom in the afternoon. Before and after school each day, we gathered for a whole school, professional learning meeting. In the morning, the host classroom teachers and I would set the stage for what teachers would be observing; after school, we met to have conversations about what teachers observed and what their takeaways and questions were.

I made it a requirement that I would only return to a school for another residency if the principal and staff engaged in continuous professional learning and ongoing professional reading and discussion. Critically, one of my most momentous learning lessons from the residency work was that unless the principal knew literacy and teachers became leaders, whole school change was not possible even as it is necessary for sustaining literacy gains. That realization led me to alter the residency model so that the whole afternoon was devoted to working with, mentoring, and coaching the principal—especially in what I call "instructional walks." That insight also led to developing with colleagues a video-based literacy series to serve as a guide and scaffold for ongoing, school embedded, professional learning. You can learn more about that on page 109. Finally, the crucial insight, "Teachers must be leaders, and principals must know literacy" propelled me to write *Read, Write, Lead: Breakthrough Strategies for Schoolwide Literacy Success* (ASCD, 2018), with its specific details and procedures on embedding a Professional *Literacy* Community (PLC) culture into the school, led by a highly functioning school leadership team.

All of the preceding discussion—going back to my early professional learning—is to say that each of us needs to seek out, read, and apply research and practices from seminal, highly regarded texts and professional learning experiences that push our thinking. In my first book, *Transitions: From Literature to Literacy*, I write:

> Where I am philosophically is based on the professional reading and reflecting I am doing, thoughtful discussions with my colleagues, direct observations of children learning, demonstration teaching I have observed, in-service-workshops I have attended, and lessons I have attempted and then assessed. All these activities are time-consuming when added to the daily teaching demands. But they are what keep me current, professional, and proud of what I do. All this needs to go on continually for me to keep growing professionally and personally.[1]

This statement is as true for me now as it was 35 years ago. To be professionally knowledgeable is the hallmark of every conscientious and expert teacher. Once I began reading professionally, and especially after attending my first reading conference, I recognized how meager my knowledge was. After the knowledge boost from that first conference, I became committed to attending local, state, and national literacy conferences—whenever possible. I became dedicated to finding out everything I could about teaching and learning and, in particular, about teaching reading where so many students were struggling to learn to read in the high poverty school where I was teaching. I also learned, as I was reading and studying the research, that research must be supported by scholarly consensus and also be relevant to our students. The decisions we make as teachers are only as good as our knowledge and application of effective teaching practices, subject matter, the learners we are teaching, informed experiences, and—not to be minimized—common sense. Lots of experiences, including mentoring—which we discuss later in this chapter—give us a feel for what works so that what we may think is intuition is really knowledgeable and sound judgment kicking in.

The most skillful and effective teachers in any domain take charge of their own professional learning, read professionally, collaborate with colleagues, and continually strive to do better. Today's times necessitate we educate all our citizenry well if we are to survive and thrive as a republic—and that includes ensuring that we educators engage in ongoing professional learning, and most of that needs to be job-embedded, on site.

We are living in a time when we are witnessing the backsliding of our liberal, multiracial democracy. If we agree that becoming an informed and activist citizen is a hallmark for preserving democracy, that must first be a goal and reality we educators and responsible adults embrace—if we hope to instill that belief and responsibility in our students and our children. I believe the goal of schooling is to educate learners who are able to think rationally and critically, set their own meaningful goals, know how to learn, monitor and assess their own progress, apply reading and writing for multiple purposes, dialogue and debate on a variety of issues, collaborate and communicate with others, and seek out, listen to, and respect differing points of view. This goal applies to all of us, not just our students and children.

Transforming teaching and learning

I've been teaching, leading, and coaching in classrooms, schools, and districts most of my adult life—studying the research, reading professionally, collaborating with colleagues, reflecting on teaching and learning, and documenting and sharing my learning. I've drawn some conclusions along the way that I hope, dear reader, may be useful and affirming to your own transforming process—in teaching, learning, and in living a good life.

When I'm talking about *transforming* teaching and learning, I mean the *process* of *changing* the culture, environment, conditions, resources, and power structure in a way that is a renewal, a change for the better for all participants, a way of being, learning, and living that adds significant value, respect, and equity to our intellectual, social, and emotional lives and wellbeing—including in our pursuit of happiness, in and outside of the workplace.

David McCullough, prolific author of prize-winning books on America's history, elaborated on what the founding fathers meant by the notion of "the pursuit of happiness." McCullough noted, "As much as anything it meant the life of the mind and spirit. It meant education, and the love of learning, the freedom to think for oneself."[2] The love of learning and the freedom to think for oneself. Doesn't that belief just say it all? Instigating a passion for learning and using that learning to reveal and express our own thoughts. Don't we desire those goals for all our students and loved ones?

Let's start with the role beliefs play in teaching, learning, and living as our beliefs shape and determine who we are and how we behave— in all areas of our lives. It took me a long time to realize how holding intractable beliefs can stymie progress and happiness, and that's as true in teaching as it is for living a good life. Throughout this book, I talk about how our beliefs—for better or worse—determine our mindsets, behaviors, and actions. Our teaching practices reflect our beliefs-in-action. So it's critical, although it's not easy, to continuously examine our beliefs about teaching and learning and to do so schoolwide. While shifting our beliefs about teaching and learning is understandably a slow process, it's a necessary one. We cannot make significant and sustainable change schoolwide, in ourselves, and in those we serve and choose to influence without a belief system—a theory of learning based on research and experience—that serves learners equitably, respectfully, and joyfully. Accompanying such a belief system must be a mindset of high expectations for *all* learners, held by the adults working with the learners.

In my five decades of teaching, in addition to educators holding low expectations for students, I've found two related beliefs that teachers and leaders hold that work against students' optimal learning. The first is the belief that part-to-whole teaching, that is, teaching skills-in-isolation, leads to understanding of the whole. In fact, that belief-in-action makes it harder for students to learn and sustain anything of significance. A colleague offered an apt metaphor: "It's like putting all the pieces of a complex puzzle in front of students but never showing them the lid of the box." Without being able to visualize the end goal and result, solving the puzzle becomes an effort in frustration.

The second belief that makes learning more difficult is that if we explicitly show students how to do something, they are ready to do it on their own. For example, we might believe that through a demonstration or explanation, our explicit teaching will be sufficient for students to be successful when they try it/apply it on their own. This is often not the case. That is why it's so important to ask students what they took away from a demonstration, such as observing our thinking-out-loud as we are reading and/or writing a text. Charting that student feedback, for all to see, is a public assessment of students' learning and a guide for next steps—whether that be another demonstration, a shifting of plans, or something else. Most learners also need shared, scaffolded, and guided experiences before we can expect them to successfully "do it." The following chapter, "Championing the Reading/Writing Connection" will expand on that belief. Crucially, we must ensure the beliefs we hold and put into action in our daily practices are supported by scholarly consensus, are relevant for our students, and are worthy of the time and effort they consume.

So how do we allow ourselves to update deeply held beliefs? I've been surprised at how rare it is and how long it takes for most of us to shift our beliefs—and our practices. It was coming to that realization over many years that propelled me to develop a schoolwide, embedded, professional learning experience—a weeklong, school residency where I demonstrate effective, efficient, and joyful practices in K–6 classrooms. That residency model proved to be highly successful—not just in literacy achievement, but in developing a trusting and joyful school culture—and led to the development of virtual residencies.

With my esteemed colleague, literacy champion Sandra Figueroa, we co-wrote the research-based *Transforming Our Teaching* Series—the professional learning, literacy-centered, video-series that goes inside culturally inclusive classrooms to demonstrate and discuss what's possible when we establish shared beliefs and apply those beliefs to principled, research-based practices. We created three projects in the series: *Reading/Writing Connections, Writing for Audience and Purpose,* and *Reading to Understand.* The students and teachers in the videos are from the actual weeklong residencies. In other words, the work is authentic. The professional Notebooks that accompany the virtual residencies unpack and make visible the how, what, and why of the lessons, the background of the students and school, the teaching points in each video, the language of responsive teaching and ongoing assessment, and how the teaching connects with required standards. Professional reading and discussion accompany each professional learning session. In my long career, the *Transforming Our Teaching* series is the work of which I am most proud.

Teaching is a political act

Transforming teaching and learning is a political act. In the 1990s, we were living through a crisis in education similar to the one we are living through in the 2020s. Then and now, policy makers, politicians, parents, and the media decried that kids today were poorer readers than in the past and that the failure to explicitly teach phonics was the major cause. I remember returning home from a literacy conference in 1995 where I'd been an attendee as well as a keynote speaker. I came away feeling disturbed by the acrimony in education, with teachers pitted against pundits, and shared my feelings with my editor Toby Gordon. "Why don't you write a political book?" she suggested, to which I replied, "I don't even know what that means." But the thought lingered along with some guilt.

I had been telling teachers *they* needed to take a stand, but beyond speaking out, *I* had not taken deliberate actions to confront the crisis. I agreed to write a "political book" if we could get it out quickly. I came to believe that with careful research, expert support, and my own teaching experiences, I could be a reliable narrator for sanity and sense in teaching reading. I wrote *Literacy at the Crossroads: Crucial Talk About Reading, Writing, and Other Teaching Dilemmas* in three months while I was teaching full time. It was released at the International Reading Association's annual meeting in 1996 and became an immediate best seller.

Book banning, censorship, what can and cannot be taught are all part of the politics of education. In many locales, school boards, parents, and superintendents seek to control what students learn and how they learn it. Teachers are increasingly being given less freedom to teach and less authority to make "acceptable" decisions—on curriculum, content, books, language—even as they are being held more and more accountable. In particular, giving students access to books and resources that encourage learners to think for themselves is seen as threatening the social order.

In today's overheated, educational climate, it takes moral courage to speak out, to not go along, to live our beliefs and stand by them, to protest. And yet, we need our collaborative audacity, resolve, and reasonable voices. We must get involved. We cannot wait for policies to change or for permission to transform. Plato said it best: "One of the penalties of refusing to participate in politics is that you end up being governed by your inferiors."

Start with doing what you can within your own classroom and setting to improve teaching and learning. For example, even with a mandated program, choose and use only the parts that are applicable for your group of students. Be quietly subversive when necessary. Keep in mind we need to raise compassionate citizens who bring high intellectual habits and critical thinking to deal with society's complex problems and political crises. We cannot waste brilliant minds on bits and pieces of "stuff" and egregious, time-wasting activities. It's well known that students who read well and write well do more reading and more writing, on authentic topics, most often of their choice. Ask yourself, "Is what I am doing helping students become engaged, determined, self-directed learners?" If not, change course. As noted throughout this book, a well-educated, thoughtful citizenry is our best hope for all of our futures.

As we know, teaching well is not just about technique; it's about integrity and compassion, engaging hearts and minds, and questioning what doesn't work or make sense. We can continue to learn from research and practitioners while not abandoning what we know to be true and necessary. The most effective teachers put students before programs and find a way around harmful mandates. That is, they are "positive deviants";[3] they find a way to make a "worthy difference." They don't change their practices on demand or because the pendulum is swinging. In *Literacy Essentials*, I write: "The educational pendulum will always swing, but we must not! We may shift a bit to the right or left, based on relevant research, experience, and the beliefs we hold, but if our foundation is rock solid, the shift will be an intentional, well-informed movement and not a full tilt."

Beginning with becoming professionally knowledgeable, to questioning research that has not been peer reviewed and independently evaluated (that is, the researchers and publisher were not involved in the study of its effectiveness), to writing letters of protest as an informed group, even small steps can make a difference. A story, a blog, an editorial, a podcast, speaking out at a school board meeting can be a radical act. Telling our stories and speaking our truths have the potential to inform our constituents, encourage activism, and change our world. But change won't happen without our relentless advocacy. Teaching is a political act.

Ask yourself: "How can I make a worthy difference?" "How can I make my work really matter?" Don't just complain; become part of the solution. Atul Gawande, surgeon and prolific author, who coined the term "positive deviant," acknowledges:

> Arriving at meaningful solutions is an inevitably slow and difficult process. Nonetheless, what I saw was: better is possible. It does not take genius. It takes diligence. It takes moral clarity. It takes ingenuity. And above all, it takes a willingness to try.

I give the last words here to renowned scholar and one of my literacy heroes, P. David Pearson: "Whatever you do, do not shrug your shoulders in the hope that this iteration of the debate, this pendulum swing, will, like its predecessors, fade into the shadows of historical curiosity. This one is exceptional, and it requires exceptional response on our part."[4]

Considering the science of reading

Like clockwork, the old rallying cry "Schools are failing to teach our students to read" returns every few decades or so with an unchanging message: "We now have irrefutable, scientific research on the most effective way to teach reading." These days that evidence is called the "science of reading," and the debate centers on the need to shift from what many call "balanced" reading beliefs and practices to "structured literacy." First of all, teaching reading has never been a fixed process or a one-size-fits-all process. Science is not a unified or final set of facts but is rather an imperfect process that is always evolving, based on the latest research and our professionally informed instruction, observations, and experiences. Uncertainty is part of the process, as it always will be when human beings are intricately involved.

The "science of reading," for those who might not know what the term means, has been used by some in the field to prioritize the systematic, explicit teaching of discrete skills connected to sound-letter relationships, skills that are quick and easy to measure. Those skills include phonological awareness (which is the ability to identify and manipulate individual sounds called "phonemes" in spoken words) and phonics (which is applying letter-sound relationships to decode—to recognize and pronounce—written words). To be clear, such skills are necessary but insufficient for becoming a reader, one who thoughtfully applies strategies to make sense of text, chooses to read (mostly) books, and who self-monitors and finds joy in becoming a discerning reader. And, scientific reading research is not limited to word recognition— plenty of scientific research exists in the areas of comprehension, vocabulary, and more. We have known all this for decades.

Importantly, we have also known for decades that—along with phonics and word identification skills—readers need to be able to access a wide range of strategies and tools to comprehend text. Readers differ and have different needs; there is no one best way to teach children to read—or to learn most things, for that matter. While evidence-based, reading research is important, translating such research into classroom reading instruction must be carefully implemented within a full and complete view of reading. Results of the research must also be supported by scholarly consensus and be relevant and meaningful for the actual readers and writers in our classrooms. Evidence-based research must also be supplemented with the observations of countless, experienced teachers—those who have consistent, clear success year after year in teaching children to read. Effective teaching of reading has always depended most on a highly knowledgeable teacher, one who has a deep understanding of reading as a complex, multi-faceted process, and one who adjusts teaching to capitalize on the strengths, interests, and the needs of the learner.

Evidence-based research studies that show the benefits and/or superiority of reading approaches dominated by phonics teaching are scanty or non-existent. If your school or district is investing in commercial reading programs with an over emphasis on phonics, check the highly respected What Works Clearinghouse: "The purpose of the What Works Clearinghouse is to review and summarize the quality of existing research in educational programs, products, practices, and policies." Additionally, if we look back on the impact of the 2001 No Child Left Behind Act (in effect through 2015), five years after implementation, the billions of dollars of NCLB funding yielded students across the U.S. who, according to standardized tests, were good at sounding out (nonsense) words and decoding but who showed no measurable growth in reading comprehension. Those same results are consistent with other research that shows students who had more explicit instruction in phonics did not show significantly higher reading achievement on standardized tests than students who received a more comprehensive approach. No surprise here. A phonics-first approach to reading is too narrow. From the start, we must view learning to read as a language and thinking process, not just a sounding-out-words process.

Reading comprehension must be our first and primary goal in teaching reading, and phonics is but one necessary tool in this muti-dimensional process. This is why professional knowledge—along with experience and collaboration with colleagues—is so important. To raise our voices and do right by our students, we have to know research and how, when, and if to apply it to our actual students. Almost 40 years ago, renowned educator and researcher Don Holdaway warned about the same issues we are facing today related to scientific claims about reading. Here are a few of his wise and cautionary statements, still applicable today:

> When a teacher is using a structured…program, whether out of conviction, insecurity, or through school policy, a number of unwritten, unsubstantiated, and sometimes quite false assumptions tend to operate:

- The series was written by "experts" and their judgments are superior to mine. (In fact, a reliable professional judgment must always be an on-the-spot knowledge-of-client judgment.)

- The sequence of skills and sub-skills has been scientifically ratified, and I should not depart from it to any significant extent for any child. (There is no scientifically ratified sequence of skills in reading development.)

- Task success for all children can be controlled by the devices and progressions built into the materials by those who are experts in readability. (No formula for readability can approach accuracy without taking into account the other agent in the transaction, the reader.)

If we view reading, as I believe we must, as reading for understanding—including for pleasure, information, enrichment, personal interests and goals—all of that can happen from the earliest stages. And, of course, decoding skills are necessary. However, there are just too many variables in teaching reading to teach all learners the same way or to simplify the teaching of reading by calling it an exact science.

The human element must be paramount in all we teach. The learners' interests, strengths, needs, choices, and how we respond to the learner are all key. Critically, and important enough to restate, science works best in tandem with the human side of reading—knowing and engaging the reader, building on the readers' strengths and interests, and embracing the "heart and mind" in teaching, learning, and living. What is also not given serious consideration in the "science of reading" is the text as a crucial factor in a reader's engagement, efforts, and success. Significant factors that affect the reader include student choice; equitable access to a wide range of books, texts, and genres (such as audiobooks, news articles, graphic texts); text features such as font size, amount of print on the page, length of text, format, supportive illustrations; background knowledge; vocabulary expertise; and language comprehension. Recent scientific research, for example, by Nell Duke and Kelly Cartwright, also includes the importance and impact of motivation and self-regulation by the reader, which is something that those of us who expertly teach readers have long known and incorporated without a scientific seal of approval.[5] As well, learning to read requires an inclusive, equitable learning environment where students feel safe to take risks, ask questions, and offer their viewpoints. Again, but important enough to re-emphasize, reading is a language process and a thinking process, not just a reading-the-words process.

In teaching an adult learner to read during the pandemic (see Chapter 6, "Championing the Reading/Writing Connection"), it was not the explicit phonics and decoding that made him a reader, although we worked diligently on that, of course. It was listening to books, reading together, discussing what we read, and reading independently-with-my-support texts he chose that lit his imagination, inspired his interests and curiosity, and confirmed he was not alone in his life struggles. He drew inspiration and hope from the real-life characters we read about and talked about; their courageous actions gave him strength and the will to keep on reading and to strive to do better—in reading and in living. It was the overlap between the "science" part of reading (including phonics as well as the focus on comprehension strategies, vocabulary, and self-regulation), and the "heart and mind" part of teaching and learning (the language, literature, and cognitive focus) that turned him into a reader. Interestingly enough, I found the same thing to be true more than 35 years ago when I was working with low-performing readers, and I document that experience in my first book *Transitions: From Literature to Literacy*.

In my five decades of teaching reading as a classroom teacher, certified reading specialist, specialist for students with learning disabilities, and Reading Recovery teacher, my colleagues and I have successfully and joyfully taught both the decoding and the comprehension—often in tandem. I have written many well-researched and well-received books on teaching reading and writing equitably, responsibly, and joyfully. I have co-authored a video-based, literacy series to explicitly show how it's done in diverse schools and classrooms and how students and teachers can do it all, right from the start—the phonics and decoding, the comprehension, the reading and writing for authentic audiences and purposes, and the love of reading. However, such an integrated outcome is only possible if we teachers and leaders are professionally knowledgeable, take ongoing responsibility for securing and growing our knowledge, and share what we learn with others.

Without solid knowledge of research and principled practices, we cannot assess the quality and usefulness of any instructional program or assessment for our students or be able to advocate for better, equitable practices. As one example, at this writing some states are requiring a reading fluency test at the end of grade 3 as a major determinant for whether or not students go on to grade 4 or repeat grade 3. What I've learned from decades of teaching reading is that fluency is an excellent predictor of reading comprehension in the earliest grades but is an unreliable predictor for older students. For example, a grade 4 student could have low fluency scores and still have satisfactory comprehension. Also, many states are requiring that *all* kindergarten through grade 5 teachers and beyond receive intensive training and certification in the "science of reading" with its focus on explicit teaching of phonemic awareness and phonics. Certainly, teachers need to have this knowledge so they can use it judiciously but, again, it's a limited focus on one aspect of reading. Teachers also need to teach kids how to be strategic as readers. Both are necessary; it's never been an "either/or" stance.

Given the over-reliance on intensive phonics these days, it's important to revisit an award-winning reading study by Sheila Valencia and Marsha Riddle Buly. The researchers examined the reading profiles of a random sample of 108 entering 5th grade readers who had failed the end-of-year 4th grade state reading assessment. Their findings showed that for 58% of the students in the sample, phonics and word identification were not an issue. Where they did need support was with meaning and/or fluency. The findings confirm that readers who struggle do so for different reasons. It's also important to keep in mind that instruction and intervention(s) meet the needs of students both in focus and intensity.

Looking across many studies of student-instruction interactions suggests that instruction targeted to students' area of need produces gains in that area. However, when instructional time was spent on skills and abilities in which a student was strong, no additional growth was detected. So, although instruction that targets a student's specific needs will increase learning, misdirected instruction may actually waste valuable instructional time. Students' areas of need change over time, and our instruction and assessment must adjust to meet those current needs.

Keep in mind that the call for phonics-first teaching has occurred before—in the 1960s, the 1990s, and now in the 2020s. Almost 30 years ago, distressed by the politics of literacy and, in particular, an exclusive focus on phonics, I wrote *Literacy at the Crossroads* to set the record straight, take a stand, and to add a voice of reason to the polarizing, national "reading wars."

The largest national assessment of reading confirms that U.S. students are competent at literal levels and incompetent at critical and analytical levels. (still true)… Our task is clear. Despite the public outcry that we are not teaching the basics, the irony is we are overfocusing on discrete skills and superficial learning at the expense of not teaching our students how to interpret, evaluate, analyze and apply knowledge.

(p. 6)

It is up to us as informed teachers, learners, and leaders to question assumptions and apply research, principled practices, and commonsense knowledge to the actual readers, writers, and thinkers we are teaching. There is no commercial reading program that can meet the needs of all learners, all the more reason for all educators and policy makers to be highly knowledgeable about research, reading processes, and reading instruction. Even when we talk about the "science of reading," we need to acknowledge that the scientific research must include a convergence on all aspects of reading, not just decoding skills, and that science can be imperfect. For helpful guidance in how, when, and why to apply reading research to inform instruction, see "The Science of Reading: Making Sense of Research" by Tim Shanahan.[6]

I am reminded of how the journalists on the Editorial Board of *The New York Times* are described as being "informed by expertise, research, debate, and certain longstanding values." Yes! Research is important, but it's only one of many factors to consider when deciding how and what to teach. And who we are teaching, the learner, is of utmost importance—the expectations we hold, our relationship, our compassion, and our knowing the person we are teaching, not just the subject matter. Keep uppermost of mind: *In meeting the interests and needs of all students, an informed teacher's research-based, practical knowledge and experience are superior to any packaged program.* Any program, at best, provides a workable framework.

Without solid professional knowledge, it's difficult to scrutinize the validity of a researcher's claims and how that research might—or might not—apply to our own particular situation and context. Without deep professional knowledge, it's difficult to determine the quality and usefulness of a commercial program we are expected to use. Finally, remember that you are the most important person for reaching and teaching your students, and you must be fully informed to do so. Value your own examined experiences, teacher research, and reflections. Expert teachers customize their teaching to fit their students' interests, strengths, and needs and to dignify students' language, intelligence, and efforts. Such teachers actualize research as they also optimize engagement, curiosity, and joyful learning.

Seeking out mentors

As part of being professionally knowledgeable, I depend on mentors to continue growing as an educator. That mentor might be a peer, an author, or a leader in the field. What's important is to look for a "proficient other," someone you admire to support your efforts and competencies as a teacher and a learner. That person need not be at the same grade level, teaching the same discipline, or even be in the same profession. What is paramount is that the mentor be someone you trust who is invested in your achievement and growth and wants you to find your own voice, vision, and victories. A good mentor will also be a careful observer, an excellent coach, and a confidence booster. Also of great import, an effective mentor provides feedback that is strength-based, timely, kind, actionable, and useful. No matter how long we've been teaching or working at a particular job, and no matter how much we excel, we all need role models and mentors to keep on growing.

To be clear, when we talk about a "mentor" we are mostly talking about a long-term, one-on-one, coaching relationship between mentor and mentee, with mutual interactions around principled practices. When we talk about a "coach," we are usually talking about short-term guidance and focus on a specific goal, as in the story that follows.

I remember reading about renowned surgeon, writer, and public health researcher, Atul Gawande, who at the height of his illustrious career realized that he was no longer getting better as a surgeon and had the data to prove it. He writes: "Professional athletes use coaches to make sure they are as good as they can be. But doctors don't. So why did I find it inconceivable to pay someone to come into my operating room and coach me on my surgical technique?" Gawande notes that opera singers, such as Renée Fleming, have voice coaches, and virtuoso violinist Itzhak Perlman relies on his wife's "outside ear," her sensitive and critical listening, to tell him how his playing sounds to an audience.

Acknowledging that a coach might be useful for increasing his surgical skills, Gawande sought out a retired surgeon he deeply admired and had a personal connection with to observe him in the operating room. Because the observing physician sat at an angle where he could see what Gawande could not, he was able to observe, inform, and guide Gawande who was then able to make enhancements, even mid-surgery—with patient positioning, lighting, better use of the surgical assistant. To be sure, these were small and nuanced improvements, but they reduced his complications rate and saved more lives. Gawande's coach, like all excellent coaches, was 100% present as observer and listener and used conversation and thoughtful questioning to discuss "What worked?" and "What didn't go well?" It is by asking relevant questions—not giving solutions— and involving the learner in thoughtful dialogue that causes learners to think and problem solve. Gawande notes, "Coaching done well may be the most effective intervention designed for human performance."

Like Gawande's coach, the most effective mentors coach and ask questions that cause us to be metacognitive, that is, to think about our thinking, which can lead to greater effectiveness and learning. In addition to questions such as, "What went well?" and "What was the strongest part of the lesson?" (focusing on strengths first), also consider questions such as, "What did you notice about your students' reactions to the lesson?" and "Is there anything you might have done or said differently?" (focusing without judgment, on practices that might be questionable). Helping the learner identify and evaluate their actions— whether it's a teacher or child—is crucial for recognizing what practices and language enhance learning or discourage learning, and what steps we might take for improvement.

My own work confirms that teachers who are mentored well are more effective and have greater job satisfaction, and their students achieve more—including on standardized tests. I have witnessed firsthand what happens when teachers no longer have a principal, teacher leader, or mentor who is invested in their professional learning. The teachers, who may already be quite effective, maintain effectiveness but don't tend to move to a higher level of efficacy. They also lose some of their enthusiasm for teaching. One teacher told me, "Without professional learning, there's no longer any sense of excitement in our school about learning." One outstanding teacher I know well, who was missing having a mentor, set up a support network to meet monthly with several trusted colleagues to discuss articles on research and practice, including their own practices. They also began observing each other and giving valued feedback.

Even if your school or workplace has an instructional coach, a mentor serves as a personal guide to your unique situation, interests, and needs. If you are working in a school without a suitable mentor, think about reaching out to someone in another school. If that's not possible, consider virtual mentoring and conversations with someone you respect. Do what you can to ensure you are paired with a mentor willing to actively listen and respond to your concerns, support your efforts, work collaboratively and respectfully with you, and help you grow professionally. If you are inexperienced or new to the profession, you might seek out a teacher who is just a few steps ahead of you in knowledge and practice. That partnership might feel less overwhelming than working with the most skillful teacher you know.

Regardless of where you work, if you are in a setting without opportunities for quality, relevant professional learning and study, seeking out a mentor will be crucial to ensuring optimal instructional effectiveness. Especially if you are working in isolation, recognizing strengths and areas for improvement is made easier with another set of eyes and ears and ongoing conversations with a trusted colleague.

The truth is that all of us can benefit from working with an excellent mentor.

CHAPTER 6

Championing the Reading/Writing Connection

- ❖ Focusing on literacy delight and meaning
- ❖ Teaching an up-and-coming reader (Ted's story)
- ❖ Reading and writing approaches that enhance learning
- ❖ Putting libraries at the center

DOI: 10.4324/9781003381242-6

Focusing on literacy delight and meaning

What does it mean to be literate? Not everyone understands literacy in the same way. The simple definition of literacy is the "ability to read and write." But if we view literacy as a human right for living a good life, as I believe we must, then knowing how to read and write must also include communication and understanding, even if the audience for the literate act is oneself. Going further, the goal of literacy must result in enrichment, empowerment, and self-determination—essential for pursuing life, liberty, and happiness—at any age.

If we expand the definition of literacy to begin at birth, with including "reading the world," I will argue that babies who experience books and being read aloud to daily have an understanding that is not quantifiable, literacy-wise. For example, the 8-month-old granddaughter of my dear friend Toby notices when her parents substitute a word in a predictable story she has heard over and over again. On occasion, she has seemed irritated until they read it in its original wording. She is not just responding to specific book language; she is demanding it. She is also fully attentive when they sing the song with her name in it; they have been singing it to her almost every day since she was born. She pays attention and smiles every time she hears it. If she is crying during the day, she will immediately stop and begin smiling when the song begins. And she loves books! She has cried on occasion when her mother stopped reading a book, then stopped crying when her mom resumed reading. When hearing a story read aloud and seeing the pages, she pats the actual characters in the book. She expects stories. It's part of her routine: "This is bedtime, this is what we do, you're going to hear stories."

Even applying a broadly accepted definition of literacy: "**Literacy is the ability to identify, understand, interpret,** create, **communicate** and compute, **using printed and written materials associated with varying contexts,**"[1] this 8-month-old child is able to apply the parts of the definition I have highlighted in bold. She is also already responding to picture books in ways that indicate her preferences, awareness of language, and delight in stories. We tend to only see literacy as the written word (writing and reading), but oral literacy (speaking and listening) is a necessity. In fact, literacy began with the oral tradition of storytelling, not just with the need to communicate but also to delight—to entertain, to inform, to tell stories that would be passed down through generations.

We are now living in a time when literacy, like so many other beliefs and concepts, has been politicized and hijacked to the point where reasonable conversations are often not possible. We are so divided as a nation that we no longer dialogue with people from "tribes" that are different from our own, for example, the political party, socio-economic group, religion, culture, viewpoints, locale. This is dangerous business, because the need to communicate clearly and respectfully and to be heard and understood is a right that undergirds every healthy democracy.

The purpose of literacy must be that the end goal of education means we graduate concerned, activist citizens who believe excellent and equitable schools, health care, housing, and justice are not just for the privileged but for everyone. That we see the human condition not just as an individual one but a communal one. That we see the "other" as our "brother," not our enemy. That we see that each of us has a role in making the world (not just our own world) a more habitable and just place. That we seek delight and meaning in all we do.

There's a lot of talk these days about "mastering the fundamentals" of reading. This is generally taken to mean everything related to decoding and phonics and knowing and applying the relationships between letters and sounds. Even though "fun" is in the word fundamentals, there is little playing around with stories and language here. These "fundamentals" are prescribed as necessary practices teachers are required to know and apply. The issue is one of proportion. I have never believed that being able to recognize words in isolation is reading; it is word calling, whether it's sounding out words or recognizing words by sight. Reading is a comprehensive and cohesive process that must include understanding. It is not an either/or process; readers need to be explicitly taught to decode, *and* they need to be explicitly taught how to read for meaning. This reading debate, previously known as the "reading wars" and more recently as the "science of reading" shows no sign of abating. (For more on the "science of reading," refer back to Chapter 5.)

What's important to keep in mind is that a full definition of reading must include books—and delight. Books are the hard currency of being a reader, whether it's a physical book, an e-book, an audiobook, or a handmade one. I would expand "books" to include comic books, graphic texts, and multimedia texts, among others. Becoming a reader does not primarily happen through getting good at phonics and word reading. While that is a necessity, of course, word solving skills are insufficient for becoming a reader—someone who chooses to read for enjoyment and information and to live a fuller life. Books provide the firm foundational bridge that makes an enriching reader-life and writer-life possible.

Not only that. Voluminous reading for pleasure results in better comprehension, fluency, vocabulary and language growth, and writing quality—including grammar and spelling. Significantly, avid reading leads to self-teaching in both reading and writing. Through reading and more reading, we discover what we find delightful, beautiful, and touching. We uncover what we might try out, imitate, or do as writers ourselves. Knowing the rules of language is not enough, not for experiencing delight and meaning. It's the nuances, unusual and surprising choice of words, phrases, and formats—the insubordination the writer instigates—that leave us wondrous, awestruck, gob smacked. As Ross Gay notes in his book of essays, *Inciting Joy*:

> The point here, from the outset, priming the pump as it were, in addition to sharing and listening, and softening and laughing, is to

free us from the prospect of doing it well or right. Let's get that out of the way so that we might instead make something beautiful.

Imagine, if we were to tell our students, once they've internalized "the rules," that what we're after is not regurgitation of those imperatives. That what we want is for them to create something beautiful as their primary goal—and break some rules along the way. Imagine if we and our students felt free enough to nurture freedom and joy on our journey to becoming fully human and literate.

One of the easiest and most pleasurable ways to provide delight and meaning is through reading aloud. Don't worry too much about kids understanding every word when we read aloud to them. Read aloud to them great literature, books with glorious language and illustrations. Make it a masterful oral performance, which will increase their engagement and understanding. Our enthusiasm and joyful reading of a picture book, for example, will enthrall listeners, and they will get the gist of the story—even at a young age. Reading aloud provides enchantment for the imagination and our very souls. We and our students seamlessly enter worlds and language previously unknown to us, and we return, again and again, to favorite read alouds. All that enchantment impacts us as writers. I often say to students after we finish a marvelous picture book or chapter in a great fiction book, "Let's listen to this part again and notice how the author did such and such. You might want to try out something similar in your writing today."

The writing connection to reading cannot be overstated. I have deliberately looped reading with writing together because being a writer depends so much on being a discerning reader and noticing what authors do. In fact, for our youngest students and our up-and-coming-readers, it's often their own writing attempts that become their first successful reading. Their story, told and written in their own words and language, is an opportunity for applying and assessing their letter-sound knowledge and for putting themselves on a path to reading. Of course, the larger students' vocabulary is, the more words they have at their disposal for writing. That's one reason why reading aloud multiple times a day and talking about stories, fiction and nonfiction, are so crucial for language development. In *Literacy Essentials*, I write:

> In working with kindergarten classes, I see that in every case in which these children excel as readers and writers, the reading-writing connection has been fundamental to that success. In such classrooms, what the children write becomes a large part of what they read. Student and class-authored stories become texts for reading, enjoying, and embedding word work.[2]

Related, almost 25 years ago, I discovered through experimentation that kindergartners could write poetry—with deliberate word choice, line breaks, white space, rhythm, repetition—delighting in making meaning even with minimal knowledge of letters and sounds. Importantly, we immersed kids in free verse poems, noticed and charted what poets do, demonstrated poetry writing by the teacher, and wrote a poem together as a class before releasing kids to write on their own. Then each child's favorite poem went into a classroom anthology for all to read and reread. Poetry writing is a great equalizer since every child is successful, which is especially important in anxious, turbulent times when we are seeking a release from life's pressures. Free verse poetry encourages kids to write about anything—and discover the extraordinary in the ordinary. One of my most crucial findings was that we made writing harder for kindergartners—and all students—when we taught elements such as line breaks, rhythm, and white space as isolated elements. It was actually easier for them to take in all the elements at once—in the hearing, reading, and writing of poems. If and when it became apparent that one element needed special emphasis, then we separated it out and taught it and made sure to connect that element back to the poem as a whole.

In writing their poems, students use their growing phonemic awareness and phonics to make meaning. In fact, looking at kindergartners' writing is a valid and easy assessment for determining their phonological awareness and skills regarding beginning and ending consonants and blends and medial vowels. As they write, using known, conventional spelling along with their best invented spelling, they are reading and rereading—to themselves and aloud to a partner—to be sure all makes sense and looks and sounds exactly as intended. This technique of reading aloud one's writing while in the process of writing is exactly what I've done while composing and revising this book, and what many journalists also do. As I go along, I read the text aloud to myself to check for meaning, rhythm, tone, and flow. I also read portions of it aloud to trusted friends and colleagues for their feedback on those specifics and others.

With the kindergartners, following my philosophy of "Do the best you can. I'll help you with the rest," we teachers do the final editing of kids' poems. We honor each child's original language and layout and limit any editing to spelling, in order that the poems can be easily read by others. In the world, once writing is made public, we expect conventions to be correct. For specific guidelines on how to get great results with your children and students, see my *Kids' Poems: Teaching Children to Love Writing Poetry*, a K–4 series. Each poem has a side-by-side, two-page spread with original illustrations. One page shows the poem exactly as the child wrote and arranged it on the page; the adjacent page shows the poem with conventional spelling.

The importance of teachers and leaders as readers and writers cannot be overemphasized. We simply cannot teach reading well or inspire a passion for reading if we don't read. If you are not yet a reader, consider starting with shorter books, poetry, and short stories on topics that interest you. Seek out recommendations from friends and colleagues who are readers. You might also check out my recommended reading lists. For the past 20 years or so, I have joyfully chronicled my reading history in a small notebook where I list all the books I read each month along with the author, genre, and a star rating if the book is exceptional. Even young children can keep similar reading histories. Semi-annually, I publish the books I've loved, highlighting several standouts along with commentary that connects my present reading and thinking to the classroom and educational issues. See my semi-annual postings, as well as Archives that date back to 2011, on my website at "What I'm Reading."

Just like you can't teach someone to play tennis if you don't play the game, or teach someone to play a musical instrument if you are not a player, you can't teach writing well without at least taking a stab at it, making yourself vulnerable in front of your students, and thinking and writing aloud. Do it even if you're scared and feel you're not good enough. You'll be endeared to your students for making the public attempt, and through your demonstration you'll understand exactly what it is you're expecting students to do.

I've been teaching reading in underperforming schools for five decades. As well, I am a huge reader. I have stacks of books by my bed, bookshelves full of well-loved books, and books assembled everywhere in the room where I write. I read book reviews, prowl independent bookstores, seek out reading recommendations from friends and colleagues, and notice what authors do. What I know for sure about being a reader is you need to be surrounded by books and authors you love, have sustained time to read and talk about books of choice every day, and have minimal book requirements beyond reading a quantity of books, because reading more makes you a stronger, confident, more discerning reader—and a better writer. I also know for sure that public, school, classroom, and home libraries foster the development of students becoming more open-minded, empathetic, activist citizens. See also "Living a reading life" in Chapter 9 for much more on what it means to be a reader.

A word here about leveling books, which is a national problem. Leveling books enforces a reductionist view of reading, that is, the belief that a formula can be used to designate an appropriate book for a reader. Leveling books does not take into account engagement, interest, motivation, complexity of text concepts, or prior knowledge of the reader. Leveling books is not a proven, scientific process; it is a subjective one. So, even if you are using leveled books as a teacher guide for working with small groups, be sure that students know—and that we have demonstrated and practiced with them—how to select books when they are reading on their own. For independent reading, that means students can read 95% of the words and comprehend at least 90% of the text, taking into consideration that the child's background knowledge, engagement, and eagerness to read a particular text can render such percentages inexact. Above all, the importance of book choice for accessing delight and meaning is a necessity. As almost all the reading students do will be on their own, in and out of school, they must know how to choose books for successful independent reading, so we demonstrate and practice how to do that. Related, ensure that classroom libraries—just like our public libraries—are not leveled. A leveled collection of books is not a library. Keep uppermost of mind, it is loving books, not leveling them, that ultimately makes a reader.

Finding delight and meaning in writing also depends on choice, or what I call choice within structure. Even with required standards and adopted programs, we can find a way to teach writing authentically, that is, writing for real-world audiences and purposes. I have learned that the only way to fit in all the requirements is to ground the teaching of reading and writing into the social studies and science standards and curriculum and into other content areas. I have written extensively about how to do that in *Writing Essentials* and *Literacy Essentials* and have included detailed lesson plans. The bonus with that integrated approach to literacy and learning is that focusing on meaningful content raises students' engagement, vocabulary, knowledge of the world, and curiosity.

The common factor in beginning all my residency work over decades has been that many students disliked reading and writing, and this dislike was directly connected to rigid requirements, little or no choice, and teaching skills in isolation. Once those barriers were removed and replaced by meaningful teaching with high expectations, kids soared as learners.

Teaching an up-and-coming reader (Ted's story)

As previously noted in Chapter 1, when 53-year-old Ted invited me to work with him on improving his reading, I had no idea how I would teach him, but I knew with certainty that we would be successful. I was guided by all my years of teaching, professional learning, and previous work with readers who learn differently and struggle with reading. My many years as a classroom teacher, reading specialist, and Reading Recovery teacher prompted me to begin with building upon Ted's strengths and interests and to develop a trusting and warm relationship. I knew in my heart and mind that teaching must be responsive and respectful to the learner—in the moment, in the process, in the plans, in evaluation—and give the learner choice, dignity, and agency.

I was also guided by my firm beliefs: Once we have signed on, contractually or otherwise, to teach students to read, we are obligated to do everything we can to ensure the student(s) becomes an engaged, successful, and joyful reader. Even when technology is severely limited—as it was for Ted and many underserved students and their families—equity issues and the right to an excellent education demand we do all we can to ensure every child and adult becomes a reader. Additionally, I knew that reading texts that are of high interest to the learner are more important than reading levels for engaging and sustaining the reader's efforts.

Reviewing what Marie Clay (renowned researcher and creator of Reading Recovery for early literacy intervention) has taught us, I attempted to create an environment of "confidence, ease, flexibility, and with luck, discovery… The teaching should not start where the teacher is but where the child is!… Share the tasks of reading and writing by doing *for* the child what he cannot do for himself." Clay believed that by creating a firm foundation for the learner to build upon, the learner becomes willing and eager to begin instruction. This belief holds true for learners of all ages and is especially relevant and necessary for remote learning in a pandemic or learning during a time of crisis.

Initially, we spent the bulk of our time reading and talking about the same book we'd "read," although for a while, that reading involved Ted listening to an audiobook while I was reading the same book in print. Our conversations went beyond basic comprehension to how parts of the text connected to our own lives. I learned how strong Ted's oral language and vocabulary were; I found his insights about a text to be deep and thoughtful. As mentioned in Chapter 1, it was through our early conversations that I learned he loved music and that he had a CD player, so that's where we began—at his comfort and interest level.

He was already listening to the audiobook *Who I Am* by Pete Townshend, the lead guitar player for the Who and a writer and composer. Ted knew lots about him. I bought the book and read it, and we had discussions connecting Townshend's life to his own—the good and bad times. Ted became my teacher as I knew nothing about Townshend, rock star and composer of an opera, which I listened to and enjoyed at Ted's urging. We followed a similar listening-reading-discussion path with *Born a Crime* by Trevor Noah, renowned comedian and late-night host. Biracial, Noah grew up in poverty under the racial oppression of apartheid in South Africa. I selected the memoir, which I had previously read, thinking Ted would enjoy the powerful story and relate to Noah's challenging years growing up.

We began each session with a "check-in" where I asked Ted how he was doing. These brief check-ins with time for him to talk seemed to lessen his anxiety, which made it easier to focus on the reading work. As Ted was speaking, I wrote his words down on my computer—as a record but mainly to document and validate his life—for him. Gradually, as his reading began to improve, I sent these dated pieces to him via U.S. mail, and he told me how happy he was to see his words "written on paper"—that seeing his spoken words written down made him "feel like a writer." At first, we read those texts together (over the phone), but he quickly took over reading them on his own. Those personal texts later became the core of our explicit word work, using his language in a context that was meaningful to him to begin to teach phonics (onsets and rimes) and important irregular words, what we called "words-to-know-by-heart," such as "though" and "there." To be clear, Ted had years of schooling in explicit decoding and phonics work that had not taken. Word work made sense to him—and he took it seriously—when we did it in the context of the text we were reading, where he needed it in that particular moment.

The very first text we read together—out loud and over the telephone—was "Father, Soldier, Son," a photo-journalism, special magazine section that I came upon in *The New York Times*. (I got a second paper copy from a neighbor, which I mailed to Ted.) The deeply affecting story of a dedicated soldier, who serves in Afghanistan for ten years while leaving behind his two sons, also became an award-winning documentary. The magazine worked perfectly for us due to the riveting story and the two-page layout of photos and text, which supported ease of reading. No page of text was longer than a few paragraphs, and each written page was supported by related photos on the adjacent page. Early on in the story, Ted requests to read a paragraph. I tell him some of the hard words to watch out for: "Afghanistan," "platoon sergeant," "tourniquet." My notes from our session include: "He read the second paragraph almost flawlessly. I was amazed."

For the second text we read, I chose the book *The Old Man and the Sea* by Ernest Hemingway and sent him a paperback copy. I chose that book for the simplicity and cadence of the language, the main character who has a life of struggle but never gives up ("like me" Ted said), and the prize-winning quality of this relatively short text. Importantly, I wanted to dignify Ted's intelligence and intellect when choosing his first ever, adult-level book that he'd be reading. Before we began, I read the back cover aloud to him, to give him a sense of the whole story. Ted followed along visually in his book. I had planned to read the book's opening pages to him with him following along, but he said, "No. I want to do the reading." After he read aloud those first pages, I asked him, "How did you do?" "I did good," he said. I added: "Remember when I asked you what kind of book we should start with first, and you said picture books. (He laughed.) And, now you're reading a book that's considered one of the best loved works of fiction ever." As his reading continued to improve, he gradually took over and did almost all of the reading. After three months, we finished *The Old Man and the Sea*. Ted was quite proud of his achievement. Although it took us a long time to complete the book, Ted's engagement and enthusiasm remained constant.

Soon after completing *The Old Man and the Sea*, Ted called me from Target to tell me he has just bought the Obama memoir, *A Promised Land*, and that "this will be our next book to read." His choice and determination stunned me as it was such a huge reading leap. Nonetheless, instead of thinking, "This book is too hard for him," I thought "How can I make reading this book possible for him?" I got him the audiobook. Then after we'd read the Preface together, he offered that he'd prefer to just listen along and follow in the audiobook for this "complex" 700-page book. "I can read all the hard words. I get mixed up by the little ones." "Good decision," I confirmed. Interestingly enough, he could correctly read words like "intercepted," "intelligent," and "occasionally," while still having difficulty with words like "though," "through," and "what."

A week later, back browsing books at Target, he purchased *One Life* by Megan Rapinoe, a biography-memoir about an American world-class soccer player that he'd heard reviewed on National Public Radio. By his actions and statements, Ted made it clear to me then and later that he needed and wanted to choose *all* the books he/we read and discussed. Making his own choices increased his efforts, engagement, and stamina. For our first meeting on *One Life,* Ted told me, "Let's do the Prologue. I've already practiced reading it out loud." Similarly, for the first time, he began to read a chapter *in advance* of our meeting—listening and following along on his own time. He told me he read ahead because he wanted to see how Rapinoe, the main character, handled a rough event in her life, which he said was similar to an issue in his life. By the time we reached the final chapter of the book, he was reading the pages fluently and almost error free. While it took us two months to complete reading *One Life*, Ted's attention and eagerness never lagged. The right book at the right time can have magical results for the reader.

One of the things both Ted and I appreciated about *One Life* is the central question the author poses in the opening epigraph by Mary Oliver and throughout the book: "Tell me, what is it you plan to do with your one wild and precious life?" Too many students don't know what real possibility might look like or that they are capable of having agency in their lives. Ted and I had some great discussions on this book, and we both came away with much admiration for Megan Rapinoe—for her world class soccer playing, her strong voice for LGBTQ rights, and her unrelenting advocacy and eventual success for equal pay for women in the U.S. Soccer Federation. (See also Chapter 10, for more on Rapinoe's influence.)

The books that Ted and I read and listened to are not just "good" books that entertain. They are also excellent examples of how the decisions and actions a real-life character makes can enhance understanding of our past to change the trajectory of our future—a future that need not automatically be pre-determined by income, status, where you live, or the color of your skin. The "best" books are pleasurable and thoughtful but also often offer insights into how we might live deeper, more satisfying lives. Picture books provide some of the most excellent examples here. In my last book, *Literacy Essentials: Engagement, Excellence, and Equity for All Learners*, I deliberately interwove personal and professional stories into the text because literacy, learning, and living are intertwined; our stories document, validate, and value who we are.

Encourage and support all students and all children to tell, write, and record their personal stories, hopes, and aspirations through podcasts, journals, interviews, books, multimedia, and more—including original forms and formats. Use these stories as reading material for all interested students and their families. Publish them for sign-out in classroom and school libraries. Not to be minimized, quantity of reading matters. Be sure classroom and school libraries have books that appeal to all cultures, backgrounds, and interests. Texts and authors that cause students to read more need to be welcomed. *Research confirms that avid reading is a strong contributor not just to depth in reading understanding but also to emotional wellbeing, empathy, and living a fuller and more civically engaged life.* During the year and a half that Ted and I worked together during the pandemic, and before he was able to get back to his full-time job, our reading sessions added a welcome reprieve from the ongoing stress and isolation from the pandemic. That time we spent reading and talking about books contributed, at least momentarily, to a sense of predictability, stability, and calm—for both of us.

I learned some powerful lessons working with Ted, and these can be applied to teaching developing readers of all ages. Again, it's loving books, not leveling them, that needs to be our focus. The quality of the text is paramount, that is, a first-rate text that is relevant, comprehensible, and engaging to the reader is more important than any technology, reading level, or reading label. I think about text differently and more broadly now—going beyond books in print and online, to include phone text messages, the written words news anchors project on the screen as they read text excerpts aloud, subtitles in movies and videos, photo-journalism articles, magazine articles, editorials, advertisements, newspaper articles, instructions, comics, graphic texts, essays, lyrics to songs and raps, poetry, the texts we write together, and more. Notice that these are mostly short texts, which can be confidence building for a reader who might be intimidated by a whole book.

Daily, I was on the lookout for text where I could easily get another print copy to mail to Ted, such as an article from the daily newspaper. My main question in planning each lesson became, "What is the text that will interest him?" not "What skills do I need to teach him?" I knew from experience that once I have the reader's engagement and motivation, the purpose of skills teaching becomes clear for the learner. Applying a whole-part-whole mindset—and not a part-to-whole, skills-in-isolation approach—the student learns more easily, and the learning is more likely to "stick."

One of my biggest "aha" moments was recognizing the power of audiobooks and seeing audiobooks as "real books." Those books were one of the most important factors in Ted's growth as a reader. I have come to believe we must expand "reading a text" to also mean hearing texts read aloud while following along visually, listening to audiobooks and books on tape, and co-creating meaningful texts that we then read together. Related, I learned that reading challenging texts aloud, and at a normal pace, improved Ted's reading comprehension. For up-and-coming-readers, this is a potent strategy and is why reading aloud to and with all students is crucial. Also related, in reading aloud to Ted as he was following along tracking the print, I would occasionally stop and have him fill in a word (what we call "oral cloze"). This was a powerful strategy for checking on and ensuring he was tracking the print and for focusing on particular words. At first, I had to read aloud very slowly, but eventually he was able to follow my voice and track the print when I read fluently, at normal speed.

Approaches and strategies that most supported Ted in becoming a reader were oral reading, repeated reading, shared reading, oral cloze, and choosing the book to read. In particular, I encouraged him to do lots of repeated reading on his own—while following along in the audiobook—to improve his word recognition, fluency, and comprehension. That strategy, more than any others, seemed to be most impactful for him becoming stronger as a reader. Seeing and saying the same words over and over, within a familiar and meaningful context, became a successful self-teaching strategy. Also of note, Ted continued to favor reading out loud for all his reading. He told me he liked hearing himself say the words, that it was comforting to hear his own voice. As it happened, at the time Ted told me that, I was reading *Leadership: In Turbulent Times* by Doris Kearns Goodwin, her chapter on Abraham Lincoln. I read aloud to Ted the following excerpt:

> Some leaders learn by writing, others by reading, still others by listening. Lincoln preferred reading aloud in the presence of others. "When I read aloud," Lincoln later explained, "two senses catch the idea: first, I see what I read; second, I hear it, and therefore I remember it better".
>
> (p. 81)

Ted was pleased to be in such excellent company. If reading out loud worked well for Abe Lincoln, this unorthodox approach was surely acceptable for Ted as well. This same reading-out-loud strategy can be applied with partner reading in the classroom, as one way to do lots of repeated reading of a familiar text.

We talked earlier, in Chapter 5, "Developing Professional Knowledge" about the science of reading—and while that science provides explicit teaching in decoding, which is a necessity, it is only one facet in the multi-dimensional approach required to produce successful, joyful readers. Even with that acknowledgment, let's not minimize that explicit teaching of decoding can occur in context. For example, in reading *The Old Man and the Sea*, Ted began applying the *ar* rime to all words, such as, "harm," "harpoon," "shark," and "sharpening." We connected our original "ar" teaching from a former story of Ted's, where I had taken dictation over the phone in our check-in and where he had used the words "dark," "hard," and "part" in his story. We pulled those words out of context, examined them, blended the letter-sounds, and practiced reading them in isolation and then, again, in the reading context.

Regarding word work, in all of Don Holdaway's books, he discusses in detail, among other goals for readers, the importance of self-correction, self-regulation, and how and why to teach phonics in meaningful context. Regarding word recognition, he notes:

> Although we don't test words isolated from context because such a practice seems to breach every principle of developmental learning, we do observe children dealing with words in new contexts, cut up and reorder very familiar sentences, match isolated words back into a standing context, reduce and expand sentences, and use basic structures to modify and make our own "literature."

Keep in mind our teaching can be explicit and systematic while still using meaning and context.

Ted taught me many things, most importantly that no book is beyond reach if an up-and-coming reader is determined to read it and can receive full support to do so. I was surprised how quickly Ted's fluency improved, how many words and patterns he learned through reading (visually following along in the text while listening to it), how easily he made connections to his life from the texts we read, how important it was to trust his choices, and how quickly he took—in fact, insisted on taking—the lead in taking over the reading. My experience with Ted affirms that becoming a reader is possible and life changing—at any age, but only if we believe it is possible—and only if we provide the necessary expertise, flexibility, resources, and patience.

I was nervous before every session with Ted. I wanted to honor his interests, meet his needs, keep him engaged, and keep expectations high. That meant I often had to change our lesson plan mid-session. Using everything I knew as a teacher and caring person, I adapted to where Ted was and what I believed he most needed in the moment. Uppermost of mind was ensuring our time together would increase his stamina, will, and desire to put forth full efforts and keep on reading. Like every dedicated teacher I know, I tried to do my best while dealing with the unpredictable—a multi-faceted, smart, interesting, complex human being. In many ways, Ted taught me as much as I taught him. I am grateful for all we learned and accomplished together.

All my working life, I have been teaching, demonstrating, mentoring, and coaching in underperforming schools with low-income populations; many of these students are students of color, and many are second language learners. In just about every case, and this was true for Ted as well, expectations by adults for what learners can accomplish remain dismally low. Perhaps, more than any other factor, it is this mindset of low expectations, together with a lack of equitable access to first-rate resources—expert teachers, caring supporters, and excellent books and libraries—that prevent kids of all ages from dreaming big and achieving big.

This "low expectations" mindset is especially damaging for students labeled dyslexic. While dyslexia is a specific reading disability that requires explicit and highly knowledgeable teaching to learn to read, too often the label and diagnosis are used to define and limit a learner's possibilities. Keep in mind that "There are no scientifically agreed upon diagnostic criteria or uniquely effective interventions."[3] Here, too, we want to be thinking about delight and meaning and raising expectations for what's possible! As we often do in education, when something isn't working, we go to an opposite extreme to "fix it." Recently, that has come to mean testing all children in grades K–3 and beyond and training all teachers to teach all students—whether they need it or not—to administer daily, explicit, skills lessons related to decoding. This time-consuming skills work translates to little time left for reading.

I worry that the present dyslexia debate is too narrowly focused on the science of reading, without also including the craft of reading and developing learners who not only can read, but who want to read. Some of the most imaginative, brilliant, and highly successful people who have ever lived are believed to have had dyslexia, for example, Steve Jobs, Thomas Edison, Leonardo da Vinci, Steven Spielberg, John Lennon, and Jamie Oliver. All were driven to learn to read by a passionate "need to know."

Share those luminaries' life stories and help students labeled dyslexic to find and follow their own passions and talents. Those passions will help fuel learners' hunger and need to know so they can find unique expression for their inspired thoughts and ideas—beyond reading and writing—through music, the visual and performing arts, inventions, cooking, and other creative means. I'll always remember what Ted once poignantly said to me: "I wish the normal people would see the genius of us disabled ones." Those words struck at my heart.

For one thing, Ted's statement underscores the need for letting go of labels as a primary identifier for a learner. When describing a reader, let's shift our beliefs and actions to reflect a positive mindset and hopeful language. Think "up-and-coming," "differently abled," "strengths," "interests," and "books," not "struggling," "disabled," "deficits," "needs," and "skills sheets." Think of delight, meaning, and possibilities. Think of brilliance.

Reading and writing approaches that enhance learning

However and wherever we teach, I believe delight, wonder, and meaning must be at the center of creating an intellectually and emotionally satisfying environment for all learners. That is, whatever resources, approaches, and techniques we employ, they are in service to promoting caring and passionate readers, writers, and thinkers. These are not empty words. This is why I teach and love to teach, and I suspect the same may be true for you. Even though. This is a challenging time to be teaching. Even though. So much is stacked against us. Even though. We are exhausted. And yet. If there is a more noble and impactful profession, I don't know what it is.

I have dedicated my learning and teaching career to making life more equitable, meaningful, and joyful for students, teachers, and principals. Through my books, articles, and resources, I have made explicit and practical how to create an intellectual and inclusive culture of high-achieving, self-directed learners.

In this section, I want to highlight the research-based and experience-based techniques, mindsets, and approaches that have paid the biggest learning dividends for engaging and teaching *all* learners. As we are all teachers of literacy and language arts, these reading/writing approaches apply across the grades and across the curriculum. My intent, dear reader, is to make your teaching-learning life easier, saner, and more enjoyable so your whole life—and the lives of your students and loved ones—are permanently enriched.

Based on years of study and experience, I believe separating reading and writing is artificial and inefficient, although it is what often happens in the classroom—in real life, not so much. For example, I read like a writer and show kids how I do it. Here the influence of riveting literature and avid reading is paramount for high quality writing, especially when we teach learners how to notice and apply what effective writers do. In paying attention to the writing style of authors I admire, I am on the lookout for what I might apply to my own writing to strengthen it, to make it more engaging and more readable. For example, it was in reading Ann Patchett's *These Precious Days*, a book of essays I loved, that I noticed she doesn't use many adjectives and how crisp and enjoyable that makes her writing. I tend to use too many adjectives, but in writing this book I have tried to be more economical with the use of descriptive words.

Also, in writing this book—as I am doing at this moment—I weave back and forth between writing a sentence or a paragraph or two, stopping to read my writing-in-process (often out loud), making revisions, rereading, and repeating the process. I demonstrate this process for students by thinking aloud and writing aloud in front of them. Then, when students write their own stories and texts, if they are writing for audiences and purposes that are relevant and meaningful to them, they will also begin to focus on rereading their writing and making revisions as they go along, not just when they are done. We want learners to come to understand that writing is much more than creating a product; writing is a process for developing and communicating ideas. That process is recursive, that is, a back-and-forth that involves rethinking, rereading, and rewriting. Once we and our students see this reading/writing connection as a natural partnership, pivotal to enhancing both disciplines, then satisfaction, enjoyment, and achievement in both writing and reading escalate. In reading and in writing, as with all we do, our beliefs drive our practices, so it's necessary that our beliefs and practices align with research, informed experience, and the learners we are teaching and supporting.

Underpinning our teaching/learning endeavors is an interactive teaching, coaching and learning model, what I call an Optimal Learning Model. The Optimal Learning Model is a flexible, non-linear, instructional framework—an ongoing cycle of responsive teaching—with the goal of providing students the support and scaffolding that makes it possible for them to become self-monitoring, problem solving, independent learners as early in the learning process as possible. Basically, the Optimal Learning Model (OLM) is about frontloading, that is, providing the necessary and explicit background information, demonstrations, shared and guided experiences, celebrations, and support that make it possible and probable that the learner will be able to independently do "the work" with minimal assistance. To be clear, the model subsumes equitable teaching on meaningful topics in a trusting environment.

The OLM serves as the lodestar for all my teaching and is applicable to all learning, whether it's learning how to read and write, play a sport, or cook a complicated recipe. As renowned educator Deborah Meier writes in *The Power of Their Ideas: Lessons for America from a Small School in Harlem*:

> There are, in the end, only two main ways human beings learn—by observing others (directly or vicariously) and by trying things out for themselves. Novices learn from experts and from experience. That's all there is to it. Everything else is in the details.

In my lifetime of teaching, regardless of the grade level or subject area, the experiences that teachers most often leave out are the shared and—to a lesser degree—the guided ones. These include, but are not limited to, the handholding; the scaffolded conversations; the shared reading and shared writing; the let's-do-it together partnerships; the knowing how, when, and what kind of support and guidance are needed and desirable—and then providing it. This support also includes knowing how and when to release assistance, so the learner gradually and confidently takes over. It's a delicate dance, where the teacher, as guide and leader, gently relinquishes the lead to the learner as the learner becomes empowered to take on more responsibility for the task, assignment, or project. This is a joyful dance; the learner knows the expert will not let him fall—or fail. Even better, because "just right" support is guaranteed, the learner is comfortable, relaxed, hopeful, and imbued with "I can do it" spirit.

Because I mean this book to be a concise one, and also because you now have extensive access to many of my explicit how-to resources, I will primarily focus on shared experiences here as they are crucial for learners' growing independence and competence. Importantly, as I note in *Literacy Essentials,* in the chapters titled "Teaching Readers" and "Teaching Writers," the approaches we will be discussing are in service to the desired end goal of helping students *be readers* and *be writers.* We are not just teaching reading and writing; we are teaching unique human beings. Whatever approach we use, its effectiveness depends on first-rate resources, trusting relationships, high expectations, and celebration of learners' strengths and efforts.

Let's start with shared reading. Practically and theoretically, Don Holdaway's brilliant conception of "shared-book-experience"—which he developed while teaching multi-age students in a one-room schoolhouse—changed my teaching and thinking. In shared-book-experience, the teacher gathers her students close-up and reads aloud an enlarged-print, oversized text (called a Big Book) while directing attention to each word or line. (Projecting text on a screen or interactive whiteboard also works well.) Shared-book-experience, now mostly called shared reading, sets out to replicate the intimate and enjoyable bedtime reading experience in the home and bring it into the classroom.

In both settings, the child is in a safe and loving environment as the parent, caregiver, teacher, or other "expert" reads aloud and tracks the print. The listener-learner can see the text clearly—the words and the illustrations—and is invited to read along. It's a bonding, collaborative, scaffolded encounter where everyone is included and joins in as best as they can. Importantly, there is no pressure to read-on-your-own or get it "right." The texts are engaging and can include stories, chants, songs—or whatever interests the expert reader and the learner child. This is equitable teaching at its finest; every learner can be intellectually active and engaged with rich literature and content even if they can't read all the words.

Over the years, I have adapted shared-book-experience to include daily shared reading and writing experiences across the curriculum. Perhaps more than any other teaching approach, shared learning experiences have informed and enriched my teaching as well as students' learning, achievement, and enjoyment. Those shared experiences have provided the learning phase I'd been missing, the "let's do it together" stage before expecting learners to work mostly on their own. Shared experiences are also about slowing down now to hurry up later, that is, providing the necessary supports, guidance, and frontloading that make independent learning possible and successful. For up-and-coming-readers, the opportunity to hear and interact with books and text they might not yet be able to read on their own is a great equalizer and reading motivator.

For both younger and older students, projecting the text on a screen while reading aloud works beautifully. In a variation I call shared read aloud, teachers can also use parts of the read-aloud text to hone in on the use of specific vocabulary, note author's intent, make predictions, and so on—all the while keeping the main focus on enjoying the book. The text can be a picture book, a page from a novel the teacher is in the process of reading aloud, pages from a content area text, a newspaper article, and so on. Significantly, "Many different forms of shared reading can facilitate language growth for English learners—who are over-represented among students who read at below-basic levels in U.S. schools."[4] Especially when these texts have familiar content and language, and some of these will be those we write together through shared writing—including bilingual texts—students experience great success.

Shared writing is an equitable, co-writing approach for turning all students into confident readers and writers. Students, with teacher guidance, create a text together. In shared writing, the teacher does the actual transcription while encouraging students to freely express their thoughts. With the teacher and other students supporting the language and thinking of the learner, students move seamlessly between writing and reading processes—going back and forth to adjust their text and build on their reading/writing skills. Where a trusting, classroom community has been established—as we have previously discussed in Chapter 4, "Co-creating a Joyful, Inclusive Culture—learners feel free to express their ideas without fear of failure or ridicule. Here is where the real power is: learners' thinking and ideas are given priority.

An important benefit of shared writing comes from its natural connection to reading and word work. Much of the explicit word work I demonstrate for teachers in my residency work comes from familiar, class-authored texts on topics connected to real-world issues, content area study, stories, and wherever students' interests take us. Once we have enjoyed multiple readings of our shared writing texts, they easily become familiar texts for shared reading. Using a screen, interactive whiteboard, or printed copies of the text for each student, we notice and direct attention to vowels, digraphs, word patterns, prefixes and suffixes, irregular words to know by sight, root words, and more. We take words out of context and explicitly study them—circling them, writing them, talking about their unique features and meanings—and then put them back in context.

Mary Beth Nicklaus, a middle and high school reading interventionist, notes: "Beginning with shared writing worked better for me than hitting students with a canned reading intervention with its skills-in-isolation and pile of books. Our shared writing eventually led to a greater interest in reading books, figuring out words, and higher literacy achievement."[5] The power of shared writing extends to all grade levels. I'll never forget working with a group of four 5th grade boys who were deemed to be two to three years below grade level in reading, according to standardized test scores and their classroom teacher's assessment. Just as I did with Ted—beginning our reading work together with his interests—I began with talking with these boys about their interests. I learned they were upset about the way the playground worked at recess. They felt some rules and procedures were burdensome and unfair. I suggested we write a text together, detailing what was "wrong" and offering specific suggestions for improvement. We discussed what form the text would take and who our audience would be—the principal, teachers at the school, and other students.

We did a shared writing, where I acted as scribe, holding the pen and helping them shape their ideas and thinking, presented orally, as I did the actual transcription. From that draft text we authored and revised together. Also, using their text later as a shared reading, I taught them the word solving and phonics skills they had never mastered. We—and each of them alone or with a partner—read and reread that text together until they could fluently read it. Because they would be going classroom to classroom (their idea) to read their call-to-action text, they were motivated to practice and reread their text over and over again until that reading was seamless. It was the competence and confidence from that successful experience that finally propelled these boys into seeking out the reading and writing life as a useful one, and ultimately a pleasurable one.

Let's briefly weigh in on guided reading here, as it is often a fraught area. Looking at the Optimal Learning Model, in guided reading the handover of responsibility has already occurred. That is, students are now doing most of the work in a practice phase, applying what has been learned from whole class, shared experiences, and guided practice. The teacher's role is as a guide on the side—nudging, scaffolding, prompting, encouraging, and explicitly teaching as necessary. Guided reading is usually done in small groups, but it can also take place in a whole class or with one individual in a reading conference.

In reality, teachers often do most of the work in guided reading, such as supplying many unknown words because the text, usually chosen by the teacher, often turns out to be too difficult. Even when using leveled texts for guided reading—which do have their place in assisting the teacher in choosing books in which students can read almost all the words and understand almost all the vocabulary and concepts—teachers still need to examine the text to be sure it's "right" for their cohort of up-and-coming-readers. The best follow-up work for guided reading is more reading, reading on in the book or series or reading ahead to the next chapter—not skills-in-isolation work. The purpose of guided reading is to ensure that when students are reading on their own—independently and silently, which is almost all the time—they can self-direct, self-correct, problem-solve, reread as needed to comprehend almost all of the text, and set their own worthwhile goals.

Independent reading is all about respecting students' choices and providing uninterrupted time every day for students to read books for pleasure and information. I recommend we let students determine, with our guidance, what genres they love best and want to feature in our jointly-organized classroom libraries and not worry so much—at least for a few months—if a student seems to only be reading one particular type of book. It's okay, I believe, to have students over-focus on a favorite genre, whether it's graphic novels, fantasy, sports books, books in a series, or even comics. I can't imagine someone telling me I need to stop reading memoir, my favorite genre. Get kids reading; give them sustained time to read; check in on them and confer to ensure they are word solving and understanding what they read; let them stay in love with their preferred genre for months, or longer, if it's giving them pleasure and they continue to read. Also, do use independent reading time for one-on-one conferences with students. Include student self-evaluations when students are ready.

Independent writing is similar to independent reading in that students have had sufficient demonstrations, along with shared and guided experiences, so that they have internalized what writers do to engage, inform, and entertain readers. Ideally, these writers are also readers who are ready to "try and apply," with some choice and parameters related to the writing topic, format, and audience for the writing.

Conferring with students while in the process of writing—getting started, revising, editing, publishing—is a necessity for excellent writing results. And public writing conferences are a great vehicle for teaching the whole class while conferring with one student.

Public writing conferences are all about noticing and celebrating the writer's strengths—beginning with the language used and efforts employed. Because it's difficult to meet one-on-one with every student, the public conference takes place with the teacher and one student while the whole class or group observes and listens in, with the purpose of thinking about and applying a technique to their own writing. Often, especially if I am working with an emerging bilingual or multilingual learner who is either silent or saying little, having a scaffolded conversation with the writer can be a game-changer. In a scaffolded conversation, I am supporting students' oral language facility by putting possibilities in the child's ear. For example, I might say, "You could say_____," or "You might want to say something like _____," or "Notice how this author worded that. How might you put that in your own words." Asking a child lots of questions as they continue to stay silent is not helpful. Providing language possibilities and choices are often enough to boost the child's thinking and confidence and get them writing.

Finally, celebration remains at the heart of all successful and joyful teaching. In my experience, it is not uncommon for a child's life to be changed inside and outside of the classroom through one honest, affirming conference. Starting with celebrating the child's strengths (they all have them!) before offering possible suggestions for improvement is often enough to jumpstart a child's lagging confidence, courage, and willingness to put forth full efforts as a reader and writer. This is the gift we educators can choose to give to all of our students. They deserve no less from us.

Putting libraries at the center

L et me acknowledge right at the start here that I could not do the work I've done in schools and classrooms without the expertise, generosity, and support of librarians, most often called library media specialists. Time after time, it has been the school librarian who pre-selected and made available books and resources related to the topic and content we'd be studying, reading, writing, and talking about. That action was separate from the books I brought with me, mostly to read aloud and leave as gifts, and the books the classroom teacher had selected for our study.

As librarians have increasingly come under attack for refusing to ban books and for standing up for our right to choose what we read, I want to give a shout-out and thank you for the incredible work they do, often under duress. I want to name names. In Westminster, Colorado, year after year in our school residency work, librarian Marcie Haloin always had piles of fabulous read-aloud books and enthusiasm at the ready. In Seattle, Washington, our granddaughters' school librarian, Anne Aliverti, nurtured their reading habit all through elementary school, and I also had the pleasure of knowing and collaborating with her. And in our Winnipeg residency work, Candace Conti had stacks of great books for me to choose from, books that were great read-alouds and books connected to our curriculum study in process; many of these titles were by superb Canadian authors who were unknown to me. In all cases, the librarian and the school library generously supplemented the classroom library, which served as the mainstay for self-selected, independent reading in the classroom.

Libraries are not just nice to have; they are crucial for ensuring equitable opportunities and joy for all students as readers. A large body of research known as the "school library impact studies" confirms that where schools have quality library programs, library collections, and resources—supported by full-time, certified, school librarians and support staff—students have higher reading and writing achievement, as measured by standardized tests.[6] A passionate, educated staff is a necessity for ensuring that librarians can be in the moment with readers as they are choosing books. (For partnerships with public libraries and students' major input into their school library, see Chapter 10.)

Access to books that are culturally relevant, well-written, beautifully illustrated, and mesmerizing in some fashion—and many of these are picture books—is life giving. Through the stories students hear read aloud, read collaboratively, or read on their own, they can begin to envision new possibilities for themselves, realize there is not one fixed story limiting what they can become, and that relatable characters in the books they are reading and listening to can help them cope with life's challenges. Here it is important to note that while there are more books being published featuring children of color and diversity, almost 20% in 2022, the characters portrayed are often "poorly executed or insignificant."[7] So it's critical we and our students examine the quality of what we are offering and not accept inferior offerings. Sometimes, that might mean using the cultural diversity in our classrooms and schools to write our own books with students and families.

An outstanding classroom library—organized with students—must be the focal point of the classroom. And it is vitally important that students, with teacher guidance, decide how to organize *our* library and ensure it is inviting and accessible to all students. That means including books, authors, and illustrators that fully represent students' interests, cultures, and languages in a respectful and accurate manner. It means considering organizing books by genres, series, authors, and topics that appeal to students so students can easily locate their preferences—applying something like a bookstore model. For example, you might group fiction, nonfiction, and poetry by their genre or category with many books facing outward, enticing readers by showcasing the covers. For young readers, housing books standing up in plastic tubs, labeled by category, allows students to easily flip through and examine many titles. Students, even our youngest ones, can do most of this sorting and categorizing, with our modeling, guidance, and practice.

Organizing an equitable and expansive classroom library is inextricably connected to providing sustained time every day to read and talk about books, not as an aside or leftover but as the main course—plus dessert. Such time allows for readers being able to preview, peruse, read an excerpt, and carefully examine a variety of accessible books, which builds excitement for reading. Of course, we want to first demonstrate and guide students in how to choose books they can read and understand. To that end, establish, with students, through a whole class shared writing, "How we choose books to read from the classroom library." You will want to first demonstrate that process and have students try it out with support, following the Optimal Learning Model previously discussed. However, before any of that, check to ensure the collection houses books that students can find, read, and understand, and that there are books, authors, and illustrators that pique their curiosity and interests.

In my demonstrating how to choose books to read in a 1st grade classroom, it was eye opening to discover most of the books in the classroom library were too hard for students to read. That led to some soul-searching with the recognition that students didn't know what was in the library. Up until that moment, it had effectively been the *teacher's* library. When organizing the library as *our* library, consider a separate section for student-authored and class-authored books. Discuss, with student input, how the library will be managed and how those jobs will be allocated—signing out books, book return, adding new books, removing books that no longer serve readers well, and so on.

When I first started working in schools in the U.S. in weeklong residencies, I was shocked that often there were no classroom libraries. In their place there might be commercial, "leveled libraries," which I deliberately put in quotes here as libraries in a democracy must always include selection and choice by the reader. There were also, often, decodable texts masquerading as real books, and often these were read by students on a tablet. To be clear, decodable texts are written to practice phonics skills; books are written to delight and inform.

In some schools today, books have been removed from classroom libraries and been replaced by decodable texts. Greta Salmi, former principal and current coach for new administrators, and my dear friend and colleague, notes that when decodable texts are the main reading fare, "Second language learners just become word callers. Language learners don't gain meaning from text unless it's in their realm of experience." So even when her former district adopted a reading program with decodable texts—what she calls "grim, lock-step, fidelity-to-the-program" teaching instead of fidelity-to-the-child—she made sure kids generated their own texts that became engaging reading materials in the classroom.

Additionally, connected to decodable texts and other non-choice reading, in some schools there may also be a "forced" home reading program. Students are assigned leveled books and/or decodable texts to practice reading with their parents, and a parent signature may be required to prove such practice took place. This forced regime, without student choice, is causing pressure and tension in many homes, turning reading into a battle. This is worrisome as well, as students are being deprived of the rich language of stories, which promotes language growth, and is especially essential for emerging English learners. My advice, after decades of teaching readers at all levels, is to keep home reading relaxing and pleasurable and to connect it to mostly student-selected books from "real" libraries and other authentic sources. Parents can read aloud to kids, read together, and discuss all kinds of texts; if we want joyful readers who choose to read, we need to keep the main focus on delighting and informing on topics that engross learners. To that end, ensure that student-authored texts and class-authored texts become part of your student-centered, classroom library.

Not to be minimized for keeping students engaged as readers, ensure comfortable reading spaces. I have several places in my home where

Championing the Reading/Writing Connection

I like to read—a big raspberry-red chair with an ottoman, a couch in our living room, and at the breakfast table because the natural light is so good there. With your students' input, ensure your classroom has some cozy and casual reading spaces. Some teachers elect to remove their desks—as they don't spend much time there—as one way to "find" additional space for readers. Others ensure student desks are grouped in pods of four or six to open up more space and optimize opportunities for conversation and collaboration across the curriculum. Also, designate a space for one-on-one conferring with students, during independent reading time, to ensure students are understanding what they are reading, self-monitoring, and setting appropriate goals. (See also "Designing spaces for living, learning, and wellbeing" in Chapter 4.)

The most important thing about a library, whether it's a public, school, or classroom library, is that it's free and accessible to all, and that it can be a haven for our imagination and our interests—including those we have not yet discovered. I love what Brian Doyle, author of the beautiful and inspiring *One Long River of Song*, writes about a library:

> Your library is where the community stores its treasures. It's the house that imagination built. It's where all the stories that matter are gathered together and celebrated and shared... Who you are as a town is in the library. People who fear freedom fear libraries. The urge to ban a book is always an urge to put imagination in jail. But in the end you cannot imprison it, just as you cannot imprison the urge to freedom, because those things are in every soul.

For many of our students, the library is where they first glimpse what might be possible and who they might become in their present and future lives, all the more reason that library book collections—in the community, in school, in the classroom, and at home—celebrate and equitably reflect the beautiful, complex, and multifaceted diversity of being human. Anything less does a disservice to our readers.

159

Learning to Live with Loss

DOI: 10.4324/9781003381242-7

Reflections on loss and healing

I've come to believe that living a good life depends on how well we are able to live with loss and the pain that accompanies it. We are all vulnerable, and the longer we live, the more loss we experience. C. S. Lewis, in *A Grief Observed*, writes, "I thought I could describe a *state*; make a map of sorrow. Sorrow, however, turns out to be not a state but a process." That process can be lifelong, depending on how we perceive and adjust to the severity of the loss.

In the autumn of our years and in the tree that is our life, my husband and I have lost many branches—family members including grandparents and parents; aunts, uncles, and cousins; a sister; and our beloved children, Elizabeth and Peter. Our beautiful Liz, full of promise and full of life, died at age 25. Twenty-eight years later, our son Peter died at age 49.

How each of them lived is their main story, and each of their life stories is one of courage, compassion, and celebration. Our daughter, Elizabeth Jo, was born in Boston, Massachusetts, so full of life as a newborn that she was featured with me on the cover of the promotional brochure for the hospital. From her earliest years, she was precocious, curious, artistic, sensitive, and kind. She was a joyful child, always singing and creating. She had a great imagination, which was visible in the stories she made up, the drawings and paintings she originated, and the handmade gifts to friends and family that were her trademark. In elementary school, she excelled as a student, artist, reader, and writer. During her high school years, dance was her passion. She was part of a well-respected, modern dance troupe that performed publicly to wide, local acclaim. She was a masterful choreographer and elegant dancer; she spent hours happily orchestrating and creating vignettes and stories through dance, which she then taught to and performed with her dance group. At the University of Pennsylvania, she graduated with a double-major in European history and psychology. During her college years, she worked a minimum of ten hours a week as a waitress to help pay for her expenses. She loved writing and was determined to become a writer. Post-graduation she worked as a journalist for a local newspaper. She was a good friend to many, a devoted sister, and a lovely daughter. Her closest friends described her as kind, empathetic, and a great listener. Also scholarly, silly, and always up for a new adventure. We've had the good fortune that Meg, one of Liz's dearest friends from her college days, lives and works in Seattle and is also now a dear friend of ours. Meg continues to share fond memories of Liz as we make new memories together, all of which is comforting and lifegiving.

After Liz died, I didn't know if my broken heart could heal. What assuaged my grief was being able to be of service. I went back into teaching, spending full weeks in residence at underperforming schools in the U.S. and Canada. In mentoring teachers and principals and, especially, in working directly with children, I found myself again. The magic of what children can do when we see their gifts, hold high expectations, and show them what's possible gave me joy in the midst of my sorrow. For those times when I was with children, I was able to lose myself in an uninterrupted literacy flow which gave me peace of mind, gratitude, and a sense of hope for the future.

Of course, we still had Peter then. He had just graduated college, was deeply in love with Claudine, and was finding his way in the work world, where he began as a newspaper reporter for a couple of years, moved on to Microsoft for 16 years, and then worked as a senior content strategist for the University of Washington Continuum College for the last eight years of his life, where he was a cherished colleague.

Peter's childhood and growing up years were marked by his close bond with his family and friends, his passion for Dungeons & Dragons, his devotion to our beloved, wire-haired dachshund Toby, and his procrastination with school assignments and home chores. Somehow he managed to get everything done on deadline and done well. His fascination with the wonders of the universe led him to chase eclipses and played an important role in his decision to apply to Cornell University, where his personal letter to astronomer Carl Sagan granted him entrance to Sagan's already-full class. His love of journalism, which began while working on his high school's newspaper, continued at *The Cornell Daily Sun*, where he became assistant managing editor his senior year.

Peter remained obsessed with all things to do with Star Wars, movies, and music. He enjoyed spending time in natural settings, playing hacky sack, and making homemade pickles. He loved playing piano—especially jazz—and passed down that jazz-piano-love to his daughter Katie. He read aloud to his daughter Brooke through her middle school years *The Hobbit* and the entire *Lord of the Rings* series. Peter adored family board games, especially Scrabble, and with his family hosted an annual Game Day family event on New Year's Day. Peter was always authentically himself, detail oriented, persistent, and principled in his beliefs and actions. He never lost his playful, adventurous spirit and his concern for others. He was kind, funny, creative, and honest. His love for his family was paramount in his life; it was a privilege to be his mom.

For Peter, we are still in the midst of sorrow and trying to figure out how to live our lives purposefully and with some grace. Writing this book is one way of finding purpose—sharing with you, dear reader, what I have learned and am still learning about teaching, learning, and living a good life.

The Covid pandemic has wreaked havoc on us all. So has the changing world order, which feels like we may be tilting more towards autocracy than democracy. As well, so many of us are living with psychic trauma from loss, even though that trauma may not be visible. The loss of a loved one, health, a job, a partnership, a friendship, safety, housing, food security, a way of life, and so much more can cause us alarm, anxiety, grief, and uncertainty. So much of life is out of our control.

World-historical calamities, natural disasters, and unforeseen events can all contribute to a loss of certainty, discomfort, and fear. All the more reason that the emotional, social, and curricular spaces we create in our classrooms and schools must be equitable, stable, loving havens where each student—and teacher—feels secure, valued, supported, and hopeful.

Teaching, writing, working with colleagues, and dedicating our lives to serving children and learners of all ages can be a lifeline not just for those we help but for ourselves as well. Certainly, that has been true for me. Being able to help others has taken me away from myself and brought me closer to my truest self.

I am thinking these days about healing. Can one truly heal from extreme trauma? I'm not sure. Time helps, being loved helps, friendships help, being understood helps. But I'm wondering if the best we can actually do, with time and patience, is to learn to cope with our wounds and to live as fully as we can in spite of unimaginable loss, tragedy, and trauma. We can find some balance, "bounce back," and move forward. We can become resilient and grateful for the good in our lives. But as my former editor and wise colleague Alan Huisman once said, "Grief doesn't go away. The volume just goes down."

Sadness and contentedness—partners in living

When my father died at the age of 94, we flew to New York City for his memorial service and his burial, right next to my mother. Dad had spent the last 8 1/2 years of his life in Seattle, close to us, where he was recovering from a brutal stroke until he wasn't. Transplanted from his home, friends, and full-time work he loved to a restricted life in a nursing care facility on the other side of the country, he never adjusted to the loss of his life as he knew it. Still, even on his saddest days, he was glad for our almost-daily visits as well as for visits from my two sisters, each of whom lived out of state and came when they could. At first, Dad was denied his sadness and was so overmedicated for "depression," he was lifeless. I pleaded with the doctor in charge: "Let him mourn his life; depression is normal for all he's lost. Let him feel that pain of loss." With fewer drugs, he gradually reclaimed a compromised but worthwhile life, in spite of severe physical limitations. We did what we could to bring him contentment—seeing him often, bringing special foods he loved, reading aloud to him from his beloved *New York Times*, discussing the news of the day, taking him beyond his small room. Also, until his final decline—using a special transport for people in wheelchairs—we took him on occasional outings to natural settings—to enjoy the beach, the park, and outdoor picnics.

When my dad died, Frank and I, Peter and Claudine, Katie and Brooke, and my dear friend Harriet attended his funeral. We were staying at a hotel near to the cemetery; the morning of the funeral, we were all having breakfast together in the wide-open lobby. The girls had gone exploring once they finished eating, and Katie—age 10 at the time— quietly approached me. "Grandma, I'm having a pretty good time here and I'm not sure I'm supposed to." I reassured her that it was fine; it was good to all be together; it was okay to feel happy—that one could be happy and sad at the same time.

I've thought a lot about Katie's statement recently. Living with some level of grief is something I've come to accept as part of living a long life. But now I also believe contentment can and must accompany that grief. When Harry, my dad's close friend and second cousin-twice-removed, told us he wanted to conduct the grave service after my dad died, we were stunned. Uncle Harry was in his early 90s when he made that offer. True to his word and just a week before he would turn 100, he conducted a religious service at the gravesite with love, grace, and humor—and was the only one of us coatless on a frigid day. After the service, we all went to a nearby restaurant. We told stories about my dad and also celebrated Harry's 100th birthday with a cake, candles, and song. If my dad hadn't died, we wouldn't have had this celebration. Contentment in the midst of sadness. My dad would have approved. He hated to miss a good party, and he loved cousin Harry, who wrote a personal letter to him every week of those 8 ½ years and, to the delight of my father, ended every letter with a joke.

After our son Peter died, we didn't socialize for a long time. It was too difficult to be with people, even those we loved. In particular, our dear friends Sheila and Walter gently let us know they wanted to have us over for dinner when we felt ready. They would take us as we were, and we knew that was true. From the time Peter was diagnosed with his rare cancer, Sheila called every week just to see how we were, and we still talk weekly, years later. When we did finally accept their invitation, what I remember most about that evening was the laughter. Because our friends accepted us as we were—sad, fragile, and uncertain—we felt safe. We talked about our grief, spoke of ordinary things, and began to relax a bit. I don't remember how the laughter started or what we laughed about but seeing Frank laugh again was a tonic for us all.

We live with both loss and gratitude every day. I think the challenge is figuring out how to live a good life in spite of the losses. While disappointments, frustrations, and anticipatory grief are ever present in our lives, so is joy. Several months after Peter died, a dear friend asked us if we were "broken." I thought for a while before responding and then said we were "broken open." We could feel more, we had more gratitude, life felt more precious, but the truth is also that some days we do feel broken. It is then that I look at what has long been one of my favorite objects—a piece of pottery, a colorful and artistic plate—bought at a local pottery sale years ago and, then, somehow the plate dropped and shattered. Frank managed to painstakingly glue it all back together, about 15 or so pieces and shards. You can see all the cracks because of the thick, white, adhesive glue he used to piece it all back together. The plate is especially precious to me now as it represents the potential of life, both the fragility and the beauty of it—and all the cracks. It reminds me that becoming whole means embracing brokenness and life's imperfections.

Shattered pottery plate beautifully made whole.

Even in our darkest and most troubling times, hope and beauty matter. The trick is, I think, to be able to see the light and the possibilities in our lives, the light and potential of our students and loved ones, the light of a moment of unexpected joy—to experience what I have come to call "something approaching happiness," appreciating slivers of happiness wherever they appear.

Restored plate as a daily reminder of life's fragility and hope. Painting by Toby Gordon.

Relying on hope (Peter's story)

It's a funny thing about hope. We need it most when things appear hopeless.

When Peter was finally diagnosed with his exceedingly rare cancer, Claudine and I made him promise us he'd stay off the Internet, and thankfully he agreed. Had he read what was "out there" he would have been desolate. By the time people with his cancer are finally diagnosed, which usually takes decades, they are already at an advanced stage. Peter was 46 when he was diagnosed, very young for a cancer that primarily is diagnosed in people aged 60 and older.

I took on the role of family researcher to explore treatment options, and Peter took to finding survivors. When he found an article about a well-known scientist who had survived 20 years and done his best work post cancer diagnosis, Peter spent months tracking down his widow, who lived in Europe, and was reassured when he was able to speak with her by phone. Every time Peter was at a severely low point in his morale, Claudine and I made sure he talked to someone who could reassure him. While all the evidence pointed to few survivors, we his family thought, "Why not him?" "Why couldn't he be one of them?"

Through extensive investigation, I learned that a complicated, all-day surgery by a highly trained, highly experienced surgeon was the only viable treatment option and that there were only a handful of such surgeons in the U.S. With Peter's permission, I contacted each of them through their nurses and staff and sent copies of the slides from his recent MRIs. I was astonished when one of them, Dr. Jason Foster, called me at home on a Saturday evening and offered to meet with Frank and me and Peter and Claudine to personally explain what might be possible.

As in any field, including education, it is not enough to have superior skills to teach content. Relationship and communication skills must be part of the whole efficacy package. Peter was initially terrified about the surgery, long recovery, and his future. It was Dr. Foster's warm and compassionate manner, his "I will give you all the time you need," "I will be present for you and your family," and his positive and hopeful outlook that led Peter and Claudine to unreservedly choose him. Dr. Foster had it all—great surgical know-how, superior communication skills, kindheartedness, and empathy—along with a "walks on water" reputation at the hospital and cancer center. He was also the same age as Peter, and we were all captivated by him.

When it became clear that a subsequent surgery would be required six months after the first one, we were still hopeful. Dr. Foster has a way of telling the truth in a manner that nurtures encouragement, trust, and hope. When the second surgery failed to slow the cancer growth, Peter gradually, courageously, and with much grace, came to accept his fate and even to feel gratitude for the adventurous and loving life he'd lived with his wife Claudine, daughters Katie and Brooke, family members, lifetime friends, and colleagues at work. I've kept in touch with Dr. Foster since Peter died. Once or twice a year I text or email him, and he always responds. In my last exchange with him, I felt it important to let him know how much the hope he gave to Peter and his family made a huge difference. The magnificent, complicated work he does, and that so many of us do in helping professions, is exhausting and oftentimes heartbreaking. Things don't go as planned; unforeseeable factors change an expected outcome; time runs out. I wanted the good doctor to know his herculean efforts were not in vain, that the hope he provided through his actions was a precious gift to Peter and to us, his family.

Here's an excerpt from my email to Dr. Foster followed by his response, shared with his permission:

Happy Holidays Jason,

It's been a while since we've been in touch, about 9 months I think. Still, Frank and I think and speak of you regularly, always with deep affection and appreciation. We hope you and your loved ones are safe and well and getting through these challenging times. I can't imagine what it's been like for you as a surgeon this past year with hospitals and ICUs constantly full. And here we go again with the latest Covid variant…

Finally, and most importantly, I want to thank you now for the gift of hope you gave us, which was vital and which is different from optimism. I look back and see clearly now that Peter's chances of survival and living his life were extremely low. And yet. The mind hopefully thinks, "Well, why wouldn't he be in the 1% who beat this rare, brutal cancer?" I remember how exhausted you looked after that 16-hours plus, second surgery. We knew you'd given everything you had. You should know that Peter thought it was worth it. He believed that second surgery made it possible to attend Katie's high school graduation and to see her off to college. He was so grateful for that.

Truly, it wasn't until about a month before Peter died that we, his family, came to terms with the fact that there was no further treatment. Time was quickly running out; the cancer was killing him and causing too much suffering. Although his body was ravaged, his mind was clear. He was himself, and each of us— Claudine, Frank and me, and Katie and Brooke—were able to say and receive a personal and loving goodbye, full of gratitude for him, and he did the same for us. He was at peace; his death was peaceful. He accepted his fate, and he believed he had lived a full life.

I know you continue to make a difference for other families, just like ours. It's a great thing you do, and you do it with humility, open communication, and compassion. You will always have a piece of our hearts.

We hope you and your family will get to Seattle one day.

Wishing you and your loved ones a promising New Year and a better 2022. Be well.

Regie

Regie,

It is so nice to hear from you.

It's great to hear that you, Frank, Claudine, Katie, and Brooke are all doing well.

Thank you for sharing your personal thoughts and the family's during Peter's battle with cancer. You have a great gift as a writer and your words, while only 2 paragraphs, reflect the complex challenge of this disease, the hope we (I) want all patients to feel as they battle their cancer, the choice of patients to fight cancer on their own terms, and to enjoy the time we have with family and the people we love, which Peter did every day. I remember feeling the love and support you all shared, and words cannot express how much it means to get an email from you like this one sharing updates on the family and reflections on Peter's battle with his disease.

Your words are so eloquent and powerful that I had to share them with my team (nurse and PA).

I hope one day in the near future my family and I will have the opportunity to visit Peter's bench and have lunch with you and family.

Please send my warmest regards to Frank, Claudine, Katie, and Brooke.

Happy New Year.

Jason

Discovering gratitude (Claudine's gift)

My birthday happened three weeks after our son Peter died. Celebration was the furthest thing from my mind. And yet. Celebrate we did due to the generosity and thoughtfulness of my daughter-in-law, Claudine—all the more remarkable because she was deeply grieving the loss of her beloved husband. Somehow she managed to set aside her own heartache to ensure I would have a birthday memory that included some pleasure.

She persuaded Frank and me to stop by later in the day and then surprised me with multiple gifts. While we'd traditionally celebrated family birthdays together, a few years earlier I'd requested "no gifts please, just a card," and that request had been honored; a personal, handwritten message has always delighted me. So, I was taken aback by the beautiful bouquet of flowers on the coffee table in the living room, the delicious and lovely chocolate cake she'd made, and the beautifully wrapped box that housed a handmade throw pillow, an especially personal and significant gift. I was overcome with emotion and gratitude for her kindness.

The story behind the throw pillow is a story that resonates with me daily. So, let me share the full meaning of it as best I can. When Peter was recovering from each of his surgeries, Frank and I were on site, living with Peter and Claudine for several weeks, to help them with the daily care and responsibilities that were required. One afternoon Claudine suggested that the two of us go to a local craft fair, which turned out to be a welcome diversion and short outing we both enjoyed. Wandering around the booths with handmade jewelry, pottery, artwork, clothing, and other crafts, we each bought a few gifts. I spotted a forest green t-shirt I thought Peter might like. In the center of it was a garden bumblebee, peacefully resting on a large, intricate golden and brown flower with numerous petals. Above that image were the words "The Good Life" printed in white block letters which were arranged in a curve above the illustration.

Peter did like the t-shirt, and unbeknown to me, Claudine fashioned it into a beautiful throw pillow after he died. THE GOOD LIFE and the bee resting on flower petals take up a full side of the pillow. The forest green, back side of the pillow includes a golden-colored zipper for housing the pillow. I look at that beautiful gift every day and am reminded how important it is to live a good life, despite the tragedies and difficulties that eventually come to all of us.

When I am not writing, the pillow sits on my red reading chair and is the first thing I see when I walk into the room where I work and write. When I am at my computer, which is at least several hours a day, I always place the pillow behind me, to support me in the desk chair I am sitting in, to comfort me, and to help me sit up straighter. I physically feel Claudine's extraordinary act of kindness, and my gratitude is constant. I have come to think of her as "daughter-of-my-heart" and have told her so. Looking back on that birthday several years ago, I now grasp the full meaning and wisdom of a line by the prophet Kahlil Gibran: "Joy is our sadness unmasked." It was my great sorrow that made these joyful moments so moving and that propels me daily to strive to live THE GOOD LIFE. Peter would approve.

The Good Life pillow on my red reading chair.

CHAPTER 8
Revitalizing Our Lives Through Friendships

- ❖ The importance of enduring friendships
- ❖ Extraordinary friendships (Peter's band of brothers)
- ❖ Work-life friendships
- ❖ Everyone needs a Juliette

DOI: 10.4324/9781003381242-8

The importance of enduring friendships

The importance of friendships for our wellbeing and happiness cannot be overstated. I've been very fortunate all my life to have enduring friendships that have created a circle of "reciprocity and sustenance." These friendships are indispensable to my wellbeing and quality of life. They are like fresh air; they lift my spirits and add virtual sunshine to Seattle's cloudy days.

Sometimes what we need most is a friend who truly "sees" us, helps us practice self-compassion, and cheers us on when we succeed and when we doubt ourselves. A true friend can be a mirror for us, seeing our strengths and vulnerabilities in an honest and compassionate way we might not be able to see on our own. A true friend sees our best and most complete selves and makes sure we also see it. Harriet does that for me. Since we've been dearest friends since our early college days, and she has also known my family over many years, she knows me better than most. She is an encouraging, non-judgmental, loving presence. She is the most generous, open-hearted person I know.

She's my go-to-person and morale booster when I need a reality check. She provides perspective, advice, and/or solace on a sticky situation, and I play the same role for her. I have known her family for many decades and have benefited from the joy of knowing and loving her remarkable mother, Mamala, a Holocaust survivor who lived to be 107 with all her faculties intact. Most of all, like all genuine friendships, Harriet and I delight in each other's company, by phone or in-person, through texts, and through handwritten cards. We live on opposite sides of the country, and in pre-pandemic days we also got together once a year for a two-day, two-person conversation fest. As we have done for most of our lives and will continue to do going forward, we talk by phone every week; we tell our stories; we listen to each other; and we celebrate our precious friendship.

Like many of you, I do my best to stay connected with friends and acquaintances. I reach out with brief texts or emails, which are more welcome than many of us realize. I know that to be true as I'm always happy to hear from someone I like and admire whom I may I have lost touch with for a while or even for years. Less frequently, I reach out with phone calls and, occasionally Zoom calls, usually scheduled in advance out of respect for everyone's busy life. I'm also a letter writer. I know. It's old-fashioned, but it's personal and affirming to write and to receive a heartfelt, handwritten letter or card. Especially for an important thank you, a text (in my humble opinion) doesn't convey the warmth and appreciation of a personal, handwritten message the way a beautiful card does. I save many of the ones I've received over the years and occasionally reread them. I have a whole drawer of blank, artistic greeting cards that I use for friendship notes, thank you notes, and occasions such as birthdays, anniversaries, congratulations, and condolences.

Attending to our relationships and friendships is a form of self-care and other-care that helps insulate us against loneliness, disease, and depression. Having social support and close relationships translates to living longer, happier lives and is more important than money or fame, even for low-income groups.[1] In fact, "One of the most powerful predictors of whether you rise out of poverty is how many of the people you know who are well off... Cross-friendships are a better predictor of upward mobility than school quality."[2] So it's critical we promote a learning and social-emotional learning infrastructure in our schools and classrooms that opens up opportunities for learners to build community and friendships, and to know love.

We all want to feel loved and validated. Friends we trust who meet us with compassion, honesty, and understanding can provide the "family" and sense of belonging we may have been missing. Someone once told me, "A dysfunctional family is a family with more than one person in it." It's a funny-sad statement, but true for many of us. If our family of origin is absent or unsupportive, creating a chosen family to share our life with is life-affirming and cause for celebration. As well, in extraordinary circumstances like the pandemic, many of us sought out a temporary family—neighbors, colleagues, service people—to help us get through the days. Kevin became part of our adopted family. For more than a year, he grocery shopped for us as we didn't feel safe enough to do so. Along with our groceries, he always brought as a gift a lovely bouquet of fresh flowers, which touched my heart. In return, I baked cookies for him, which he loved. During each drop-off delivery, we talked and got to know each other. We do all our own shopping now, and Kevin remains a special friend. We stay in regular touch. I still bake cookies for him. He still brings flowers.

"Friends see us and believe in us in ways we'd like to see and believe in ourselves. Friends provide the comradeship that is the crown of a good life."[3]

Friendship with Renzo

My youngest friend is Renzo, a neighbor who lives down the street. At this writing, he is about to start high school. Our unexpected friendship began when he was 11, rang our doorbell, and said, "I've heard that you are the tart master of the neighborhood. I wonder if you would teach me to make a fruit tart." I hardly knew Renzo but was immediately charmed by his forthrightness and enthusiasm and happily agreed to his request. We set up a day and time for us to make a fruit tart in my kitchen. He asked what he needed to bring, and I said I'd supply all the ingredients and tools we would need. It was June, and the apricots in our local farmer's market were gorgeous and juicy. Just like teaching in the classroom, only first-rate resources would suffice for a delicious result. You can't make a great fruit tart from second-rate fruit, just as you can't teach reading well without first-rate literature.

In fact, I follow the same instructional framework for tart making as I use in the classroom when teaching a new concept. That is, we usually start with a demonstration, then move (when the learner is ready) to a shared demonstration/experience where we do it together but I'm still taking the lead. Next, the learner takes the lead but I'm right by his side, supporting and guiding his actions and not letting him fail. Renzo was a fast learner. He had already been baking sourdough breads from scratch and creating elaborate pastries. He loved to bake! His first fruit tart was a triumph, and we had a great time creating it together. Truth be told, he required minimal help from me to make the pastry crust and cut and arrange the fruit in a beautiful manner. After that venture, he began ringing our doorbell regularly—to bring us something he'd just baked or to borrow something he needed for the baking or cooking he was doing at that moment. His request was as likely to be almonds or herbs as it was to be a chicken breast.

It was several months after our fruit tart experience that our son Peter died. Renzo and his mom showed up at our front door a day later. As he'd been instructed by his dear and kind mother, he immediately said,

"I'm sorry for your loss." Being the irrepressible soul he is, he moved right into our hallway, asked to see some photos of Peter, and started examining Frank's rock collection in the living room. We were not ready for this "intrusion." It was way too soon. Our emotions were raw. I told Renzo, "I can't show you any pictures now." We talked for more minutes than felt comfortable, and then they left. But Renzo kept showing up, always with some excuse to be there, and always saying at the start, "I'm sorry for your loss." He wore us down with his genuine kindness, empathy, and generous heart. It wasn't long before we showed him photos of Peter, and Frank let him choose several rocks from his collection. It wasn't long before I gave to Renzo, from my collection, some beautiful, gourmet cookbooks I was no longer using and that I knew he'd appreciate. It wasn't long till our relationship felt like a genuine friendship.

Renzo recently turned 14. I was honored to be one of two non-family members he invited to his birthday party. I think of him as a friend, neighbor, and fascinating, highly curious person. We care deeply about each other, and we are learning from each other. These days he stops by mostly just to talk. He knows I am a teacher and a writer, and we talk a lot about education, his in particular, but we also we talk about history, plants, religion, politics, cooking, you name it. I have responded to some drafts of his writing and encouraged him to aim high and to let the people who support his ambitious efforts know how much he appreciates them. As of now, he has firmly decided he wants his life work to be a chef, one who creates original masterpieces in the kitchen. I expect we may all be reading about him some day.

Extraordinary friendships (Peter's band of brothers)

One of the most remarkable friendships I know about involves my son Peter and his best friends, a close bond that began in childhood and continues through adulthood—even without his presence. In Chapter 3, "Promoting Equitable Opportunities," I write about how school and housing integration efforts made these lifelong friendships possible and, even, likely. The importance of cross-racial friendships cannot be overstated. In *Literacy Essentials*, in the section on Equity, "Seek and Value Diversity," I write:

> Most children still form most of their friendships in school, so we need to do all we can to create deliberate access for diverse friendships to form—through mixed grouping, conversations, invitations, language use, opportunities to work and play together, and ensuring that all children feel good about who they are. Students in diverse classrooms who experience cross-cultural dialogue demonstrate increased civic engagement, are more likely to be open to alternative points of view, are less likely to stereotype "others" and are better prepared for working in our increasingly diverse, global economy.

In recent conversations with Peter's closest friends –Matt, David, Jonathan, Keith, and Ken—we discussed their integrated school's experience and how it led to the solid and lasting friendships they formed. A friendship that began by spending time together in and out of school and engaging in their mutual interests led to deep social and emotional bonds and a sense of wellbeing as adults. (See Chapter 3 for the influence of integrated schools.)

Each of them credits Peter as being the "glue" and "driving force" for keeping the group together, which was especially true post college years when the friends lived in different cities, as they do now. In a recent conversation, Matt told me:

> Pete knew how to do friendship. He was caring and believed it was important to stay in touch and to be there for each other. He was always there for us. I became closer to Pete than anyone because he modeled how to do that.

Of their close friendship, Jonathan says:

> Peter didn't take his friendships for granted. Eventually, I got better at that. He was the only person who was consistently present in my life from 2nd grade on. He wrote letters, he called me, he kept in touch. Even though we wound up living on opposite coasts, he always made the effort. He was there for me even when things weren't so great in my life.

David notes:

> These guys changed my life for the better. I don't know what I'd be without them.

Keith weighs in:

> I felt very close and connected to Pete as someone who was, also, an ongoing music maker, who also chose the West coast to live, and as someone who also was really trying to expand emotionally, ideologically, and culturally. I felt a lot of kinship in that way, that I could call Pete any time and talk about anything with him.

> One of the most important things in my life has been the opportunity to develop and grow with this group of friends who have been with me my entire journey of becoming. I had just turned 12 when we got together, and that was when I first realized there was a lot more complexity in community, in the world, and in relationships.

Ken told me:

> We just fell in with each other and really bonded. We just jelled.
> We never had to work to stay friends. There was a natural affinity
> among us. Even when we hadn't seen each other for a while, we
> would easily fall back into patterns of how we always behaved with
> each other. We had found the people we loved and just enjoyed
> hanging out together.
>
> These are my oldest friends in the world. I've known them for
> over 40 years. We can talk to each other about anything. It doesn't
> matter how long we've been apart. We just pick up where we left off.

When it mattered most, Peter's friends were there for him. A poignant
memory is top of mind. The night before Peter was to go into an all-day
surgery for his rare cancer, all five guys showed up for him, big time.
Claudine, Frank, and I were sitting in the living room of the house we'd
rented together in Omaha, to support Peter and Claudine through the
surgery and recovery process. Peter was on speaker phone in an adjacent
bedroom. While we couldn't hear the conversation, the laughter was
unmistakable and constant. David, Matt, Ken, Jonathan, and Keith were
on the other end of the phone shoring Peter up with stories, memories,
and jokes. To my surprise, Matt later told me, "Pete cracked some good
ones." I've no doubt that hour-long-plus conversation and laughter eased
the terror Peter was feeling about his surgery and lightened his mood.
Such a generous and loving gift from his friends.

Dungeons & Dragons deserves its own special mention in the formative
friendships of these men, as it was D&D that dominated the time they
spent together, starting around the age of 12. While each of the men
is unique and has different perspectives, it was their love of gaming
that drew them together and has kept them together, beginning in 7th
grade and continuing to this day. While they played many types of

games growing up and into adulthood—including word games such as Scrabble, Boggle, and historical and fantasy-based board games—it was Dungeons & Dragons, a role-playing game, that most held their attention.

Considered a nerdy game when they were kids, decades later there's been a surge of interest and popularity; D&D has gone mainstream and is considered "cool." These young gamers were onto something important. The game gave them a space to have agency in their lives. In a face-to-face game fueled by collaborative storytelling, players create characters who navigate fantasy worlds where they can be heroes who have control over their lives. David spoke of how the game transformed and shaped him and the group.

> With teamwork, you can be anything you want to be. D&D literally allows you to shape the world you're in and have a direct impact. You can vanquish what's causing you problems. A lot of it is cathartic. You can set the victory conditions. The fantasy-game allows you to explore adventures you can't explore and talk about in real life. Who wouldn't want to be a fighter, a wizard, a gnome!

Keith further noted:

> We loved playing D&D together in the safety of something enjoyable that connected us. D&D played a big role in developing our shared history, trust, and loving relationships. Our gaming conversations expanded over the years to include thoughtful conversations about what's going on in the world.

Jonathan, who was not part of the D&D group, played Scrabble regularly with Peter for many years. Jonathan fondly recalls:

> Scrabble was more than a game Peter and I started playing in high school. Over the years, it came to symbolize our enduring friendship and love of words. We lived on opposite sides of the country and treasured any opportunity to play Scrabble in person. That Peter would find time during a family trip to play a game of

Scrabble meant more to me than I can express in words. Later, online Scrabble not only allowed us to play more frequently but helped us stay connected in each other's lives. I am grateful for Peter's life and the happy moments we shared together.

In a tradition that Peter originally fostered and organized, all these years later, the men still take time off from work, family, and obligations to meet annually for four to five days of strategy board games including Scrabble and Boggle and, especially, Dungeons & Dragons. They no longer worry if the house they rent has a view or if their location has special amenities and points of interest. Enthralled by their gaming obsession, they almost never leave the house! Keith has now taken on the job of meeting organizer and ensuring the group continues to get together each year. As well, every month Keith, Matt, David, and Ken meet via Zoom to play their favorite game, Dungeons & Dragons.

Notedly, Dungeons & Dragons is being used in some schools these days to motivate up-and-coming-readers and help develop literacy skills along with social, emotional, and cooperative ones.[4] D&D requires critical thinking, problem solving, teamwork, and math to masterfully play the game. Storytelling is also central to playing the game, and as previously discussed in Chapter 2, storytelling is vital to literacy, learning, and sense of self. Also, while the accompanying reading materials, rules, and detailed reference guides can be daunting, if kids want to be a player, they will make the effort. In fact:

Dungeons & Dragons is a gateway drug to reading… Children who do not read regularly or read for pleasure will start reading the gaming books almost as soon as they sit down, and they carry that outside of the game.

As well, some creative high school teachers integrate D&D into their language arts and literature classes to teach and meet mandated curricular standards, a great example of using authentic materials to engage and inspire learners.[5]

Importantly, Ken also notes:

> The literacy component of this game can't be emphasized enough. The terminology and definitions of words used, though common to the game, are typically uncommon in regular speech. A high-level vocabulary, dictionary knowledge, and overall understanding comes in to play frequently.

In Chapter 2, "Telling Our Stories," we talked a lot about the importance of storytelling in our lives, in and out of school. The storytelling component of D&D, creating a believable fantasy world, is an improvisational, interactive, and collaborative one that transfers to increased interest in reading and writing. Players of D&D compare this gaming experience to "starring in their own movies or writing their own novels."[6]

An important perk of D&D is the opportunity it provides for establishing close friendships, like those Peter and his "band of brothers" developed, all the more reason to create opportunities in the classroom for selective gaming opportunities. Also, now that D&D is "cool" and no longer considered nerdy, girls and women are getting involved as players. The positive influence of D&D cannot be overstated. Creative and literary luminaries, such as Ta-Nehisi Coates, Robin Williams, Stephen Colbert, and George R. R. Martin, the mastermind of *Game of Thrones*, give credit to Dungeons & Dragons for being a storytelling apprenticeship that helped jumpstart their narrative writing and storytelling careers. You can't get a better recommendation than that!

If an important goal of schooling includes, as I believe it must, the freedom to become your truest self; to have your unique voice heard, accepted, and celebrated; to welcome and appreciate disparate points of view, then these friends have thrived and prospered. Jonathan, David, Matt, Ken, Keith—like their dear friend Pete—are hopeful, curious, creative, playful, and kind. Each one of them continues to make a unique contribution to making the world a more equitable, kindhearted, enjoyable space where everyone is welcome. It was effective, integrated schooling—going beyond the literacy basics, required curriculum, and testing to include ongoing conversations and interactions at the heart and mind level—which continues to make these wonderful friendships possible.

Finally, and not to be minimized, these close interracial friendships made what might have been a difficult conversation a natural one. Keith notes that the first conversation he ever had about race with Peter—and Claudine was there too—was in 2014 after Michael Brown, an unarmed Black 18-year-old was shot and killed by a white police officer in Ferguson, Missouri, and who was later acquitted. This was just a couple of years after the acquittal of George Zimmerman in the shooting death of Trayvon Martin, and the rise of the Black Lives Matter movement, all of which inspired a national conversation on race and civil and human rights.

Keith explains the naturalness of the conversation:

> I never had a conversation with Pete that was explicitly about race until after Michael Brown died. Because of our long and trusting friendship—and that we'd embraced different conversations over so many years—I knew we were on the same side, even though mainstream culture would tell me that my Blackness and his Whiteness meant we were not. Racial prejudice is making a snap judgment about someone based upon one—and only one—aspect of who they are. The key part of that practice is in the prefix, "pre" in the word "prejudice." By then, I'd already been friends with Pete for 35 years. We'd had innumerable conversations about politics, climate change, food systems, health, education, sexuality, etc., as well as the best, new two-player games to play with our wives. There was no "pre" judging involved from either of us; I knew I could trust him in a conversation explicitly about race.

Let's each of us commit to doing our part to promote and champion interracial, multicultural friendships in our classrooms, schools, and communities. Importantly, reducing racism begins with non-judgmental conversations between people we trust and, also, our willingness to listen to people outside our inner circle. Loving, trusting friendships are the magical elixir that make life more meaningful, worthwhile, and glorious.

Work-life friendships

Having a friend at work is beneficial to our health at work and at home. In *The Good Life: Lessons from the World's Longest Scientific Study of Happiness* by Robert Waldinger and Marc Schulz, the authors document that quality relationships are essential to human wellbeing, and that positive relationships at work carry over into our home lives. It was confirming to read that research as I've lived the results, a happy interdependence with colleagues that has enriched my whole life.

If I'm honest, I would say I fall in love with the people I work with and admire. Not all of them, of course, but many. I have always found I work best with people I come to know well and care about. Some of my dearest, lifelong friends are teachers, principals, and leaders from different parts of the United States and Canada that I've had the privilege of knowing on many levels. I met each of them when we worked together in their respective schools, districts, and provinces where I had been invited to raise expectations, achievement, and enjoyment in reading and writing.

Most of these professional learning experiences were residencies. Over the course of several days or a week devoted to professional learning, I led educators through demonstrating, mentoring, coaching, guiding, or co-teaching in a side-by-side collaboration. Once I commit to a residency, I am all in. That means taking time to get to know people before, during, and after our work together. That might include planning calls before we meet and—once on site to do the work—early coffees before school begins and after school socializing, all with the purpose of ensuring our conversations are about getting to know each other and not just about literacy. We work better, all of us—more efficiently, effectively, and happily—when we know, like, and trust our colleagues.

Many decades later, these friendships endure—through letters, emails, texts, phone calls, Zoom calls, birthday cards, and in-person visits. We "show up" for each other. We have been present for each other for life's ups and downs—celebrations, loss of a loved one, and support of all kinds. I am reluctant to name these dear friends for worry of leaving someone out. So let me just say, you know who you are, and you know how much your friendship matters to me because I've told you. We continue to share from our hearts our experiences, life stories, and perspectives on education, equity, our families, and the fragile state of the world. These friendships, which began with a sense of community and support in the work environment, have stood the test of time and remain cherished friendships today, decades later.

My most significant work-life friendship has been my extraordinary, 20-year friendship with Sandra Figueroa. I think of her as "sister of my heart." We met shortly after Frank and I moved to Seattle. Sandy was the new K–12 Literacy and Curriculum Director in nearby Bellevue, Washington, and she invited me to do a residency in one of the two high-poverty schools in the district. That turned out to be a life-long, enriching experience on so many levels. Not only did we learn how much we had in common literacy-wise, but we also connected deeply at the heart level. Our loving friendship has made us a strong team for collaboration and good. Over the years, Sandy has pushed and expanded my thinking, for which I am most grateful.

Although Sandy and I hadn't met until we were in Seattle, she says she knew me from my book, *Transitions: From Literature to Literacy*. "I did everything you advised with my 1st graders, except I did it in Spanish." Sandy is bilingual and bicultural and has fought her whole life to make school and life better for underserved students. She got certified as a principal so she could take the lead in an elementary school, just like Lincoln Elementary School she attended in Nogales, Arizona, and make a difference for children like herself.

I got to spend a day with Sandy at the pre-K–grade 6 elementary school where she was principal. Her school was in a nearby locale to where Sandy went to school as a child, and the school had the same demographics—students from poverty whose first language was Spanish. In a cruel twist of fate, children who did not pass the state's English language assessment—which was most of the school's students—were required to be segregated daily for four hours of isolated instruction. Sandy worked tirelessly to try to overturn that inequitable requirement.

I have several standout memories from spending the day with Sandy at the elementary school where she became principal. First, she knew the names of all 540 students and their families, and warmly greeted each one by name at the start of the day and throughout the day. Second, one of the most impressive classrooms was the pre-K class, which was filled with rich and authentic literacy work. Third, by the end of her first year as principal, due to her leadership and ongoing professional learning, the school went from underperforming to performing. Fourth, and disappointedly, the assistant superintendent had no expectations for what students could accomplish. When I asked him, "How many of your students go on to college?" he responded, "Our students don't go on to college."

That poverty of low expectations was limiting students' potential for seeing possibilities for their future lives. These promising children needed what all children need—high expectations, expert teaching, loving support, guidance, and conviction that they could handle the academic, social, and emotional challenges life presents to each of us. Sandy teaches and leads as if all kids are gifted, and in that realm she excels. She enthralls students, teachers, and leaders at all levels. In a recent workshop, one participant wrote to Sandy, "Thanks for giving us your time to embrace and encourage the child's soul for reading."

On a personal level, some of our best times together have been over good food, wine, and conversation—just the three of us, Frank, Sandy, and me. We love to cook together, tell stories, and travel together. She has stayed at our home for a week, even though our usual limit for a guest is three days. As she is so easy and enjoyable to be with—so respectful, kind, and loving—visits with her are never too long. Sadly, due to the pandemic, we went a long time without seeing each other.

Another exceptional friendship has been my 30-year-plus friendship with Joan Servis, who taught 4th grade in Shaker Heights, Ohio, for 25 years. Remarkably, half of her Facebook friends are former students, many of whom are now in their forties and have children in college. These former students still write to tell her she was their favorite teacher. One wrote, "You were a breath of fresh air after what we went through in 3rd grade." Simply put, her students adored her and have never forgotten her. When I asked her what she did to inspire such affection and loyalty and what she might advise other teachers, she notes:

> I always developed a sense of community first. You have to earn students' trust and respect. You have to bond with them in the first six weeks of school, which means revealing yourself and your life to them on things they can relate to. I told stories about my love of cats, Michigan football, and living with snakes, as my son was a budding herpetologist. You also have to have a great sense of humor!

I witnessed the joyful community Joan created as we worked closely together in her classroom when I was the district's instructional coach for the elementary grades. She was such an inspiring, outstanding teacher in all domains that when I learned she would soon be retiring, I said to her, "Joan, you have to write a book for teachers. Otherwise, all your teaching wisdom will be lost when you leave." Initially she said "I can't write a book. I'm too busy teaching." But then Joan's principal kindly interceded and found a way for Joan to teach half-time. She took two years to write the acclaimed *Celebrating the Fourth: Ideas and Inspiration for Teachers of Grade Four* (Heinemann, 1999).

Along the way, our friendship blossomed into a close, personal one. Joan lives her life with a deep sense of empathy and caring. For 20 years, she sent us flowers on the day our daughter died, letting us know, "She will never be forgotten." Even now, commemorating that loss, she sends a handwritten letter or card every year. We remain in close contact through letter writing and occasional phone calls. After Joan's beloved husband Jim died, she visited with us in Seattle on what happened to be the one-year anniversary weekend of his death. We honored his memory through personal and professional stories. Joan's friendship remains a cherished gift, for Frank as well as me. We remain in close contact through letter writing and occasional phone calls.

A friendship that blossomed into a superbly close relationship happened a few years ago when Nancy McLean and I were in Winnipeg together, co-leading about 50 administrators in a multi-day, professional learning and leadership workshop. Before the trip, we planned our lessons together by phone. Once in Winnipeg, staying at the same hotel, we met each morning for breakfast, and after the workday we had a long, conversational dinner together every night. While Nancy and I had previously collaborated in Winnipeg residency work—along with our dear friend and colleague Sandra Figueroa—this was the first time we'd had the opportunity to spend so much one-on-one time together. I also knew Nancy from previous residency work in Colorado, where she was a 1st grade teacher and literacy coach. But this was different.

Our extended time together meant we could go beyond lesson planning and casual talk to really get to know each other and delight in each other's company. Nancy is a kind, gentle, and loving soul, and she brings that gentleness and calm—coupled with a wealth of knowledge—into the classroom and school. She easily engages students, teachers, and administrators as she leads them on a powerful, literacy-learning journey. Nancy and I bonded on a deep level as we shared stories from our lives—she, talking about caring for her beloved mom in the final years of her life, and me, talking about dealing with Peter's struggles with cancer. We had developed enough trust over the years that we allowed ourselves to be vulnerable with each other, to talk at the heart and soul level. These days we keep in touch by phone, and even though we don't talk that often, we easily pick up where we left off and engage in meaningful and loving conversations.

If we want to encourage close friendships with colleagues—and students with students—we need to deliberately build in time for people to get to know each other better, that is, to deliberately set up situations—social events, book clubs, inquiry projects, professional learning—that include time and space for deep conversations. Nancy and I were already close friends from years of working together in Colorado and Winnipeg. But it was not until we had that sustained time, just the two of us, that we got to talk of the bitter and the sweet— not just in our work but in our full lives.

An additional relationship I want to spotlight is our loving friendship with Sheila Valencia and Walter Parker, both of whom are professors emeriti at the University of Washington in Seattle. I first knew Sheila professionally, through her work as an acclaimed reading researcher who had published many articles. She also had written a book on portfolio assessment, *Literacy Portfolios in Action* (Harcourt Brace, 1998), which I had read and applied to the literacy work I was leading in Shaker Heights, Ohio. I'd heard Sheila speak at IRA, the International Reading Association (now called ILA) and was impressed with her depth of theoretical and practical knowledge. I invited her into our school district for a full-day workshop. Frank and I picked her up at the airport, brought her back to our condo for drinks, and liked her immediately—her honesty, curiosity, sense of humor, and kind spirit.

When we moved to Seattle many years later, I contacted Sheila. She and her husband Walter, a professor of social studies education and much-admired author on that subject, invited us to dinner at their home. And that was the beginning of a beautiful friendship. For 20 years now, the four of us—Sheila and Walter, and Frank and I—have been alternating dinners at each other's homes on a regular basis. What's delightful is how well the friendship works as a foursome. We are all quite different, but we share similar interests in good food, cooking, politics, history, reading, and much more. The conversation never falters; the food is always delicious; the wine flows freely; a good time is had by all.

Notably, during and after Peter's long illness, when we were unable to reach out to friends, they—and especially Sheila—reached out to us with phone calls, homemade meals, and compassion. What was remarkable about Sheila is she never flinched, never hesitated to ask how we were, never seemed uncomfortable when we spoke. She "showed up," week after week, and her loving presence brought some sense of normalcy when life felt unruly and unknown. Close friendships like this, when we can be ourselves and depend on others to look after us and care for us, are healing. That friendship has been a lifeline when we needed one.

Just as having a friend at work whom we can count on makes doing the work a better experience, the same is true for our students and loved ones. When we allow ourselves to be open to and respectful of others' lived experiences, unlikely friendships are possible. Let's make every effort to ensure our students have at least one friend, one peer they can count on. That may mean asking students without friends whom they would like to be friends with and physically arranging seating to nurture that possibility. If a classmate as a friend seems unlikely, perhaps pair up that student with a younger student, and have the older student mentor the younger one in an area where the older student excels. Friendships make our lives richer, more meaningful, and more joyful. Friendships can restore—at least for a time—our sense of self, possibility, resilience, and happiness.

Everyone needs a Juliette

When Frank and I were in our late 40s and still figuring out how to live our best lives, we began what would become the most remarkable friendship we have ever known. The person of our affection was 78-year-old Juliette Hamelecourt, an indomitable force for what it means to live a full life in spite of ongoing hardships. Our friendship spanned just over a decade, and even in the midst of it, we knew how fortunate we were and felt profound gratitude.

At the beginning, we had just moved from a house into a nearby condominium in Cleveland Heights, Ohio. Juliette lived down the street in a small residential hotel called the Alcazar, where she lovingly restored, beautified, and cared for the hotel's large, courtyard garden in exchange for a lower rent on her apartment. Although my husband Frank knew Juliette casually through the art scene around Cleveland, he did not know her beyond their mutual interest in art, and I had never met her.

Until our friendship with Juliette, Frank and I had never had a joint friendship that included spending time with that friend several times a week. We got together at planned and unplanned times, at her apartment, in the hotel garden, in our home and backyard—sometimes for just a quick hello, sometimes for a cocktail, other times for a shared meal. We learned that for a friendship to thrive, frequent contact was not just beneficial but necessary.

Juliette was both an ordinary person and an extraordinary one. She could relate to everyone no matter their status, ethnicity, quirks, or past history. She cultivated and cherished friendships with people of all ages and walks of life. Her friendships included people from their 20s to their 90s. She had figured out that if she wanted friends around when she was in her 80s, she needed younger people in her life, and young people were drawn to her. A gregarious person, she made their acquaintance at bars, neighborhood restaurants, museums, her church, fundraisers, everywhere she ventured out on her own. She had an insatiable curiosity and independent spirit. People fell in love with her; she was charming, kind, honest and outspoken, at times outrageous, interested in others, and always gracious. She was always, comfortably and magnificently, herself.

She made the best of whatever life threw her. In her tiny, one-bedroom she cooked, entertained, read, and created art. After making her bed each morning, she transformed her bedroom into an artist's studio where she painted. When she invited guests for a home-cooked meal, she turned a portion of her living room into a dining area. Frank and I marveled at how she could take a small space and beautifully transform it depending on her whims, interests, and occasions. She was the most interesting person we'd ever known. She was intellectually curious and knowledgeable about "everything," from the profound to the mundane. She loved to laugh and have a good time. She was charismatic, warm hearted, and generous. I never heard her speak ill of anyone; she respected the dignity of each individual.

When Juliette walked into a room, she lit up the room without saying a word. You knew you were in the presence of someone remarkable just by looking at her. Although she was only about five feet tall, her small frame belied her enormous energy and influence. Fashionably dressed in a long skirt and jacket, jewelry from previous lives enhancing her outfit, and with her long hair piled on top of her head, she was a vision of confidence, boldness, and playfulness.

Everyone who knew her wanted to be more like her—more interesting, more curious, better read, wittier, a better cook, a better conversationist. She had that effect on people. She left behind, for all who knew her, a legacy of great memories. Being in Juliette's presence brought out the best in people. She inspired and challenged people to become their best and most interesting selves. As one of her close friends and admirers said of her, "Maybe I can never be like Juliette, but I've got a glimpse of what's possible to do with my time and feel encouraged to go on with this or that project."

Over a decade of what became an intimate friendship, we came to learn about her adventures and accomplishments; she had lived many lives. She was born in Brussels, lived ten years in Mongolia, ten years in Haiti, and ten years at the Chelsea Hotel in New York, a favored residence for avant-garde, struggling artists. She had also lived in France for a time, been a freelance writer, an editor for a small, women's newspaper, the author of many cookbooks, and the star of her own television cooking show. She was well known for her tapestries, embroideries, and paintings and wrote articles on those topics. After she moved to Cleveland, Ohio, she became active and well known on the local art scene. She regularly lectured on art and history, in French and in English, and she actively promoted local women artists.

She had been married and divorced. She had raised three children, mostly on her own. She had often struggled to pay her rent and moved in and out of poverty. She had lost an adult daughter to cancer. As she aged, she suffered with varying aliments and diseases. But she never lost her inexhaustible spirit, her joie de vivre—her zest and enthusiasm for life. She radiated joy. Simply put, she was fun, entertaining, and uplifting to spend time with. And we always learned something new—about history, eating, gardening, art. She seemed to have boundless energy. She loved spending time at the renowned Cleveland Museum of Art and thought nothing of walking there and back, about four miles round trip, well into her 80s.

We learned so much from Juliette's wisdom. She often said, "Gossip is not conversation" and she lived by that admirable belief. Relatedly, she also believed that in general, people will tell you what they want you to know. Even when we knew her very well, she never peppered us with personal questions. She had overwhelming positivity but was also a realist. "Everyone is subject to intense pain and loss," she said.

She took everything in stride, with measure and balance. When she lost an eye to cancer she said, "I can live with one eye. I can still have quality of life. I can read. I can listen to music." She continued to take pleasure in small things—feeding the birds, tending the garden, visiting with a friend. She saw life as a work in progress, and "be yourself" was a credo she lived by. She knew who she was and didn't flinch on standing up for herself and speaking out to support causes and people she believed in. She believed in the importance of doing work you love.

As she got older and frail, we took care of her. We went with her to doctor appointments, took her home after surgeries, looked in on her daily, and cooked for her. None of this was a burden, not even the sadness and relief of taking her to hospice to lessen her suffering. She had given us so much; we were happy to give back to her what we could. She was not afraid of death. She told us, "But, darlings, it's the same for all of us. We cry when we come into the world, and we cry when we go out."

A year or so before she died, she gave us a handcrafted book of art— an original story she penned by hand and illustrated with whimsical, watercolor paintings. The book's dedication reads, "To Regie and Frank who gladden my old age." I had never heard the word "gladden" before and thought, perhaps, she made it up. But, no, it's a real and wonderful word. Here's one dictionary definition I found via Google when I queried, "Is gladden a real word?"

> To gladden is **to make someone happy by delighting them** or cheering them up... The verb gladden means "to make glad," from the Old English glæd, "bright, shining, gleaming" and also "joyous." So when something gladdens you, like running into your beloved kindergarten teacher, it brightens your whole day. (bold type is in the original)

I began writing this book you are reading—or listening to—on the day Juliette died, at age 89, exactly 20 years ago. As beginning a new book is always the most difficult part of writing for me, it seemed fitting to begin writing with this section about our beloved friend as a way to honor her and remember the gifts and joys of our unique friendship. When Juliette's family asked me to deliver the eulogy at her memorial service, my opening words were: "We had an uncomplicated relationship. We loved her and she loved us." I wish for you, dear reader, at least some relationships in your life that are uncomplicated, enriching, and joyful. Such relationships need not be our closest relatives but can also be the family we create with those we love unconditionally and who similarly love us back. Everyone needs a Juliette, a unique friend who is steadfast, interesting, kind, wise, and full of laughter. A friend who expands our possibilities for what it means to live a full and flourishing life.

CHAPTER 9

Becoming Our Truest Selves

- ❖ Living with gratitude and generosity
- ❖ Prioritizing soulful pursuits
- ❖ Finding balance
- ❖ Living a reading life

DOI: 10.4324/9781003381242-9

Living with gratitude and generosity

My husband and I have been married more than five decades, and despite times of great sadness and loss, this is one of the happiest times in our marriage. In fact, it is largely because of so much sadness and loss that I have been able to prioritize and focus on gratitude. This gift of thankfulness has been a mindset shift, from a focus on what was/ is missing in my life to fully appreciating all the goodness and love in my life, starting with my dear husband Frank. This has felt less like a choice than a necessity, the responsibility, need, and desire to live a more generous and productive life—not just a busy one—a life focused more outwardly on loving and caring, on shifting my understanding and mindset around "self-care" to largely mean "other-care." The question I now constantly ask myself, in all situations, is this one: "What is the most generous thing I can say or do at this time?" Think about that: A student fails to turn in an assignment; a friend forgets a birthday; a loved one makes an unkind remark. "What's the most generous thing I can say or do?"

I was 20 years old when we married, and Frank was 22. Although we were and have remained deeply in love, there were times when I wondered if I'd married the wrong person. Looking back, I clearly see that was mostly because I'd not yet become my truest self. I was the good daughter, the straight A student, the easy-to-get-along-with young woman who did not take criticism well. I lacked confidence in many areas and was tentative about making certain decisions. Having spent my childhood and teenage years as a people pleaser, I was determined not to go overboard in the same way in my college years and marriage. I would make my own choices and decisions now. So, I stubbornly insisted on doing things "my way." I resented being told how something might be done differently and wasn't yet smart enough to fully appreciate the gem of a guy I had married.

"They come to us already wonderful." So wrote George Saunders, Professor of Writing at Syracuse University, about his students, in the Preface to his wonderful book, *A Swim in a Pond in the Rain*. That line struck a chord with me, reminded me how crucial it is to look for, acknowledge, and promote the unique assets each one of us possesses— our children, our students, our colleagues, our loved ones. Saunders' words brought me back to being newly married and having spoken the words "I do" while mentally thinking "redo." While I adored my spouse and found him charming, generous, and incredibly loving, I invested daily energy into trying to "fix" the traits that bothered me. It took me decades to let go of that mindset, to appreciate his already-wonderful qualities and to set aside, in word and deed, the truly small things—most often a way of his doing or responding to something differently from the way I might have done it. Most of all, I gave up being "right," stopped challenging him and correcting him, and adopted an attitude of "let him be himself."

Mindset shifts tend to be slow and hard, in living and in teaching, and this has been true for me as well. In my family and in Frank's too, we are all pretty stubborn, which in many circumstances can be a sign of strength and resolve regarding important principles on which we are, rightfully, not willing to compromise. But stubbornness can also be a negative, self-defeating trait when it makes us unable to compromise or respect points of view different from our own. It was mostly stubbornness on small things that worked against our harmonious relationship. Once I acknowledged and took responsibility for my own behaviors, our marriage culture shifted in positive ways I could not have predicted.

To be honest, my desire to change happened later in life, only after many losses, when I was reminded, yet again, of life's fragility. Especially after Peter died, I began living each day with an anticipatory grief, an awareness that in the autumn of our lives, we could not count on years. We had only the guarantee of this moment in this precious day we were living. I resolved to do better. Mostly, I stopped micro-managing, rarely a good strategy, and stopped nagging about little things. If it wasn't important, I held my tongue. And as I grew more tolerant and accepting of Frank's quirks and annoying behaviors, without my saying a word he became more accepting of my annoying actions and began ignoring small things that previously had bothered him (or at least he stopped verbalizing them to me). That made me behave more generously with him. Our circle of generosity led to a more peaceful, loving environment. We listened more with our hearts, not just our minds. Our conversations became more interesting and focused on topics outside ourselves—people we cared about, world events, art and history—as well as what to eat for dinner and how to beautify our garden.

These days I make sure I thank my husband every day for his many acts of loving kindness: fixing a wonderful breakfast, making the bed, ironing our sheets (Yes! This man loves to iron!), doing the dishes, and bringing me coffee while I'm writing (I know; it's as wonderful as it sounds). I show my gratitude for him daily by cooking and baking for him (Yes! This woman loves to cook and sees cooking as an act of love), by being open to his suggestions, by being quicker to forgive, and by saying "yes" to all I can comfortably say yes to—that is, in seeing possibilities even if they're not my possibilities.

Late afternoon plum torte with Frank.

So, what does this all mean for the workplace, our schools and classrooms, our relationships with those we hold dear? For our students and loved ones, it might mean becoming a better listener, not being too picky about choices they make that aren't really important in the long run, being open to a different way of having students "show what they know," and shifting our mindset to strengths-based rather than deficits-based. Such shifts in our behaviors will improve our relationships, and as we've previously discussed, everything begins with relationships.

If we want our students to become their truest selves in all ways— emotionally, socially, and academically—they have to feel that they are safe with us and valued by us; that we acknowledge and welcome their presence, their intellect, their language and culture; and that we "see" them. They have to know we have their welfare at heart, that they can trust us, that we will offer choices—not just requirements—and that we will do all we can to support their efforts and interests. They also need to know there are second chances—to revise writing, to redo an assignment, to make things "right." To that end, let's ensure our feedback and actions to students and their families are fair, thoughtful, and "do no harm." Think: "What is the most generous thing I can say and do at this time?"

At the memorial service for Peter, beautifully organized by our daughter-in-law Claudine, we his family were surprised by all the heart-touching stories, qualities, actions, and behaviors about Peter that we were hearing about for the first time. This was also true in the many condolence cards we received, the most comforting of which told a story about Peter, a fond memory of him, or a kind action or event which illuminated his unique character, adventurous spirit, and sense of humor. I was particularly struck by the fact that Peter never got to hear what we heard—how much he was valued by his colleagues at work for his leadership and communication skills, how many lives he had touched, and specifically how he had positively impacted others. Since that time, I have been telling my friends and family, while they are alive to hear it, how much I love them, care about them, and value them. Sometimes I do this orally; most often I put it in writing. At first, it felt a bit awkward being so openly sentimental and personal, but I've overcome that. Most important to me now is that the people in my life that I deeply care about know how grateful I am for their presence, now.

Gratitude and generosity need to be part of our curriculum and to ground our important conversations. We can let our colleagues, students, and our families know, orally or in writing, what we appreciate about them. It need not be a long message, just a few, heartfelt lines. When we look back over our lives, we want to know our lives and actions mattered, not just to ourselves but to others. "What is the most generous thing we can do at this time?" It might be shifting our thinking to "Why not?" when a learner offers a preference or action we hadn't considered. It might be extending recess or independent reading time. It might be welcoming spontaneity and changing our plans to maximize learners' engagement. Or, it just might be that teaching with empathy and leading with our hearts is the best gift we can give these days. And that is a magnificent gift indeed!

Prioritizing soulful pursuits

I was the oldest of three girls in our family, and our futures were set by our parents. We were brought up with what we should do and become, not what we could do, might do, and become. The message I received was to become somebody other than myself, to deny my true feelings even as I didn't know what my true feelings were. Or, put another way, I could choose my own identity as long as it conformed to what was expected of me.

I was a responsible child and a rule follower, so I never questioned my parents' beliefs or rebelled. My parents proudly proclaimed that I was such a good child, I practically brought myself up. At the time, I beamed. When I was older and wiser, I cringed. My parents were loving and kind, but this was the 50s, where middle class women—at least the ones we knew—didn't work outside the home. My mother's days revolved around ordinary things—housekeeping, cooking, shopping, volunteering, taking care of her mother, catering to my dad's requests, ensuring we physically had all we needed for school, visiting with friends, and reading.

While it was assumed I would go to college, it would be to get my degree in teaching or nursing "as something to fall back upon." The real purpose of going to college, while not explicitly stated, was to find a husband; marriage was the end goal. It did not occur to me that I could look after my family and also use my intellect to contribute to the larger world in a meaningful way. I talk about that journey, from wife and mother to *also* teacher, leader, and author in Chapter 2, p. 25.

Finding my true self has been a lifelong process. It has been about finding, valuing, and listening to my inner voice (not just listening to others), speaking honestly, and setting my own goals. It has been about being vulnerable and tolerating uncertainty, and about setting boundaries for what I can and cannot do, for example, leaving work at a reasonable hour and saving some time for myself.

Teaching has helped me find my truest self. When I was at my lowest point, teaching brought out the best in me. Loving the work and the children helped me accept and love myself too. Valuing the crucial work we do and knowing the truth of our values continue to make it possible for me to have a clear compass for what I believe and am willing to do now and going forward. Of course, I am still working on becoming my truest self, but I am closer to being who I want to be and was meant to be.

Here I want to talk about mindsets, actions, and soul filling pursuits that have brought me closer to becoming my truest self. You'll notice that these chosen pursuits occur mostly outside of the workplace, but I bring what I've learned from living my life into the classroom. My personal and professional lives intersect to form a complete whole. I share my thoughts with you, dear reader, with hopes you may become your truest self as well, that you will discover and embrace pursuits that bring you joy. Let's start with embracing simplicity.

Embracing simplicity makes my life easier, more efficient, and more enjoyable. I look after myself—and others—through cooking, walking, gardening, spending time with a friend, reading at the end of the day, and keeping things as simple and doable as possible. I try to avoid doing hard things, things that take a lot of time that don't have a big payoff. I gravitate towards actions and activities that make me feel alive and present, not just busy. This is as true in my home life as it is in my teaching life.

I remember flinching years ago when a colleague called me an ordinary teacher, but embracing that truth has been a gift. Over the years, I have told teachers, "I'm an ordinary teacher. I don't do anything you won't be able to do." When I demonstrate for teachers and friends and then we "do it" together with hand holding and guidance, I am proven trustworthy. When they go off to "do it" on their own, they are successful. The task, whether it be a reading lesson or baking a fruit tart, proves doable. The simplicity of it also makes it joyful.

I often get asked by teachers why I am not generally a fan of "centers," activities created for students to do on their own or with a partner, so the teacher is free to meet with a group—often a guided reading group in the early grades. Three factors can be problematic. One: Creating these "learning centers" can take a lot of teacher time and effort. Two: Often, the tasks are "busy work," worksheets and skills-in-isolation practice. Three: What students are "learning" during their center time is rarely assessed, so we don't know what students learned and if center time has been meaningfully productive. One shortcut that teachers appreciate is to substitute independent, choice reading for "centers."

Simplicity does not mean simple. I look for shortcuts to accomplish the same goal—for example, I no longer roll out a pie crust or crust for a tart, which can be messy and time consuming. I pulse all the ingredients in the food processor and then pat the crust down by hand into the baking dish. Instead of filling the baking pan with rice or some other item to keep the crust from rising in the pan as many recipes suggest, I just pat the crust down as necessary, with paper towels or a clean dish towel. Also, embracing simplicity, I prebake the crust, for about 15 minutes just until it's turning golden, and then add the filling. That action promotes a shorter baking time for the filled tart or pie, which allows the fruit to retain its freshness.

So what does this mean for the classroom? Sometimes we inadvertently make things harder for ourselves and our students. Be thinking: "Is what I am asking students to do worth the time and effort it takes?" "Have I provided the necessary demonstrations, shared experiences, and guidance that will enable learners to be successful?" "Will this feedback or action inspire students to put forth their best efforts and want to go on learning?" If the answer to any of those questions is "no," rethink the goal and intent of the lesson, approach, or activity, and be willing to change your plan and direction to benefit your learners.

Soulful pursuits help me find and value my inner voice, which sometimes gets lost in the flurry of life's demands and insecurities. But listening to ourselves, trusting ourselves is a necessity. If we deny our inner voice for too long, after a while it will stop speaking to us, and we won't hear it anymore. Find the soulful pursuits that help you to become and be your truest self, those beliefs, behaviors, and actions that define and inspire who you are, and who you strive to be, at your core. Share those pursuits with your students and loved ones, as I share mine here, for inspiration and reflection.

Gardening is a pursuit that brings me joy and perspective. As I am writing this section, it is mid-May in Seattle, and I have just been in the garden. It's a beautiful, sunny day, the kind of day people move to Seattle for but one we've not had for a long time. I am taking deep breaths and breathing more easily. My body has relaxed. It's been an unusual spring, lots of cool, wet weather with scarce breaks of sunshine. Too much time indoors, too much rain. Yet, all is forgiven with this one dazzling day. The irises are about to bloom; beautiful azalea bushes in bright pink and pale pink are gorgeous against a field of purple flowers and blue forget-me-nots. Two crab apple trees are a putting on a festival of myriad, majestic light pink flowers with specks of red and white in the center of each bloom.

Something about a garden is magical and happiness giving. Partly, I think, it's because the magic doesn't last. We know the blooms are temporary—no time to waste in enjoying them. Must appreciate and savor them now. Also, there's no guarantee they'll be back next year or even tomorrow. Blooms die; plants die over the winter and need to be replaced; an unexpected freeze kills a favorite bush. A fierce, overnight rain may wipe out some flowers on the cusp of blooming. Gardening is all about gratitude and loss, hard work and sacrifice. It's a metaphor for life really. Nothing lasts forever; change is inevitable; what worked one year may not work the next. We persist as best we can to create a sense of beauty, order, and whimsy. We hope for the best and do what we can to make it happen.

Having a garden has also taught me patience. Even with best efforts and care, some plants take many years to take hold. We planted a fig tree on a hill in our backyard about 18 years ago. We got our first and only fig after about 8 years. Over the next several years, we got between 5 and 12 figs each season. We talked about removing the tree, giving up on it for failure to thrive. Then, unexpectedly, last year there were about 30 figs on the tree, still unripe when we picked them in late fall but good enough that I was able to make three jars of delicious, unripe fig jam, which was a delectable accompaniment with our breakfast toast and some main dishes. I'm looking at that fig tree right now. It looks spindly and fragile with just a few leaves on it. And yet. It's likely, though not guaranteed, that with some luck and favorable weather, we'll harvest even more figs this year. Some plants, like our students and children, just need more time to bloom.

The most unusual tree in our backyard is a peony tree, which we bought and planted when we moved into our Seattle home 20 years ago. It's a slow growing tree that produces magnificent, big, lacey pale pink flowers, with touches of deep pink and yellow at the center of each flower. We get about 30 such blooms each spring, and although they only bloom for a week, even with favorable weather conditions, they are spectacular and spirit lifting.

May garden with peony tree in bloom.

As the peony tree grew it began to lean, and we did some research about what to do. We were advised that staking it would stall its growth, that to become strong it needed us to give it time to learn to stand on its own. Just like the learners we may teach, including our own children, we have to be careful not to give so much support that they never become independent. And sure enough, with enough sunlight and water and some fertilizing and faith, the tree straightened up on its own. I wouldn't have believed it if I hadn't seen it. But this year, years later, the tree is leaning so far over that not staking it was not an option. Common sense and the need to care for a beloved living thing have kicked in and superseded applying the research—"let it stand on its own in order to thrive"—which has worked well, until now. So it is in our lives and in our classrooms and homes. What once worked may not always work. Circumstances change, we change. We have to apply any research and advice to fit with reality and the actual living beings we are working with.

Cooking is another pursuit that calms, energizes, and centers me. It is one way I show family and friends how much they matter to me. In fact, I have long seen cooking as an act of love. It's a lesson I learned from my mom. I don't ever recall her serving a store-bought dessert (her apple pie was legendary), and I still remember how elegant and artful the table looked for our guests. Especially today when life seems to move so fast, it's fun and relaxing to slow down once in a while, cook at leisure, and put a wonderful meal together for ourselves, family, and/or our friends. Good cooking, like a good life, requires patience, flavor, ingenuity, and great care. Good food, lovingly prepared, can be healing.

Throughout the Covid-19 pandemic, cooking gave me respite and a sense of purpose, took me away from daily concerns and into a worry-free zone. The world was in despair—the pandemic, war, violence, democracy in crisis—but I could still create something to soothe the soul. In the silence and warmth of my kitchen, I could banish negative thoughts and become a version of myself I favor—creative, organized, with just a bit of chaos thrown in, as well as capable and content. I love putting wonderful dishes together from scratch or by following and, often altering, a recipe. I adore the colors, textures, and possibilities of the fresh ingredients paired with the spices in my cupboards. When I'm creating in the kitchen, I revel in my cooking space. I'm transported to another zone. The anxious part of me disappears.

Typical daily view in my kitchen.

Like the other day. The writing was not going well. I was having difficulty focusing and organizing my thoughts. I had written barely a word after a couple of hours. Frank suggested I take some time off, put the writing aside for a while. Good advice. My thoughts went right to a recipe from a recent *The New York Times* Sunday magazine that I had set aside to try—"spicy coconut greens with tomatoes and shrimp." I love pleasing my husband Frank with a delicious, home cooked meal, and he was not disappointed. In fact, I will modestly tell you he said it was the best meal he has ever had (although he has said that before).

Just like teaching, the more experience and success I have as a cook, the more confident I am to adjust and revise a recipe or framework. I don't feel bound to exactitude except when I have limited knowledge or familiarity with the process or intended outcome. This is where being a continual learner is so important, no matter the field of endeavor. While I have a complete, organized file drawer of recipes I consult, I don't like being bound by recipe cooking only. For one thing, my deepest pleasure comes from "knowing" enough about a recipe or desired dish that I don't need to consult the recipe. I can add whimsy, spice, and variety with a fair degree of confidence. The same is true in the classroom. While of course I adhere to standards and required curriculum, once I have internalized the framework of a lesson— "what," "why," and "how"—the more brain space I have to play around with ideas, divergent thinking, and meaningful conversations. That's where the joy is for us and our students.

Let me add here that we don't need lots of ingredients or resources to cook well or teach well. Some of my finest meals have been when we have very little in the refrigerator. Those constraints can bring a kind of freedom, a challenge that pushes me. Less choice makes me focus and become more creative. It's the same in the classroom. Too many choices can be overwhelming for students, which is why I favor "choice within structure." Far from "anything goes," some limitations on wide choice are actually a relief for students and are easier on us teachers as well.

Finally, I love stories that go along with certain recipes, for example the fascinating story that goes with the greens and shrimp recipe I made a few days ago. The recipe is inspired by a childhood in the Philippines by a now-famous head chef in a London restaurant. I relish books by writers that include recipes throughout the text. In fact, in the early days of the pandemic, like others who had a similar reaction, I found it difficult to read and concentrate on a fiction or nonfiction book. I went back and reread several cooking memoirs by well-known cooks that combined riveting storytelling with home cooking favorite recipes. Those books are not only inspiring, but they left me with an "I can do that" spirit—exactly the mindset we want for our students and loved ones.

Baking is also a passion. I have a chocolate chip cookie recipe that everyone loves and that I am happy to share with you. It uses double the chocolate, double vanilla, less sugar, less flour, 2 cups of nuts, and almost 3 cups of quick-cooking oatmeal. I always have these cookies in the freezer as my husband loves desserts, and he eats one or two of these cookies almost every day, either straight out of the freezer or microwaved for about 30 seconds. Not to brag, but I am also known for my beautiful and delicious fruit tarts. Happy to share a fruit tart recipe with you as well.

Raspberry and apricot fruit tart and just-made apricot jam.

Going to local farmers' markets is a weekly ritual Frank and I savor. We are fortunate in Seattle to have year-long farmers' markets, and we take full advantage. I go crazy, in a good way, over a perfect head of leaf lettuce, ruby red Swiss chard, carrots in a riot of colors, a gorgeous head of cauliflower, cherry tomatoes in shades of orange and yellow. The latter wind up on my kitchen counter, and I eat them by the handful. But, in the Northwest, it's the berries of every kind—marionberries, blueberries, strawberries, raspberries, and too many varieties of berry to name—that keep on giving all summer long.

Making jam and preserves is a summer ritual I embrace. Rhubarb, strawberries, apricots, peaches, all kinds of berries—especially the wild blackberries we often pick in local fields—are dizzying in the colors, smell, and texture. I cook in small batches, savoring the slow, handmade process. I make enough jam to last until the following summer, and I love giving jam away to friends and neighbors. But primarily I make jams and preserves for Frank, because he loves them with his morning toast.

Walking grounds me. Daily walks in our neighborhood reduce my stress and help me relax. I walk without devices, savoring the sights around me as well as the silence, the light, and the shadows. I walk, not just for the exercise, but also for the pleasure of being surprised and awed by nature's rewards, just for paying attention, for example, to the glorious variety of trees—red oaks, magnolias, redwoods. When it's early spring, I'm noticing dandelions now, as lovely flowers and salad greens, not just as weeds. In early September, I'm amazed by the intricacy and majesty of spider webs being spun. If the light hits the web just-so, I catch the spider furiously working on a miraculous creation. I am careful not to interfere and walk carefully by. In fall, I am awed by leaves in magnificent colors, many of which seem newly invented. How can it be I never noticed these sights and colors before? As I go along, I may pick up the pace and listen to my breathing, slow down to observe a lovely garden, or stop to chat with a neighbor. There is something soul cleansing and invigorating about a walk, even when the weather is less than stellar and the world is in turmoil.

Finally, celebrations are a necessity, even in tough times. During the pandemic years, Frank and I celebrated New Year's Eve, just the two of us, by dressing up, preparing a wonderful dinner, setting a beautiful table, and listening to favorite music. There is almost always something to be grateful for and to celebrate, even if we have to create that celebration ourselves. In our children's growing up years, with Frank and I both working full time at demanding jobs, we had parties—lots of them. We had a dress-up New Year's Party, complete with strobe lights, loud music, dancing, and fabulous food in our small, rental house almost every year.

I recall spending my entire two-week vacation from teaching preparing and cooking for the party. And it was worth it. I still recall the carefree time we had, the delicious hors d'oeuvres we served, and the festivities going on into the wee hours. Among our friends, we were also known for our "come-as-you-are" parties. Mid-afternoon on a Sunday, we would call some friends and invite them to "come-as-you-are" and "bring what you have"—including any kids—to a casual, potluck dinner "tonight." The adults loved these impromptu parties, and so did the kids. Nobody we knew had spontaneous gatherings, so these were a hit. Why not add celebrations to our classroom and school lives? If you already have a celebration culture, as discussed earlier in this book, adding planned and last-minute classroom or whole school celebrations can be invigorating and life giving. A few examples, in the classroom at the end of the day, might be recognizing a student(s) for acts of kindness, trying out something difficult for the first time, or taking an action that positively impacted others.

Figure out what gives you pleasure, relaxes you, makes you feel more alive and generous. What makes you feel like your truest self? Pursue those avenues and make space for our children and students to become their truest selves as well.

I remember complimenting our son Peter years ago, when his daughters were in elementary school, on what great parents he and Claudine were. He brushed that aside and said something like, "We just try to stay out of their way and let them become who they are meant to be." Good advice. Let's ensure we create time and space—physical, social, and emotional—to promote self-discovery, in-depth inquiry, and expanded possibilities and choices for all learners.

Finding balance

Finding balance in our work lives and our personal lives is tricky and difficult. In fact, I've yet to meet anyone who claims to have found it. My dearest friend Harriet and I have talked about finding that elusive balance our entire lives. Our conversations on what we called "finding the balance," which we viewed as an important life goal we needed to achieve, used to go something along these lines: "I'm running around in circles; I'm going as fast as I can, but I haven't been able to catch it yet. Have you?" Some form of chasing balance was always present in our talk. We thought if only we tried harder, moved faster, and were better organized we would succeed, feel happier, be more fulfilled.

What were we thinking? We were wives and mothers who worked full time at demanding jobs and who also assumed most of the responsibility for running our households. We were family members, devoted friends, and responsible community members and citizens. Our insistence on wanting to do it all and do it perfectly kept us from recognizing and appreciating that, given all that was on our plates, we were doing pretty darn well. Now, Harriet and I each look back on our younger selves and congratulate her for her tenacity, work ethic, and determination to try to do it all. But we also wish that less experienced self would have gone easier on herself, been less demanding, and been more appreciative of all she was ably accomplishing.

Today, older and wiser, we realize that "balance" as an ideal is mostly unworkable. Life is too unpredictable and uncertain, even day to day, to focus on seeking balance. Now we embrace doing the best we can as being "good enough." Everything doesn't have to be optimally achieved. Every standard doesn't have to be met with exactness. Sometimes, satisfactory is good enough, especially when best efforts have been applied. Here's a story that brings home the point.

Some years ago, at the end of a weeklong residency to improve the teaching of writing in an underperforming school, a teacher presented me with a large, handcrafted, colorful necklace with the words "Good is good enough" prominently featured. In giving me this lovely gift, which I treasure to this day, the teacher explained that her biggest teaching-learning takeaway from the week was those four words, "Good is good enough," which I'd spoken in relation to what teachers were expecting from their students. These were students who disliked writing and whose efforts were typically lackluster. The writing the students were doing the week of the residency was the best they had ever done—in terms of quality, engagement, and efforts. The teachers recognized that reality, along with the crucial role that choice played, as well as the powerful impact of writing for an authentic audience and purpose. And yet. Despite all their insights and positive intent, the words they spoke and conveyed to students were mostly negative messages such as these: "Improvement needed." "Not good enough." "Go back and fix up those misspelled words." "Add juicy words to your story." "Tell me more." "You need to work on…" and on and on.

A reminder to focus on students' best efforts.

What this teacher and others came to understand, through our whole group, public writing conferences, was that teachers needed to first notice, name, and celebrate each student's strengths and efforts with positive and specific language such as, "That's the most writing you've ever done." "When you wrote …in your first sentence, that lets the reader know right away what your piece is all about." "Your use of humor, when you said…in your ending made me laugh. That shows you are thinking about your reader." "You skipped lines which makes it easier to read and to add in other thoughts." For so many of the students, specific acknowledgment of what they had done well—in particular, the specific language they had used—without mention of what needed improvement, was a first. The shift in teachers' mindset from "more work needed"—which was almost always focused on isolated skills—to "good is good enough" was the catapult that eventually led students to raise their writing standards and willingly revise their writing-in-process. Once their teachers viewed them as writers instead of writers-with-deficits, everything changed for the better.

Just to be clear, sometimes as-close-to-perfect as we can get it is in order. I believe, for example, that letters, editorials, requests and the like that go out to a specific audience need to be published with correct spelling, grammar, and punctuation out of respect for the reader; errors distract from focusing on the message and reading it easily. Once students have put forth best-efforts, I gift them with the needed corrections. They have reached the "good is good enough" stage on their learning continuum that moves from good to better to excellent, which is largely true for our progress in whatever it is we're learning. Excellence is an end goal, but not yet. The learner requires more demonstrations, more practice, and more opportunities to "try out" the desired outcome and receive useful feedback. Lots of demonstrations, guidance, support, and practice working in the "good" zone will eventually lead to "better" and, eventually, "excellent," with the learner assuming increasing responsibility. On a personal level, there are times I settle for no less than excellence and aim for perfection. As an example, we recently celebrated our granddaughter Katie's graduation from college. I made her two large fruit tarts, and I wanted them to be fabulous, flawless, and superb in design, color, and taste. Given my years of experience in tart making, this was a reasonable goal. The tarts were not perfect, but they were beautiful and delicious.

Today Harriet and I subscribe to the words of author and philosopher Voltaire: "Don't let the perfect be the enemy of the good," that is, by insisting on perfection, we can fail to appreciate the actual progress we are making. I didn't understand or appreciate the significance of those words until recently, that is, accepting what is "good" as a necessary part of the process and journey of moving toward "excellence." In becoming our truest selves, perfection and being able to do it all are no longer our goals. My house is dusty, so many things need fixing, and I am still not as organized as I'd like to be, but I am more content. I have come to realize that seeking balance as an absolute is unrealistic. Life is too unpredictable; we do better when we are flexible and open to change and uncertainty, which are inevitable. We do better when we make space for silence, being in nature, being with friends. We do better when we accept our limitations.

The best we can do, I believe, is to seek to live a well-integrated life where our professional lives and our personal lives intersect and are aligned with our core values and beliefs. And when we put forth our best efforts but still fall short, we need to go easy on ourselves. "Good is good enough" is sufficient much of the time. Finding some balance in our teaching and learning lives is ever changing and situational; it depends a lot on our perspectives at the time, our ability to prioritize what's most important to do now, and our self-compassion and acceptance for being imperfectly and gloriously human.

Living a reading life

I read to become more hopeful, to glimpse what might be possible, to be exposed to universal human experiences, to understand other cultures and other lives, to see myself and my life more clearly. Award-winning novelist Chimamanda Ngozi Adichie notes, "Literature is the last thing that we can depend on to tell us the truth about who we are."[1] Surely, that has been true for me in reading fiction, nonfiction, and poetry to interpret our world. I read to become more than I already am—more knowledgeable and compassionate. More empathetic, kinder, gentler. More fully human. Wiser. I read for the language authors use to wrestle words and phrases into unforgettable sentences and original formats. I read because I am curious—about history, science, education, philosophy, and more. I read for the pleasure and joy of it, the escape, the solitude. I read because I love stories, essays, poetry, and books, especially memoir and narrative fiction and nonfiction. I find that if a book—or any text, for that matter—is elegantly and honestly written and pleasingly organized—even if the book deals with tough issues or topics I might not typically read about, it becomes a gift, a work of art, a soul pleaser.

These days I am reading more nonfiction. The world is so complicated, and I want to understand it better. In particular, books that have raised my consciousness on race, equity, and gender have changed me, made me more informed, reflective, and compassionate. Memoir, in particular, is a favorite genre as I love being able to peer into other people's lives—for the unique stories they have to tell and for insights into my own life. At the same time, I find riveting fiction powerful for expanding my thinking, challenging my assumptions about who we are, questioning my place in the world, and—again—considering what it means to be fully human. Making time for some semblance of sustained reading defines my life, especially early morning and at the end of the day.

I wake up hoping that our daily newspaper has already been delivered, as having breakfast with *The New York Times* has been part of my morning ritual for decades. Later in the day, I often read *The Morning Newsletter*, a daily, digital digest for insights and highlights on several major news topics from that day's *The New York Times*. I also read in bed for about an hour each night before calling it a day. Usually that reading is a book, but sometimes it's an article from a journal, a story, magazine, or long newspaper or article I've set aside to read. Reading relaxes, inspires, informs, and often dazzles me. Reading can be, as Daniel Pennac famously wrote in a book with the same title, *Better Than Life*. Heartfelt thanks and profound gratitude to all the authors who have carried me to another realm, to places and people I've never met or visited with before, to ideas I've never before encountered. What a gift! Storytelling, whatever form it takes, is one of the best and most vital things about being human. I've never met anyone who didn't enjoy a good story, and I'll wager that's true for you as well.

Books are always on my mind—what I'm currently reading, what I plan to read next, and what was most memorable about the book I just finished. Most often, when I've finished a book I've loved, I let it linger with me for at least several days before I pick up a new book—to think about the characters, the story, the language, the influence the book has had on me. When I'm deciding what to read next or when I'm just wanting some book love, I turn to my home library, a treasure chest that brings me joy and solace. I love to browse the bookshelves and run my fingers over beloved books and authors, search my current stack for what I might read next, and make room for books I have not yet purchased.

Once a month, at least, I winnow my shelves to include only the books I love, that is, those books that have impacted and informed my emotional, intellectual, and reading-writing life. The rest I give away, a few at a time, to friends and to the "Little Free Library" down the street. Refer back to Chapter 6, "Championing the Reading/Writing Connection" for setting up equitable and accessible classroom libraries.

For those libraries, students can decide, with our guidance, which books are favorites and need to be featured; which ones are tired and "boring" and need to be donated elsewhere; which are new arrivals and need to be reviewed; and so on. See Chapter 10, "Becoming a Significant Influencer" for one school's inspirational, student-led effort to make the school library meet the interests and needs of the student body.

Think also about setting up rituals and routines for book recommendations, for making students aware of titles and authors they might not find on their own. That might be through book talks, a podcast, or a short, handwritten summary placed underneath a book facing outward—much like we often see in bookstores. So many of the books I choose to read are recommended by a friend or book review. Fortunately for me, I have a reading soulmate, Toby Gordon. She is a former editor turned painter who has also been a cherished friend for decades. Among other things, we depend on each other for book recommendations and, remarkably, we have 99% agreement on the books we love. Our friendship is comforting and healing; we know each other so well, in large part because of our discussions about the books we read.

I keep a record of all the books I have enjoyed in a smallish, plain notebook that serves as my reading log. Each month I list the books I've read (title, author, and genre), and I put a star next to those I have found outstanding. That's it. I love having a simple record of my reading over the months, years, and decades; it's my reading history, my reading identity writ large, and a crucial part of my life. I share my current reading notebook with students and teachers as an example of how I record my reading history, which reflects my reading identity. With their teacher, students often opt to adapt a similar model, and they collectively revise it to suit their purposes. They appreciate that what we're recording is a celebration of their reading history and identity, not an evaluation of how many pages we read, a required summary, or book report. I also share on my website, for all who might be interested, "What I'm Reading, With Commentary," a semi-annual listing of my favorite books with descriptions of my top favorites, along with an opinion piece related to reading and literacy.

Let me be honest here. I have a serious book addiction for which I make no apologies. My habit is supported by a lovely, little independent bookstore in our town. Madison Books, located in the Seattle area, is a member of Bookshop.org, a worldwide, online bookstore with a mission to financially support local, independent bookstores: "We believe that bookstores are essential to a healthy culture and we are a benefit corporation, a company dedicated to the common good." I happily support this mission. In fact, I now order almost all my books through my local, independent bookstore and delight in knowing some of the money from sales gets funneled back into the community in the form of rent, wages, and so forth instead of going into the pockets of distant shareholders.

Madison Books, my lovely neighborhood bookstore.

This fairly new bookstore in our small community has literally changed my life. It has become my place of tranquility and happiness amidst pandemic anxiety, dreary weather, and uncertain times. I visit the shop often—to peruse new books, pick up books I have ordered, and purchase books for myself and as gifts for others. Although the bookstore is tiny, about 400 square feet, it is wonderfully organized and somehow manages to have almost everything I am looking for. If not, the bookseller, most often the general manager James Crossley, cheerfully orders what I am looking for and gives me a call as soon as the book or books arrive. Other bookstore amenities include complimentary gift wrapping; weekly newsletters with new releases, best sellers, recommendations, and "first lines that last"; a monthly book club; story times for kids; and other public events. Having this magical bookstore so close by is a joy, in large part due to James Crossley, who is the most well-read and thoughtfully-read person I know. We have become book friends, which is a delight. I seek and trust his recommendations, and we chat about what we are reading. Walking into Madison Books is like being welcomed home.

Seattle is a reading city; I also enjoy Elliott Bay Books, a nationally, renowned independent bookstore. If you get to Seattle, be sure to visit both these enchanting community spaces. Finally, it is noteworthy that during the pandemic and beyond, book sales have increased along with the rise of more independent bookstores, and many of these are run by non-white booksellers, featuring books by multicultural authors for children and adults.[2] I should mention here, that while I am only discussing books for adults in this chapter, my book addiction and book love extend to children's books. Separate from my adult collection, I have an entire wall of floor-to-ceiling bookshelves devoted to them.

Reading as respite

The same way I find cooking for pleasure and baking relaxing—a time when I do not focus on how long it will take, what mistakes I might make, or looking for the "perfect recipe"—reading provides a similar pleasure in that I slow down, really slow down, and just savor the pleasure of the process. I give myself over to being fully present in an activity I enjoy, without concern for meeting a deadline, understanding every detail, or meeting someone else's expectations. I have set the goals and standards for myself and chosen what I want to create and what I want to read. It's liberating!

So it must be for our students. We must not forget amidst the noise of standards, high stakes testing, and the push for the "science of reading," that reading for enjoyment, choosing texts that are relevant to us, gaining new knowledge on topics of interest, and taking pleasure in all of it as a whole—not in bits and pieces and isolated skills—is a human right. So do what you can to create a reading culture of respite for yourself and your students. Consider as a classroom teacher or as a principal starting off the day with everyone reading a self-chosen text—and let's include all school members—the secretaries, custodians, parents who might happen to be there, lunch crew, librarians. Some of those self-chosen texts might be class-authored and student-authored. Imagine the stress flowing out of all involved by starting the day quietly, slowing down, breathing easy, and deciding what you want to read and how you want to read it.

To keep reading as respite, we have to make it a priority. There is never enough time, but how we choose to spend our time shows what we most value. Perhaps most of all, when we devote sustained time(s) each day to uninterrupted reading—and make it the mainstay of any reading program or curriculum—we are validating the importance of a love of reading, curiosity, and all the peace and joy reading a self-selected text can bring. As noted in the Introduction by Maria Popova and Claudia Zoe Bedrick in their magnificent book, *A Velocity of Being,* reading "will remain an elemental hunger" because "the dignity and authority" of the written word can never be replaced by technology and new inventions.

What are you reading now? Share your own short lists of favorites with friends and colleagues. If you're like me, I bet you wish you had more time to read. Finding that time is hard, I know, but I encourage you to "steal" it from your schedule. I also encourage you not to feel guilty when you go through a period when you don't read a lot. During the pandemic, I was only able to focus on reading mostly short pieces—magazines, journals, favorite parts from recently completed books.

It's important that we also value rereading books as a worthwhile and even necessary goal for our students as readers, from our emerging readers to our most sophisticated ones. For young readers, it is the reading and rereading of favorite books, including songs, chants, and poems, that can be the catalyst for them becoming readers. Once they can read a book fluently without stopping to figure out words, they are free to give over their efforts to understanding the text. Do think about how to deliberately embed reading and rereading for pleasure into your school, classroom, and home reading culture and rituals. Reading is like oxygen; it's necessary for our bodies, minds, and souls to thrive.

Prioritize sustained time for reading for yourself and your students. You will be providing a priceless gift—living a reading life. I give the last words here to Natalie Goldberg, in her classic and beloved book, *Writing Down the Bones: Freeing the Writer Within*:

> That's why we have to go back again and again to books—good books, that is. And read again and again the visions of who we are, how we can be. The struggle we go through as human beings, so we can again and again have compassion for ourselves and treat each other kindly.

CHAPTER 10

Becoming a Significant Influencer

- ❖ Learning how to make a worthy difference
- ❖ The *Transitions* story
- ❖ Becoming an opportunity maker
- ❖ Fostering resilience
- ❖ Providing hope and possibility (Crystal's story)

DOI: 10.4324/9781003381242-10

Learning how to make a worthy difference

I never expected to become an influencer, someone whose actions and views earn the respect of others and impact thinking and behaviors on important issues and human lives. To be clear, I am referring here to becoming a positive influencer, one whose impact improves teaching, learning, and living so all stakeholders benefit. Most often, such influence involves collaboration, taking collective action with trusted others over shared interests and goals. To be clear, I use the term "significant influencer" in a personal, caring educational context, and not in a commercial one, such as an "influencer" seeking to sell a product or plan.

I was a shy child who hid behind my mother's skirt when others came into the room. In elementary school, I was an obedient and diligent student. In high school, I got As, kept to myself with two close friends, and admired the popular crowd from afar. In college, I started to think more for myself and of myself. Mostly it was the courses in the arts— literature, fine arts, history—that unleashed my intellectual curiosity and potential. It was not my education major. In my four years as an education major at Syracuse University, only one course—a terrific philosophy of education class—caused me to think deeply about teaching and learning. I did not become a rule breaker or a "positive deviant" until I was in my late 30s and early 40s.

My first success as an influencer happened when I was working mornings as a one-on-one tutor for students with "learning disabilities." There were about a dozen of us across the school district, and our hourly pay was $8.00, which was meager even decades ago. We tutors were only paid when the student showed up. That meant, for example, that if a student was out sick or on a class field trip, we didn't get paid. I organized the group at an evening meeting at my home, and together we successfully lobbied the superintendent to increase our pay to $12.00 an hour regardless of whether the student showed up. What we asked for was reasonable; we made our case politely but firmly; it was a small but sweet victory.

My most significant professional event, which wound up changing the course of my life, was attending the International Reading Association's annual conference in New Orleans in the spring of 1981. It was the first time I realized that a teacher, if she was knowledgeable enough, research-informed, and dedicated enough, could have a positive influence on teaching and learning that went beyond one classroom and one school. It is no exaggeration to say that insight was a revelation to this isolated teacher. This was not only my first reading conference and my first international conference, but it was also my first time away from home on my own since I'd been married. The fact that I was at the conference at all was a stroke of luck. My school district sent two reading specialists to this conference every year, and my turn had come up. I could not have afforded to go on my own, nor would I have been granted release time if I could.

The experience was life changing and expanded my thinking in ways I could not have predicted. For the first time, I saw clear possibilities of influence beyond my structured, pull out, small group teaching I'd been doing as a reading specialist; I felt affirmed for my emerging beliefs about teaching reading and writing using children's literature. (At the time, I was reading books out of Australia and New Zealand that had made me question my skills-first approach.) At the conference, I heard speakers talk about writing being connected to reading, the importance of quality literature in teaching reading, print awareness and literacy in young children, honoring children's language, and how to create a "literate environment."

I knew I had to find a way to go back to the annual IRA conference (now called ILA for International Literacy Association), that I couldn't wait another seven years for my turn to come up again. But how to make that happen? It occurred to me that if I wrote a proposal to present at IRA and it was accepted, my district—believing I was bringing honor and recognition to the district—might feel obligated and proud to sponsor me. And that's exactly what happened and how I wound up attending and presenting at that conference for many years. The most beneficial part of the conference was not the sessions I attended, but the thoughtful conversations I had with other educators. If you are fortunate enough to be able to attend an educational conference, see if you can go with a colleague to continue expansive conversations post-conference and to make it easier to share out what you learned with teachers at your school and in your district or province.

One of the most valuable life lessons I learned and took to heart was how important it is to be generous, to share our knowledge with others. At my second IRA conference, in the spring of 1982, I met Don Holdaway, noted New Zealand educator and author. He made time to meet with me, and that initial meeting was the start of our decades-long professional learning and treasured friendship. Don became my most significant, lifetime, mentor-friend. I dedicated my book *Reading Essentials* to him—"in appreciation of your enormous contribution to literacy, and especially for bringing joy into learning"—and he invited me, years later, to co-author a book with him. I will also never forget the generosity of Barbara Watson, then Director of Reading Recovery in New Zealand, who spent several hours teaching me and a colleague how to take a running record, a record and analysis of a child's oral reading. These are just a couple of the educators I wrote to in advance of the conference who agreed to meet personally with me and have a conversation. It was rare to have an educator I requested to meet with turn me down. Two important things I learned here: 1) Don't hesitate to ask "famous" people in the field to meet with you or connect with you, and 2) Pay it forward when you can; extend that generosity to other teachers and colleagues. Do your best to elevate and credit others.

Regarding that generosity of distinguished, educational leaders, I am reminded of something Frank Smith, literacy and language expert, said to me many years ago, when I expressed that I was hesitant to give away my ideas to anyone who asked. I've never forgotten what he said: "Where those ideas came from, there are many more yet to come." In other words, be generous. It changed my thinking and behavior. As long as proper credit is given, I am happy to share what I know and have created.

The *Transitions* story

My first book, *Transitions: From Literature to Literacy*, and its unexpected success, gave me a glimpse of what might be possible in terms of becoming a significant influencer. I share that story here with hopes you may be inspired to connect the power of the written and spoken word to see possibilities for yourself. There will always be naysayers, including yourself, who will tell you it can't be done and give all the reasons why. But keep dreaming and dream big. Imagining what could be and who you might become is the first step in making the impossible possible.

In my early 20s, I was a traditional classroom teacher with good intentions but limited knowledge. I knew I needed to know more to teach effectively, especially in reading where my expertise—believe it or not—was limited to being an expert in phonics and teaching sounds and words in isolation. I went back to school to earn a Master of Education Degree with certification as a reading specialist and as a specialist for teaching students with learning disabilities. Most importantly, at around the same time, I also became certified as a Reading Recovery teacher, following Marie Clay's brilliant work and still-valid-research that takes vulnerable 1st graders before they fail and provides them tailored, intensive one-on-one teaching of reading for up to 20 weeks, resulting in great success in grade 1 and beyond.

Working as a reading specialist in a high-poverty school with almost all Black children, I was pulling out children in small groups and relying on worksheets and other materials to teach skills development. There was no joy in this work for me or the children, so while our sessions were limited to 30 minutes, I "sneaked" in books whenever I could. What I now knew to be true—from knowledge gained through my latest educational certifications, ongoing professional reading, and the delight of sharing enchanting books with my own children—weighed on me. The majority of 1st graders at the school where I was working were failing to learn to read, based on standardized test scores. The curricular materials being used were commercial, core texts with stilted, abridged language for "stories" and consumable workbooks for practicing skills-in-isolation. I resolved to do better for all children. We weren't talking much about equity, authenticity, or joy in those days, but we should have been.

In the spring of 1983, with the full support of my principal, Delores Groves, I submitted a proposal titled "First Grade Book Flood" to our superintendent of schools. The proposal championed children's literature and stories as the mainstay for teaching reading and included not just the specifics of how and why to do so but also the research supporting the stated objectives. I remember meeting with the superintendent after he'd reviewed the detailed proposal. At the end of our meeting he asked, "How much money would you need to get this going?" I hadn't thought about that. I hadn't believed I might actually be taken seriously. I blurted out "$4,000" to which he said, "No problem." And I immediately wished I'd asked for more.

In the fall of 1983—after I'd attended my first two international reading conferences—1st grade teacher Karen Shiba and I devoted each morning to co-teaching reading and writing to her students. We relied on a literature-based approach that used the best of children's literature, mostly predictable, natural language texts and children's own stories— class-authored and student authored—as the mainstay. We created an extensive classroom library with hundreds of books, including Big Books, enlarged and illustrated texts, that originated in New Zealand and Australia and that were just becoming available in the U.S. We did lots of shared writing and shared reading for fluency and pleasure and also for explicit phonics and word work. For writing, we relied on journal writing and children's original fiction and non-fiction stories, many of which were published into little books by parent volunteers and made available for sign-out from the classroom library. The children—as children do when the work is meaningful, engaging, and joyful—exceeded our expectations. They became such accomplished, comprehending, fluent readers that the district gradually moved to a literature-based approach for all students in the elementary grades. Teachers, administrators, and parents from around the district and neighboring school systems came regularly to observe and participate in our joyful literacy classroom.[1]

The success of our work gave me the courage and impetus to tell and share our story through my first book, *Transitions*. It was my growing knowledge and confidence, seeing what kids were actually capable of, when we relied on wonderful children's literature—plus the extensive research I was reading and applying—that made me think about writing a book for teachers. Let it be known I was not a writer. I had not written so much as an article, but I felt compelled to share our success so others could replicate it with their students. I was an avid reader, and I recognized that professional books and resources on teaching with a literature-base were coming from New Zealand and Australia, and while these were outstanding, they did not quite fit our American context or offer the kind of personal experiences, practical support, and range of issues our teachers might need to rethink their teaching and their beliefs about how children learn.

I had no idea how I might find a publisher, but someone suggested I prepare an outline, write a couple of chapters, and bring half a dozen copies with me to the annual meeting of the 1981 IRA. So that's what I did, walking from booth to booth in the convention center, seeing if I sensed a need or a match. Someone suggested Rigby Australia was looking for a book by an American teacher, so I left one set of drafts with Sue Donovan, its publisher. I stopped by the booth the next day, as she had requested, and the first thing she said was, "What do you think of *Transitions: From Literature to Literacy* as a title?" I loved it; she wrote me a handwritten contract on the spot, which left me excited, stunned, and terrified. I did not feel I had the confidence to pull this book off; I felt like a fraud, but I knew I had to give it my best shot. Too many of America's students were being badly underserved, and these were—just as they are today, 50 years later—mostly our Black and brown kids from economically challenged backgrounds.

What made writing that first book possible was the support from my husband Frank, who physically took me by the hand and sat me down in front of my computer when I was frozen with fear. "You can do this. Put aside all the professional reading you're doing. You know enough." That boost got me started writing. Beginning a new book is always the hardest part for me; it's when I have the most self-doubts, but I hadn't learned that lesson yet.

What made the book better—more relevant, readable, and engaging—was my hands-on-editor, Andrea Butler, who was sent to me for a week—a gift from the publisher, direct-from-Melbourne, Australia—to my home. I knew who Andrea was, an internationally known and respected author and speaker, a rock star in parts of the literacy world. And she was coming to my home to support me. This great bit of luck, generosity, and hands-on guidance was life changing. I have often thought that everyone needs that type of mentor—an expert who can offer us exactly what we need even when we have no idea what we need and what that effort might entail. Isn't that what we strive to do for our students and people we deeply care about—support them in every way we can, advise gently, and step out of the way when they're ready to try flying solo?

As it happens, Andrea was due to arrive at our home on the day Frank and I were leaving home to drive our son Peter to Cornell University, where he'd be an entering freshman. There was no way I would miss that rite of passage with my son and his dad. Also, none of us had visited the university beforehand, and I wanted to be part of the memories and photos that would emerge from that inaugural visit. But I was torn and stressed. How would I explain to Andrea, a woman I'd admired but never met, that she would be spending a few days in our house, alone? Frank and I had only a couple of days to get the house ready for her stay and to help Peter finish up his packing. We cleaned, shopped, cooked, and left lots of good food for our honored guest. We notified a few close friends and neighbors, and several stopped over to welcome Andrea and see how she was getting along. During the time we were away she read my complete book manuscript, made notes, and marveled at seeing her first squirrels ever, in our backyard!

When we returned home, I was eager to get started working—right away. I will never forget Andrea's wise response: "How can we begin working together before we get to know each other?" Of course, she was right. We took, I believe, a couple of days of "play" time—walking in the neighborhood, sharing life stories, meeting some friends, and enjoying local adventures. Just like with our students, we teach better and they learn better when the relationships and bonds between us are trusting and caring. We had fewer days to work together, but once we knew each other we were quickly productive. We had to slow down first so we could hurry up later.

Andrea taught me so many things I would not have figured out on my own. "Start with a story to immediately engage your reader." That was a big one. And "You tell teachers they need to have a philosophy of education and know what their beliefs are. Well then. Where's yours? Get it in there." And, later on, when I had written several books, I reached out to her in distress: "Andrea, there's something terribly wrong with the tone of this new book, and I can't figure out what it is." Quickly she sized up the issue, which was a crucial one: "You use the word 'should' throughout your book. Teachers 'should.' Students 'should.'" That was a huge revelation and one that was a game changer. I stopped using "should" in all my writing, instead saying something like: "You might think about…," "You could try…," "You might consider…" "Should" is a command, and I'm not a commander, at least not anymore.

In 1988, *Transitions: From Literature to Literacy* was jointly published by Rigby in Melbourne, Australia, and Heinemann in Portsmouth, New Hampshire. It was one of the first books by an American teacher written in personal, conversational, and practical language on how and why to teach reading and writing using the best of children's literature. The cover photograph was groundbreaking as it featured two Black students. In the late 1980s, the prevailing wisdom amongst publishers was that a more marketable cover image would include one Black and one white student. I disagreed. It seemed to me that since the majority of my students were Black, my book should reflect that reality. I had, in fact, worked with the two students featured in the photograph and insisted that they appear on the cover. Ultimately the publisher honored my decision, and the book went on to become a bestseller.

A new and unexpected reality became available to me. I began to get speaking invitations even though I'd never spoken publicly in my life. I came to understand the power of the written and spoken word as a potential, significant influence on people's thinking and changing. While I relished the opportunity and privilege of speaking to small and large groups of educators, it also petrified me. I had no experience speaking to an audience. Afterwards, I would silently thank the person who gave the talk as I did not recognize her. Public speaking felt like— and still often does—an out of body experience.

I understand the terror of becoming a public figure when you're used to being behind the scenes. I felt it keenly when *Transitions* was first released at the International Reading Association Annual Meeting in Toronto, Canada, in 1988. I was standing at the Heinemann booth when Delores Groves, my principal, who was attending IRA to participate in the celebration of *Transitions,* approached me: "Why are you dressed in all those dark colors? Go change into something colorful." Her statement made me conscious of the fact that I was trying to hide, to become invisible, so people wouldn't know that I didn't know enough, wouldn't find out I wasn't worthy of being an author. It took me many years to call myself a writer.

Over the years, I've had lots of support from great editors, educators, and students. That generous support has enabled me to write multiple books and resources. Today, I am trying to pay it forward, to support teachers and students to become the authors of their own history and their own lives and to write about it. No one has told your story in your voice in your unique way. We need to hear, tell, write, and read more authentically diverse stories so that all educators and children see themselves, their families, their languages, and their cultures, represented in a positive and respectful way. We need more stories that illuminate and validate who we are and who we might become.

Becoming an opportunity maker

At our core, what the most influential teachers and leaders do for up-and-coming changemakers—which, by the way, are all of us—is to make the road ahead less scary, less bumpy, and more doable, more predictable. While there will always be potholes along the way, there are also alternative routes for a smoother journey *if* we, who are helping to steer the ride for others, have the will and commitment to pave the way. Then, all learners might have the opportunity to find and celebrate their unique talents and become their truest selves.

Remember soccer star and equity advocate Megan Rapinoe? We talked about her in Chapter 6 in regard to my reading sessions with Ted and the way her memoir *One Life* and current advocacy work inspired both of us. Well, in 2022, Rapinoe was awarded the Presidential Medal of Freedom, America's highest civilian honor for her significant influence on several fronts. Former President Obama said during the award ceremony during his tenure:

> It's a tribute to the idea that all of us, no matter where we come from, have the opportunity to change this country for the better. From scientists, philanthropists, and public servants to activists, athletes, and artists, these individuals have helped push America forward, inspiring millions of people around the world along the way.[2]

How about considering a similar award or special recognition for students who change their classroom, school, neighborhood, or larger community for the better? Think with students: "What can we do, for example, to ensure fair access to…, to improve…, to make our voices heard on…?" Kids are never too young to become activist citizens, those who inspire others to become their best selves by going beyond themselves. In the Prologue of Rapinoe's memoir, she refers to herself as an "opportunity maker." She assists team players to score; she sets them up for probable success. That's what the most dedicated teachers, mentors, and leaders do—and that includes students.

Alexandra Mason is such an opportunity maker. In her junior year of high school, she combined her love of writing, art, technology, passion about climate change issues, and working with kids—which she calls "my favorite thing ever"—to create and self-publish an outstanding picture book for elementary school students, *The Circle of Climate Change: We Can Help.* To encourage student participation in the book project, she solicited, selected, and digitized 200 drawings for her book. The book empowers youth to make a positive impact in reducing climate change.

As a high school senior, Alexandra took her climate change advocacy work into community outreach. Working with 600 students in grades 1–4 across Winnipeg, she built and distributed elevated, wooden garden boxes with the goal of helping students see the positive impact plants can have on creating a healthier climate. By planting and caring for flowers and vegetables, students observed how growth and changes in plants impact the environment. Alexandra also wrote and taught a science unit "Growth and Changes in Plants" for all grade 3 students.

Her talents have been well recognized and rewarded. As a freshman at the University of Manitoba, she is the first ever, first-year student selected to run a program at the University in the Faculty of Science and Engineering, called UMEarth. Earth Sciences is committed to, among other efforts, how humans can shape the environment to combat climate change. Alexandra notes, "Whether you're in kindergarten or university, the smallest things we do can make a difference. My goal is to give youth the opportunity to see how they can make a positive impact on our world."

Lois Bridges, Executive Director of the non-profit organization Bring Me A Book (BMAB), is a literacy opportunity maker of the most wonderful kind. Lois has dedicated her life to opening up literacy opportunities for teachers, children, and families in underserved communities. She has worked as stellar book editor and publisher on hundreds of professional books for educators, has championed many literacy initiatives, and has strived to create a collective mindset around the equitable need for books. Her generosity on behalf of others is exceptional. Her leadership at BMAB, along with leadership and contributions from many educators and supporters, has made it possible to bring "book abundance" and book choice to children and families living in under resourced communities and schools where students have typically been denied book access and book ownership due to such factors as poverty and homelessness. Nationally, BMAB at bringmeabook.org—founded in 1997 by former middle school teacher Judy Koch, a tireless champion for uniting all children with the very best of children's literature—raises funds for purchasing thousands of books for classroom and home libraries; engagement workshops that foster close, working relationships between school and public libraries; and resources and offerings for students, teachers, and families to help students attain a sustainable reading habit. To that end, BMAB provides the opportunity for students and communities to move from book scarcity to book abundance—in school and at home—and to become joyful readers with strong and positive reading identities.

Bring Me a Book access-partners include school and public libraries, First Book, and the socially responsible, online, independent children's bookstore, Bookelicious, which allows students to create their own bookmoji (personalized reading avatar)—from a culturally responsive collection of over 30,000 books—to suit their reading interests and preferences, to use as an expansive wish list at the public library, and/ or for choosing several books to own. Also to be celebrated, BMAB provides the materials and guidance for students and their families to easily assemble free-standing Book Cubbies for housing a child's home library. Having designated shelves for self-selected books is as important for honoring children as readers as it is for us adults as readers. Those well-placed, carefully chosen books improve the quality of our lives; they make the magic of reading a daily and visible reality and joy.

Related, Matt Renwick, principal, and Micki Uppena, library media specialist at Mineral Point, Wisconsin, Elementary School have organized an extraordinary library project, The School Library Book Budget Project. Supported by funds from Bring Me a Book, they have inspired and led about 50 4th and 5th grade student volunteers, who had to apply to be part of the project. The students' collaborative task was/is to examine and audit the current selection of texts in the school library and make recommendations for acquiring new texts that represent their and their peers' interests, identities, and needs as well as to rethink how the library might optimally be used.

It's a remarkable project in that the students, empowered and trusted with the authority to make important decisions for the whole school, took their responsibilities seriously, needed little redirection, and thrived. They shared data they collected and analyzed, ordered new books and resources, unpacked and shelved new deliveries, considered library design and display in book placements, and deeply engaged in all aspects of the project. Students honored personal and peer interests and diverse cultural identities to create a more inclusive, equitable, and welcoming school library. Kids loved becoming trusted decision makers and remained highly engaged throughout the process. They became self-directed, self-determined, activist learners, which is what we want for all our students. Micki comments on how students went beyond the original, auditing-the-library opportunities to see and seize bigger-picture opportunities for how the library might best serve all its users.

> What I've really seen from these kids is the ability to accept different perspectives and their willingness to look beyond themselves. This happens as they debate and prioritize the books that are purchased, as they divide the work, and as they expand the project beyond the book buying experience. One of the most powerful experiences for them is when they interview each student in our school about their reading preferences and then advocate for

these students. Another thing that really stands out for me is that they want to go beyond the book buying and reorganize the library in a way that makes sense for kids! It is their library after all.

This sustainable equity project is one of the most impressive I've seen for creating opportunities for students as leaders, influencers, and responsible citizens. If education is about making good citizens who care about each other and who respectfully work together for a common purpose that benefits everyone, then these students have an uncommon level of awareness, knowledge, and commitment on how that can happen. "A functioning democracy needs citizens who know how to make decisions together."[3] These young citizens are well on their way to becoming positive changemakers in areas that extend way beyond a school library. They are learning how to create something meaningful together, to reimagine how things might be better, not just for themselves but for the greater good.

Terri S. Thompson, who has been a 1st grade teacher for almost 30 years, is an opportunity maker and influencer of great significance. She has that rare gift of making every child—no matter their label, past experience, or challenges—feel loved and capable. This, in spite of the fact that the children with the most severe emotional and learning issues are placed with her, year after year. Unfailingly, she uncovers their gifts and helps them to heal and thrive. I have known Terri for 25 years, since we met and worked together when I did a weeklong residency in her school and classroom for several consecutive years. She was and is one of the finest teachers I have ever had the privilege to work with. We have kept in contact over the years, as both dear friends and colleagues.

I recently spoke at length with Terri about how it is that all of her students do well, academically and emotionally. She notes, "I grew up with a significant amount of trauma," and throughout her life she has suffered many losses of people she loved. Nonetheless, through her indomitable spirit and support from caring people, she has been able to turn trauma into triumph and to embrace the positivity of life. There are no "yes, buts" with Terri; she makes sure every student succeeds. Kids step up to do the work and want to do it. I saw this up close, and it was a remarkable and joyful thing to see. Although Terri has also served as a Title 1 teacher, a literacy coach, and taught literacy courses at a local university, her heart remains with teaching and spending time with six-year-olds. Her grandmother had a lot to do with that.

Terri's grandmother was a strong and loving influence in Terri's life. Her grandmother's favorite book was a huge dictionary with golden edges that glistened. Every day they were together, she would have Terri flip open the dictionary and pick a page at random, and her grandmother would then choose a word she thought would resonate with Terri. Then they would talk about that word in context. Her grandmother also read aloud pieces from the newspaper and excerpts from books she was reading. Terri learned the joy of words and language and entered kindergarten as a fluent reader and academically advanced learner. That turned out to be a problem for the kindergarten teacher who was focused on "letter of the week" and skills-in-isolation teaching. As Terri says, "I got kicked out of kindergarten because I ruined her lessons. Once you learn to read, you can't unread." A seasoned 1st grade teacher intervened: "I know what to do with her. Give her to me." Terri's grandmother taught her the value of loving language, while her 1st grade teacher taught her that all students have needs that matter.

Terri's humane and loving manner, accompanied with high expectations, deep professional knowledge, and sense of humor, have made it possible for students to experience how to be successful in all aspects of their lives. Her calm accountability with a tone of "I know you can do this" inspires students' best efforts. At this writing, it is mid-school year, and all her students have made more than expected growth, with 20/24 of students who have already met or exceeded their end of year projected score in reading and 19/24 who have met or exceeded their end of year projected score in math, according to standardized tests. She notes, "Had I taught just what was required, we wouldn't have reached this goal." She is no longer "permitted" to do guided reading groups, so she teaches her reading groups outside of mandated reading time.

A big part of what makes Terri a significant influencer is how she creates a caring community of kindness. She simplifies things for kids. For example, in establishing rules of behaviors, rule number 1 is to be kind. Rule number 2 is to follow rule number 1. And, you guessed it, all other rules fit under rule number 1. She tells her kids, "If you're being kind, you're going to get my attention." Kids also notice when their peers help each other, and they emulate that behavior. If a child is struggling with making a friend, Terri finds out who that learner would like to be friends with and then seats him next to that person and helps nurture a budding friendship.

Here is some wisdom from Terri for creating opportunities for all learners:

- Be sure you know the strengths and interests of your students. Talk to them, not at them; have genuine conversations.

- Never ask a student to do something you're not willing to do, regardless of the age of the student.

- See people beyond any label. Treat them with empathy, not sympathy, which can be condescending.

- Reading aloud is the number 1 way to get kids calmed down. "Nobody wants to miss out on a great read aloud."

- Affirm kids for what they're doing well; tell them, "Keep doing that."

- Make sure your decisions put what's good for kids first. "So many school decisions put adults' needs and schedules first," such as everyone being on the same page, literally.

Terri is insistent I include this quote from her regarding our years-long collaboration:

> You helped me understand high expectations for each student and taught me how to teach writing. The key thing I learned from you is that you have to truly listen to what people are saying and process that with empathy. Listening to hear vs. listening to respond.

And I am equally insistent in including the key thing I learned from Terri: "Every child is redeemable, lovable, and capable if we can see their gifts, teach to their strengths, and nourish their souls. In a joyful classroom, every child knows they are loved."

As testimony to Terri's significant influence on her students, many come back to see her years later, in college and beyond. When Terri and I spoke, Maddy, one of her former students who is now in college, had just visited with her and was planning to talk with Terri's 1st grade class about writing. Maddy decided she wanted to be a writer because of her joyful experience as a writer in Terri's 1st grade class. I still have the handmade card Maddy gave me when Terri had students make their own business cards. I was there that week, coaching and collaborating with Terri, as students dreamed big and considered their futures. Maddy's card says, "Maddy S., writer and artist." Maddy is planning for a career in journalism. No doubt she is following in the footsteps of her beloved 1st grade teacher; she is already acting as an opportunity maker.

Never underestimate the power of one teacher to change a child's life for the better. Often we never know whose lives we've impacted, but if we have honored and celebrated children's strengths, culture, and intelligence, we have touched their lives in ways that will resonate and significantly influence them—perhaps for a lifetime.

Fostering resilience

> Resilience is learned…for children anywhere who bear the
> brunt of life's hardest blows, and live with poverty, violence, and
> hopelessness, resilience is the key, the deciding factor between a
> child who overcomes adversity and thrives and a child who never
> makes it to a healthy adulthood.[4]

One of the ways we provide hope is by helping students develop
resilience. We don't have control over many life events, but we do have
some control over our behaviors in how we respond, especially if we
can practice resilience. By resilience, I mean having the will, energy,
and inner resolve to persevere in spite of adversity, obstacles, loss,
and failure. It's about reckoning with the broken pieces of our life and
attempting to forge a strong path forward, even as we may despair
over what we can't control. Although we may never be the same again,
we can adapt and grow. It is resilience that allows us and drives us to
revisit, revise, rewrite, and reclaim our life stories with dignity, courage,
and hope.

I think of Judge Ketanji Brown Jackson and how she persevered and
triumphed with grace and grandeur through the Senate confirmation
hearings to become the first Black female Supreme Court Justice of the
United States, and then to make her wise voice immediately heard. I
think of the Ukrainian soldiers and civilians who have fought with grit
and resolve against overwhelming odds to push back against Putin's
horrific, unconscionable war. I think about a dear friend and her
husband, whose illness has made him a quadriplegic and how, each day,
they bravely face enormous challenges with love and humor. I think of
all the teachers who show up every day for their students, even when it
is personally difficult to do so. What each have in common is a strong,
resilient spirit that cannot be quantified. Severely hard times, such as a
pandemic, tragedy, or life-changing misfortune—make us more aware
of the fragility of life and the importance of making our lives matter in
ways that give us meaning and purpose—and even moments of joy.

In particular, the pandemic has demonstrated instances of remarkable resilience by individuals, companies, and cultures. Recognizing a new reality, which requires flexibility and putting new possibilities into action, we have seen how people can and do adapt to change—not just with trauma and frustration—but also with strength, leadership, courage, and cooperative teamwork. Consider just a few examples: the lightning-fast development of effective vaccines to fight Covid-19; the record high employment for many disabled people who can now work from home; increased book sales and a substantial increase in the opening of new independent bookstores; teachers and health care workers giving their all to accompany in-person, hybrid, and remote instruction; cities reconfiguring traffic patterns to re-envision more open streets and spaces for pedestrians.[5]

Things are different now. We need each other more. We need to work together and see each other's potential and gifts. Human relationships still matter most. We need to teach with empathy and lead with our hearts. Whether it's fighting a war, engaging students in work they find meaningful, or leading an organization, how people respect and respond to each other is paramount. A culture of suspicion, closed thinking, and inflexibility is a culture doomed to failure. By contrast, a culture of shared beliefs, fresh ideas, achievement, and work satisfaction promotes equity and success for all.

Resilience doesn't happen in a vacuum. It needs to be demonstrated and promoted, through examples and deeds of relentless striving that lead to a goal once thought to be unachievable. Sharing stories of resilience through organized and unrelenting group effort (César Chávez, Martin Luther King Jr.), through strong leadership (Volodymyr Zelenskyy, Winston Churchill), and through personal stories of triumph (Harriet Tubman, John Lewis) are a necessity. Stories of unbroken spirits in spite of broken bodies and unimaginable hardship inspire us. Oral and written stories of resilience from history and life's traumas can be game changers for our children's futures and our own as well.

I am continually struck by triumph over travesty, perseverance over defeat, and eventual success in spite of overpowering obstacles. One example of supreme resilience in the face of setback after setback—including extreme physical and emotional pain—involves the thousands of women who worked to secure the right to vote through passage of the 19th Amendment to the Constitution. Another example of supreme resilience is the huge numbers of people of all ages in the U.S. and around the world who lobbied for equal justice under the law for Black men and boys and came out to support Black Lives Matter. The entire history of enslaved people and marginalized populations is a powerful story of resilience that continues to this day. *The 1619 Project* and others make it clear that we can only keep our democracy if we recognize, learn from, and apply from the lessons of history. Where people thrive, resilience is present. That is a universal truth.

So how do we foster resilience in ourselves, our children, our students so more of us can thrive? Through stories, through our own examples, through perseverance, through speaking out and forming coalitions of action that make meaningful change possible. Through providing equitable opportunities—including second chances—that make resilience possible. Through fostering caring relationships, conveying high expectations, and promoting opportunities for meaningful participation. Given the fraught times we have been living through, we need to prioritize an additional set of 3 Rs: Relationships, Responsiveness, and Relevance, all of which are discussed in this book and make resilience possible even in times of crisis and hardship.

Providing hope and possibility (Crystal's story)

Hope is perhaps the greatest gift we can provide our students and our loved ones. It's not a guarantee everything will turn out well but rather the possibility for a quality of life and some joyful moments, even in the midst of difficult times with unsurmountable odds. In his remarkable memoir, *When Breath Becomes Air*, author and neurosurgeon Paul Kalanithi and his wife determine, "one trick to managing a terminal illness is to be deeply in love—to be vulnerable, kind, generous, grateful." And I would add, to be hopeful, even for small things such as peaceful moments, a smile from a loved one, a sunny day. Hope has the capacity to make a tough situation more bearable, to allow us to see possibilities, and to make each day matter.

Hope isn't a choice; it's a moral and human obligation, a necessity for living. It is hope that can give us courage and the will to keep going. It is hope that can preserve our identity and give us the determination to move forward. Sometimes hope is created by physically showing people what's "out there" and what might be possible in their future. Some of us have heard stories of a student who was not considered college material—often a student of color and/or a student who suffered from poverty, homelessness, and other life inequities—who wound up attending college and graduating. Most often it has been because a significant influencer, a positive, caring, and knowledgeable person, got involved and changed the trajectory of the child's life. They took the time to get to know, "see," and mentor this person, encourage them, boost their confidence and competence, take them to visit a college campus, help them through the application and financial aid process, and follow up to ensure they know how to get the support they need once accepted to college.

More than a decade ago, when my dad was in the rehab hospital in Seattle, we heard a remarkable story. This particular hospital had a whole floor dedicated to people on ventilators. Typically, the percentage of those who permanently got off ventilators in U.S. hospitals was very low, but in this hospital it was high—something like 70%. How did they do it? Staff literally got people outside of the hospital setting into the wider world. Weekly, hospital staff loaded patients with their ventilators onto buses and took them on outings—to the beach, local parks, Seattle's famous Pike Place Market, the zoo, and much more. Patients saw a world beyond their severely constricted one and envisioned what might be possible. Their will to live surfaced, breathing hope and revitalized efforts into their futures.

Related, Atul Gawande, noted surgeon we discussed earlier, did a study to find out why people with the same disease had much better outcomes in different hospitals and locales around the U.S. The common factor was effort; where patients did better, staff were relentless in finding ways to improve patients' health and morale. These fortunate patients beat the recovery odds.

That is what we do—and must do—as educators, family members, friends, and caretakers—support learners at all levels and in all disciplines to see possibilities and realities for living a worthwhile life. For many, especially those in underserved communities, that means helping learners to re-story, that is, to envision and create a revised life story, one that includes a brighter and healthier future. That means providing hope. Most often we do not know how many lives we have changed by our actions, our caring, our providing of hope. But rest assured, you have done that. Even if you have just changed one life for the better, for that person the difference has been immeasurable. You have been a significant influencer.

Crystal was such a student. The daily encouragement and expert guidance she received from her interventionist teacher, Mary Beth

Nicklaus, changed her life. Crystal, a high school student who was struggling mightily with reading and writing, began to rethink the story of how she sees herself through poetry writing. Through emotional and heartbreaking poems, she details her life of toxic stress and abandonment while beginning to imagine a different future for herself. Mary Beth notes: "Her words and the stories created from this darkness wrangled the reader's heart and soul and squeezed until you couldn't breathe… couldn't form words yourself." Crystal's path to finding her way forward comes in no small measure from the positive feedback she receives on her use of poetic language to express her emotions and, eventually, to guide herself in a positive direction. The facts of her life didn't change, but she is able to see herself and her life differently, more hopefully. Given the chance to write the story of her life, she transforms from a silent, despairing student with low confidence to an insightful, well-spoken young woman with growing confidence.

When Mary Beth first shared some of Crystal's poems with me, with Mary Beth's approval, I wrote to Crystal. I was overwhelmed with the way Crystal used language to describe her pain, suffering, and trauma. Her emotions on the page were raw, devastating, and brutally honest. I told her how impressed I was with her self-awareness, her taking control of her life by owning up to her reality, tough as it is. We began a correspondence that lasted throughout the school year. Here is an email I sent to her after we'd been corresponding for about a month:

Hi Crystal,

I've been thinking of you a lot. Mrs. Nicklaus shared, with your permission, your poem, "This is a story about a girl." It touched me deeply. It made me sad and scared for you but also proud of you, the way you are able to put your life into poetry that tells an emotional, compelling, heartbreaking story.

I love the title of your poem, the way you call yourself "a girl." It feels like you are looking back at the girl you were and telling her story, bearing witness to all she endured. I love the way you conclude each stanza, beginning with, "And this was the girl at the age of 5." "And this was the girl at age…" It feels like you are acknowledging all that the girl—you—endured, all the pain without let up, all the horrible suffering. And yet. That girl is strong and brave, even if she doesn't feel that courage. She—you—has endured in spite of all the cruel adversity suffered. I say Bravo! to her and to you.

I think, Crystal, that writing your life story as poetry may eventually help you change your future story and how you see yourself. I see you as a remarkable survivor. Keep taking one day at a time and showing up at school. Keep writing. You are a stunning writer already.

Wishing you a decent week and sending admiration and all my best wishes to you,

Mrs. Routman

With Crystal's permission I shared several of her poems in a keynote talk to hundreds of teachers. In granting permission, Crystal wrote: "I have never been the one people talk nice things about, but because you did it, I feel so much better… I am speechless and have no words to describe the happiness I feel right now."

Some of the teachers who heard Crystal's poems wrote to her through Mary Beth to say how moved they were by them. Mary Beth notes:

> She is a different girl than the quiet soul I met a year ago last fall when she first came to my class. She is also fixing herself up more with hairstyles and clothes, so I feel she has gained confidence that will stick… Once the two of you began interacting around her poetry, I watched her grow from a girl who could look like she was at one with the wall, to a girl who became fully Crystal. My raucous

boys learned to cower from a few short words and a disgusted look from Crystal when they acted like idiots. She suddenly became a humorous, powerful, tough presence in the classroom. It changed the whole dynamic in the classroom... My whole room became one obsessed workshop of sharing and writing, and the gift lasts until this day.[6]

I first met Mary Beth at Wisconsin Reading in 2016 where we bonded over lunch together and began an ongoing collaboration and warm friendship. When she shared her frustration about engaging her "special ed" students in reading and writing, I suggested she have her students write their own books and publish them. In her own words, that was the beginning of a shift for her, to personalizing the curriculum so that students' ideas and interests became the authentic "scope and sequence," not just teaching "essential skills." Mary Beth noted, "I became more of a facilitator, building on their ideas and contributions. I came to realize how powerful students were in offering ideas that could teach all of us. I became a different teacher because of that." So, when Crystal shared with Mary Beth that she liked writing poems, Mary Beth encouraged her and made time for Crystal and all her students to write poetry in the intervention classroom. The end result for almost all of Mary Beth's students is that they tested out of her intervention class but requested to stay with her; they had come to love learning and writing and the learning community they had all created.

Even as we follow required standards and curriculum, our primary job must be to find a way in, to use each student's strengths and interests to provide hope for their futures, to hold a steady belief in what students might become. The pandemic and its aftermath—and other catastrophes—have been life-altering for all of us, but for those students whose lives were already filled with trauma, we're compelled—I believe—as responsible educators to reorder our teaching and our lives. Focusing on learning loss is not productive. Again, we need to prioritize these 3 Rs: Relationships, Responsiveness, and Relevance, which makes resilience, intellectual curiosity, and learning possible and likely—even in times of crisis and hardship. This is the time to practice radical empathy, to lovingly care for people, to seek out their gifts and their strengths. This is the time to provide hope and possibility, to become a significant influencer.

Dear Reader, let me say this emphatically and compassionately. If you have changed even one life for the better, you have been a significant influencer. If you have opened up an opportunity for a child, helped make a possibility a reality, or served as a cheerleader for a student who didn't have one, you have made a notable contribution to that person's life. You are that changemaker whose love, kindness, and determination have made teaching matter.

Afterwords

Here's what I know for sure. Living a good life is about developing, nurturing, and sustaining caring relationships—in our teaching lives, our home lives, and in the happy intersection of both. I also know for sure we are most whole and content when we can live all aspects of our lives with authenticity, generosity, and hope and embrace the noble work we do. For many of us, despite all the challenges and uncertainties, teaching is that work.

In becoming my truest self and a significant influencer, it turns out that teaching was exactly the right profession for me, although it took me many years to figure that out and make it work. Ultimately, it was my frustration with the inequities in my work situation and my sense of "we can and must do better for students failing to learn to read," that led me to write the "First Grade Book Flood" proposal. Acceptance of the proposal by the superintendent of schools catapulted me into a thrilling role, which eventually led to opportunities I could never have imagined.

In teaching children to read and write with children's literature and daily journal writing—and abandoning, rigid commercial programs and worksheets—we provided an explicit and joyful foundation for literacy learning. Students' resulting high achievement, including test scores, eventually led to guiding and coaching teachers across my school district, writing books for educators (even though I wasn't a writer), public speaking opportunities nationally and internationally, and creating a weeklong residency model in underperforming schools in the United States and Canada.

Along my journey, I learned that teaching and coaching are what I'm good at and what I love doing. I am honored to be part of this profession, even as it is fraught with ongoing challenges. It's the what's-possible-with-*all*-learners that keeps me awe-inspired. Put me in front of a group of children and—regardless of their grade, abilities, and quirkiness—I see their potential and promise; I fall in love with them and adore teaching them, learning from them, and learning with them. It's where I experience a state of flow; I don't see anything but those children, even when there are 20 or more visitors observing. Time ceases to exist. I become my best self—loving, caring, listening, changing course as needed, flexible, confident, joyful. While this state of flow is not an everyday occurrence, it has happened regularly enough that I know I was meant to be a teacher. Best of all is seeing a student who was floundering start to flourish. Owen was such a student. When I asked him what had changed that made his success as a reader and writer possible, he said with a big smile, "'I can't do it' went to its grave. 'I can do it' rised up."

What we do, what you do matters. Changing the life of even one child is monumental. Here's a crucial lesson I learned over many decades. I have had many encouragers along the way but some naysayers too. There will always be people telling you it can't be done, that it's too risky, too costly, too difficult. Ignore those voices. Listen to your inner voice. Start dreaming. It hasn't been done yet—until you do it.

Also by Regie Routman

Literacy Essentials: Engagement, Excellence, and Equity for All *Learners* (Stenhouse)

Read, Write, Lead: Breakthrough Strategies for Schoolwide Literacy Success (ASCD)

Literacy and Learning Lessons from a Longtime Teacher (IRA Publications)

Teaching Essentials: Expecting the Most and Getting the Best from Every Learner, K–8 (Heinemann)

Regie Routman in Residence: Transforming Our Teaching, video series with accompanying PD Notebooks *(Reading/Writing Connections, Writing for Audience and Purpose, and Reading to Understand)* (Heinemann)

Writing Essentials: Raising Expectations and Results While Simplifying Teaching (Heinemann)

Reading Essentials: The Specifics You Need to Teach Reading Well (Heinemann)

Conversations: Strategies for Teaching, Learning, and Evaluating (Heinemann)

Literacy at the Crossroads: Crucial Talk About Reading, Writing, and Other Teaching Dilemmas (Heinemann)

Invitations: Changing as Teachers and Learners K–12, 2nd Edition (Heinemann)

The Blue Pages: Resources for Teachers from Invitations: Changing as Teachers and Learners K–12 (Heinemann)

Transitions: From Literature to Literacy (Heinemann)

Kids' Poems: Teaching Students to Love Writing Poetry (four-book series—K, 1, 2, 3/4) (Scholastic, Online)

Notes

Chapter 1

1 Belsha, Kalyn, Asmar, Melanie, and Higgins, Lori. "Covid's Lasting Toll on Our Schools." *The New York Times*, Sunday Review, March 20, 2022, p. 10, for last sentence.

Chapter 2

1 Sacks, as quoted in Popova, 2022.
2 Koblin, John. "TV Show Finds a Hit in Podcasts." *The New York Times*, October 3, p. B2.
3 StoryCorpsU. A non-profit organization dedicated to "collecting, preserving, and sharing stories" to build connections between people and showcase our shared humanity.
4 Doris Kearns Goodman made this statement on the *Rachel Maddow* show, 1–6–22.

Chapter 3

1 Oct. 20, 2022, email.
2 Hughes, Virginia. 2022. "Want to Change Minds? Consider Talking It Out." *Science Times*, *The New York Times*, September 20, D3, quoting Thalia Wheatley, a professor and social neuroscientist at Dartmouth College.

3 Popova, 2022. Popova is an essayist, poet, and commentator on the literary arts and all aspects of life.

4 Manitoba Education and Early Childhood Learning. *Framework for Learning*. Province of Manitoba, 2022. www.edu.gov.mb.ca/k12/cur/framework/index.html; Manitoba Education and Early Childhood Learning. (n.d.) *Education and Early Childhood Learning*: English Language Arts: Curriculum Supports. https://www.edu.gov.mb.ca/k12/cur/ela/cs.html.

5 "For Reading, Writing, and Oral Communication Learning Progressions Kindergarten to Grade 3" see regieroutman.org, Resources for *The Heart-Centered Teacher*. A similar document for grades 4-6 is in press.

6 Hartocollis, Anemona, Dana Goldstein, and Stephanie Saul. 2023. "College Board Is Under Fire for A.P. Class." *The New York Times*. February 14, p. 1, 12.

7 Patel, Eboo. 2022. "What I Want My Kids to Learn About American Racism." *The New York Times*: Opinion. May 14.

8 Smith, Clint. Jan. 28, 2022, tweet.

9 Ibid.

10 Weakland, Mark. 2022. "They Tried to Ban My Book." International Literacy Association, Feb. 18.

11 I tell this story in *Transitions*, 1988, p. 9–14.

12 Kamin, Debra. 2023. "'Change Is Hard': Leaving an Integrated City." *The New York Times*: Real Estate, B8, January 15; for last two sentences and following quote.

13 Roosevelt Alumni for Racial Equity. 2022. "Roosevelt High School: Beyond Black and White." Public Broadcasting Service (PBS) video documentary, May 25, for lines 2–5 this paragraph.

Chapter 4

1 Mair, Debbie Lenhardt. Email.

Chapter 5

1 *Transitions: From Literature to Literacy*, Heinemann, 1988, p. 28–29.

2 McCullough, David. 2017. *The American Spirit: Who We Are and What We Stand For.* Simon & Schuster (short collection of speeches).

3 Here, I use the term "positive deviant," which means "making a worthy difference" and originates with Atul Gawande in his book *Better,* p. 246 for quote. See more in his "Afterword: Suggestions for Becoming a Positive Deviant," p. 250–257.

4 Pearson, P. D. 1997. *The Politics of Reading Research and Practice.* The Council Chronicle: Commentary. NCTE, summer, Vol. 7, No. 1, p. 8.

5 See "The Science of Reading Progresses: Communicating Advances Beyond the Simple View of Reading" by Nell K. Duke and Kelly B. Cartwright, *Reading Research Quarterly,* International Literacy Association, April/May/June 2021, and "The Science of Reading Comprehension Instruction" by Nell K. Duke, Alessandra E. Ward, and P. David Pearson, *The Reading Teacher,* International Literacy Association, May/June 2021.

6 See "The Science of Reading: Making Sense of Research" by Timothy Shanahan. *The Reading Teacher,* International Literacy Association, September/October 2020. p. 119–125. See, also, for research on the science of reading, Reinking, D., Hruby, G. G., & Risko, V. J. (2023). Legislating phonics: Settled science or political polemics? Teachers College Record: The Voice of Scholarship in Education, 125(1), 104–131.

Chapter 6

1 Definition from https://uis.unesco.org/node/3079547.

2 *Literacy Essentials,* 2018, p. 170. See also, Chapter 4, "Embracing the Reading Connection," p. 169–191.

3 Literacyworldwide.org/statements; see ILA's *Research Advisory: Dyslexia.*

4 Mitchell, Corey. 2018. Reporting on the research "Shared Book Reading Interventions with English Learners: A Meta-Analysis," which included 54 studies and almost 4,000 students. August 13.

5 Nicklaus, Mary Beth. Email.

6 Kachel, Debra. 2013. "School Library Research Summarized." School Library and Information Technologies Department, Mansfield, PA University.

7 Shaffi, Sarah. 2022. "One in Five Children's Books Features Character of Colour—but Fiction Lags Behind." *The Guardian.*

Chapter 8

1 Pink, Daniel. 2022. *The Power of Regret: How Moving Backward Moves Us Forward*. Riverhead Books, reporting on results from the Grant Study, p. 142; for ideas in last two sentences.
2 Brooks, David. 2022, "What Is It About Friendships That Is So Powerful?" *The New York Times, Opinion*. August 5, A20; sharing results of a study led by Raj Chetty at Harvard University.
3 Brooks, 2022.
4 ILA newsletter, 2022.
5 Darvasi, Paul. 2018. "Leveraging the Lore of 'Dungeons & Dragons' to Motivate Students to Read and Write." MindShift, Oct. 8, quoting York University Professor Ian Slater; for last quote and line following quote.
6 Gilsdorf, Ethan. 2014. "A Game as Literary Tutorial." *The New York Times*, July 13.

Chapter 9

1 Adichie, Chimamanda Ngozi, as cited in Packer, 2022.
2 Alter, Alexandra and Elizabeth A. Harris. 2022. "Diverse Bookstores See a Boom No One Was Expecting." *The New York Times: Business*. July 11, p. B1, B3.

Chapter 10

1 For more on the 1st grade proposal, its research base, and its results, see *Transitions: From Literature to Literacy*, p. 9–14.
2 Samuelson, K. (2016, November 22). "Watch President Obama Award 21 Medals of Freedom." *Time*. https://time.com/4580275/barack-obama-medals-of-freedom/.
3 Packer, George. 2022. "The Grown Ups Are Losing It." *The Atlantic*, April.
4 Hannah-Attisha, Mona. 2018. *What the Eyes Don't See: A Story of Crisis, Resistance, and Hope in an American City*. One World, p. 14 for resilience quote.
5 Nir, Sarah Maslin. 2022. "The Pandemic Brought Seismic Changes. They Changed With It." January 3, P. A1, A2.
6 Nicklaus, Mary Beth. Email. March 29, 2019.

References and Quotations

Ackerman, Diane. 1998. *A Slender Thread: Rediscovering Hope at the Heart of Crisis*. Random House, p. 233.

Alter, Alexandra and Elizabeth A. Harris. 2022. "Diverse Bookstores See a Boom No One Was Expecting." *The New York Times: Business*. July 11, p. B1, B3.

Applebee, Arthur. 1996. *Curriculum as Conversation. Transforming Traditions of Teaching and Learning*. The University of Chicago Press, p. 52.

Belsha, Kalyn, Melanie Asmar, and Lori Higgins. 2022. "Covid's Lasting Toll on Our Schools." *The New York Times*, Sunday Review, March 20, p.10.

Bishop, Rudine Sims. 1990. Concept of "Mirrors, Windows, and Sliding Glass Doors" originally appeared in *Perspectives: Choosing and Using Books for the Classroom*. Vol. 6, No. 3, Summer.

Bowles, Meg, Catherine Burns, Jenifer Hixson, Sarah Austin Jenness, and Kate Tellers. 2022. *How To Tell A Story: The Essential Guide to Memorable Storytelling from the Moth*. Crown.

Brooks, David. 2022. "What Is It About Friendships That Is So Powerful?" *The New York Times, Opinion*. August 5, p. A20.

Burns, Catherine. (ed.) 2017. *All These Wonders: True Stories about Facing the Unknown*. Crown.

Burns, Catherine. (ed.) 2019. *Occasional Magic: True Stories of Defying the Impossible*. Crown.

Campbell, Marcie and Corinna Luyken, illustrator. 2018. *Adrian Simcox Does NOT Have a Horse*. Dial Books for Young Readers

Clay, Marie. 2016. *Literacy Lessons Designed for Individuals: 2nd Ed.*, The Marie Clay Literacy Trust, p. 29.

Coates, Ta-Nahisi. 2015. *Between the World and Me*. Random House.

Crouch, Debra and Brian Cambourne. 2020. *Made for Learning: How the Conditions of Learning Guide Teaching Decisions*. Richard C. Owen Publishers.

Darvasi, Paul. 2018. "Leveraging the Lore of 'Dungeons & Dragons' to Motivate Students to Read and Write." *MindShift*, Oct. 8, quoting York University Professor Ian Slater.

Doyle, Brian. 2019. *One Long River of Song*. Hachette Book Group, p. 141.

Duke, Nell and Kelly Cartwright, 2021. "The Science of Reading Progresses: Communicating Advances Beyond the Simple View of Reading." *Reading Research Quarterly*. April/May/June.

Gay, Ross. 2022. *Inciting Joy*. Algonquin Books of Chapel Hill, p. 164.

Gawande, Atul. 2007. *Better: A Surgeon's Notes on Performance*. Picador, p. 246, for quote on p. 112.

Gawande, Atul. 2011. "Personal Best: The Coach in the Operating Room." *The New Yorker*: Annals of Medicine, October 3.

Gilsdorf, Ethan. 2014. "A Game as Literary Tutorial." *The New York Times*, July 13.

Goldberg, Natalie. 1986. *Writing Down the Bones: Freeing the Writer Within*. Shambhala, p. 82.

Gonzalez, Valentina. 2022. "4 Practical Ways to Make Instruction Accessible for Multilingual Learners." *Edutopia.org*, February 28.

Gonzalez, Valentina. 2022. "How to Use English Learners' Primary Language in the Classroom." Edutopia.org, December 13.

Goodwin, Doris Kearns. 2018. *Leadership in Turbulent Times*. Simon & Schuster, p. 81.

Graves, Donald. 1983. *Writing: Teachers and Children at Work*. Heinemann.

Hammond, W. Dorsey and Denise D. Nessel. 2011. *The Comprehension Experience: Engaging Readers Through Effective Inquiry and Discussion*. Heinemann (independently re-issued in 2019 and available at amazon.com), p. 192.

Hannah-Attisha, Mona. 2018. *What the Eyes Don't See: A Story of Crisis, Resistance, and Hope in an American City*. One World, p. 14 for Resilience quote.

Hannah-Jones, Nikole. 2021. *The 1619 Project: A New Origin Story*, created by Nikole Hannah Jones, with many contributors, essays, photographs, literary timelines, poems, stories. Edited by Nikole Hannah-Jones, Caitlin Roper, Ilena Silverman, and Jake Silverstein. One World. Preface, xix.

Hartocollis, Anemona, Dana Goldstein, and Stephanie Saul. 2023. "College Board Is Under Fire for A.P. Class." *The New York Times.* February 14, p. 1, 12.

Holdaway, Don. 1979. *The Foundations of Literacy.* Ashton Scholastic.

Holdaway, Don. 1980. *Independence in Reading.* 2nd Edition. Heinemann.

Holdaway, Don. 1984. *Stability and Change in Literacy Learning.* Heinemann, p. 64 for quote on p. 115; p. 42 for quote on p. 143.

Hughes, Virginia. 2022. "Want to Change Minds? Consider Talking It Out." *Science Times, The New York Times,* September 20, p. D3, quoting Thalia Wheatley, a professor and social neuroscientist at Dartmouth College.

Kachel, Debra E. 2013. "School Library Research Summarized." School Library & Information Technologies Department. Mansfield PA University.

Kalanithi, Paul. (2016). *When Breath Becomes Air.* Random House. Epilogue, p. 216.

Kamin, Debra. 2023. " 'Change Is Hard': Leaving an Integrated City." *The New York Times*: Real Estate, January 15, p. B8.

Kendi, Ibram X. 2019. *How to Be an Antiracist.* Random House.

Koblin, John. "TV Show Finds a Hit in Podcasts." *The New York Times,* October 3, p. B2.

Lewis, C. S. *A Grief Observed.* 1961 with pseudonym, and in 1994. HarperCollins, p. 59.

Lewis, Daniel. 2022. "Spellbinding Author Who Took His Audience to 1776 and Back." *The New York Times,* August 9, p. A1, A21.

Manitoba Education and Early Childhood Learning. *Framework for Learning.* Province of Manitoba, 2022. www.edu.gov.mb.ca/k12/cur/framework/index.html.

Manitoba Education and Early Childhood Learning. (n.d.) *Education and Early Childhood Learning*: English Language Arts: Curriculum Supports https://www.edu.gov.mb.ca/k12/cur/ela/cs.html.

Manitoba Education and Early Childhood Learning. *Reading, Writing, and Oral Communication Learning Progressions Kindergarten to Grade 3.* Province of Manitoba, 2023.

McCaulley, Esau. 2022. "My Teachers Made Me Who I Am." *The New York Times: Opinion*, September 25, SR, p. 8.

McCullough, David. 2017. *The American Spirit: Who We Are and What We Stand For.* Simon & Schuster (short collection of speeches).

McGhee, Heather. 2020. "Racism Has a Cost for Everyone." TED Talk, May 8.

McGhee, Heather. 2021. *The Sum of Us: What Racism Costs Everyone and How We Can Prosper Together.* One World.

Meier, Deborah. 1995. *The Power of Their Ideas: Lessons for America from a Small School in Harlem*, Beacon Press, p. 181.

Mitchell, Corey. 2018. Reporting on the research "Shared Book Reading Interventions with English Learners: A Meta-Analysis," which included 54 studies and almost 4,000 students. August 13.

Morrison, Toni. 2004. Commencement address to Wellesley College graduating class. Wellesley, MA, for quote on p. 29.

Morrison, Toni. 2011. Commencement address to Rutgers University graduating class. New Brunswick, NJ, June 11.

Nir, Sarah Maslin. 2022. "The Pandemic Brought Seismic Changes. They Changed With It." January 3, P. A1, A2.

Ottolenghi, Yotam. 2022. "Journey to the Plate: Spicy Shrimp-and-Greens from an Ottolenghi Head Chef." *The New York Times*, Sunday magazine, September 11.

Packer, George. 2022. "The Grown Ups Are Losing It." *The Atlantic*, April.

Patchett, Ann. 2022. *These Precious Days: Essays.* HarperPerennial.

Patel, Eboo. 2022. "What I Want My Kids to Learn About American Racism." *The New York Times*: Opinion. May 14.

Pearson, P. D. 1997. *"The Politics of Reading Research and Practice."* *The Council Chronicle*: Commentary. NCTE, Summer, Vol. 7, No. 1, p. 8.

Pearson, P. D. 2007. "An Historical Analysis of the Impact of Educational Research on Policy and Practice. Reading as an Illustrative Case," in Rowe, D. W. Jimenez, R.T. et al., 56th *Yearbook of the National Reading Conference*, National Reading Conference, p. 56.

Pennac, Daniel. 1999. *Better Than Life.* Pembroke Publishers (currently Stenhouse Publishers).

Pink, Daniel. 2022. *The Power of Regret. How Moving Backward Moves Us Forward.* Riverhead Books, reporting on results from the Grant Study, p. 142.

Popova, Maria. 2022. Quoting Oliver Sacks in Jan. 18, 2018, in *The Marginalian*: Highlights, from a link in reference to George Saunder's *A Swim in the Pond in the Rain.* Jan. 28.

Popova, Maria. 2022. Quoting Parker Palmer in *The Marginalian*, weekly email digest, October 20.

Popova, Maria. 2022. The *Marginalian,* weekly email digest. Or *Literacy Today,* "What Kind of Talk? Exploratory Talk Versus Presentational Talk." (6–15-15) for quote on p. 48.

Popova, Maria and Claudia Bedrick. 2018. *A Velocity of Being: Letters to a Young Reader.* Enchanted Lion Books.

Rapinoe, Megan with Emma Brockes, 2020. *One Life.* Penguin Press.

Reynolds, Jason. 2022. In CBS interview with Jane Pauley. July 16. Accessed via Twitter @Larryferlazzo.

Roosevelt Alumni for Racial Equity. 2022. "Roosevelt High School: Beyond Black and White. Public Broadcasting Service (PBS) video documentary, May 25.

Routman, Regie. 2018. *Literacy Essentials: Engagement, Excellence, and Equity for All Learners.* Stenhouse, p. 263 for quote on p. 51; p. 390 for quote on p. 58; p. 260 for quote on p. 183. (For all of her books, see "Also by Regie Routman.")

Samuelson, K. (2016, November 22). "Watch President Obama Award 21 Medals of Freedom." *Time.* https://time.com/4580275/ barack-obama-medals-of-freedom/.

Saunders, George. 2021. *A Swim in the Pond in the Rain (In Which Four Russians Give a Master Class on Writing, Reading, and Life).* Random House.

Servis, Joan. 1999. *Celebrating the Fourth: Ideas and Inspiration for Teachers of Grade Four.* Heinemann.

Shaffi, Sarah. 2022. "One in Five Children's Books Features Character of Colour—but Fiction Lags Behind." *The Guardian.*

Shanahan, Timothy. 2020. The science of reading: Making sense of research. *The Reading Teacher,* 74(2), p. 119–125.

Simpson, Alyson, Neil Mercer, and Yolanda Majors. 2010. "Douglas Barnes revisited: If learning floats on a sea of talk, what kind of talk? And what kind of learning?" Editorial: *English Teaching: Practice and Critique.* September.

Smith, Clint. 2021. *How the Word Is Passed.* Little, Brown and Company. p. 83.

Tannen, Deborah. 2021. "In Real Life, Not All Interruptions Are Rude." *The New York Times, Opinion.* September 25.

Valencia, Sheila. 1998. *Literacy Portfolios in Action.* Harcourt Brace.

Valencia, Sheila and Marsha Riddle Buly. March 2004. "Behind Test Scores: What Struggling Readers Really Need." *The Reading Teacher* 57(6), 520–531.

Waldinger, Robert and Marc Schulz. 2023. *The Good Life: Lessons From the World's Longest Study on Happiness.* Simon & Schuster.

Weakland, Mark. 2022. "They Tried to Ban My Book." International Literacy Association, Feb. 18.

Wilkerson, Isabel. 2020. *Caste: The Origins of Our Discontents.* Penguin.

Then and Now, 1988 and 2023

Celebrating my first book and celebrating this one!

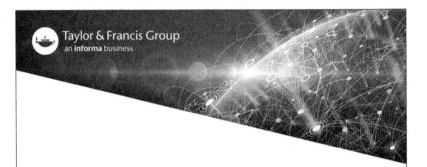